Dresden

the Bradt City Guide

Tim Burford

www.bradtguides.com

Bradt Travel Guides Ltd, UK
The Globe Pequot Press Inc, USA

Zwinger, home to several fine
branches of the State Museums
(SF) page 152

Frauenkirche (Church of Our Lady) with the Art Academy in the left foreground (ADI/Tips) pages 193 and 156 respectively

Dance of Death frieze in the Dreikönigskirche (Three Kings Church) (SF) pages 228

Detail from the *Procession of Princes Wall* (SF) page page 156

The Golden Rider statue (SF) page 162

Semperoper (Opera House) (CM/DTB) page 152

Sculpture on top of the Art'otel (ADI/Tips) page 85

Transparent Factory
(B/Tips) pages 175–6

The International Congress Centre
(ADI/Tips) page 167

UFA Cinema Center or
Kristallpalast (Crystal Palace)
(ADI/Tips) page 137

The Yenidze building (SF) page 167

The Hofkirche (SF) pages 206-7

View of the Altmarkt from the Rathaus (City Hall) (SF) page 159

The Jägerhof – home to the
Museum of Saxon Folklore
(SF) page 221

Residenzschloss (Royal Castle) (SF) page 155

Schloss Wackerbarth, Radebeul
(SW) page 240

Basteibrucken (Bastei Bridge), Saxon Switzerland
(TSS) page 268

Schloss Moritzburg (CM/DTB) page 233

Author/Acknowledgements

AUTHOR

Tim Burford studied languages at Oxford University. In 1991, after five years as a publisher, he began writing guidebooks for Bradt, firstly on hiking in East-Central Europe and then on backpacking and ecotourism in Latin America. He has now written eight books for Bradt, as well as the *Rough Guides to Romania* and *Alaska*.

ACKNOWLEDGEMENTS

Thanks to Christine Ross, Antje Muller, Michael and Dirk at Lollis Homestay, Danilo at Die Boofe, and Rebecca Lack for linguistic aid.

Having spent the last decade and a half writing about the mountains of Chile and the Caucasus, I was keen to turn my attention to a winter destination that would be rather more cultural and also within reach by train from Britain. I suggested Trieste to the good people at Bradt; they misheard and signed me up to do a guide to Dresden. No matter, both are wonderful destinations, redolent of Mitteleuropa, Kaffee und Küchen and Austro-German music. When I got to Dresden (not having visited since the early 1990s) I was bowled over by the sheer beauty of the place and by the way in which all the rebuilding efforts are coming to fruition, with a population looking to the future and no longer back to the awful events of 1945. Although some museums were closed for refurbishment or about to change location, new attractions are opening all the time, making this book a joy to research.

Germany being Germany, everything works as it should, but any excessive seriousness was leavened by the city's modern multi-cultural nature and by its real love of music and other cultural activities, of course including food and drink. And when I missed the Andes and the Caucasus it was just a short train ride to Saxon Switzerland, with its very enjoyable hiking and cycling.

Contents

Hofkirche

How to Use this Book

MAP REFERENCES (eg: [map 3]) refer to the colour maps at the end of this guide. Where a map reference is alongside a main heading that refers to the majority of places under that heading – any exceptions are marked separately. There are also many cross-references to other pages throughout the book.

HOTELS are listed by price range within each area, from luxurious suites to camping by the Elbe.

RESTAURANTS AND CAFÉS are listed by area, followed by bars and beer gardens, listed in the same way. Prices were verified in December 2006, but should in any case serve as a useful comparative guide.

OPENING HOURS are included for museums, shops, sights and for most restaurants and bars.

TIME is given in local German style, using the 24-hour clock.

Introduction

For the second half of the 20th century Dresden was known mainly as a city that had been largely flattened in World War II and then somehow been lost within communist East Germany. However, with the reunification of Germany and the application of large amounts of money, the city has been reborn as the perfect blend of Baroque architecture and high-tech infrastructure. Much of the city has been restored to its 18th-century glory, as epitomised by the iconic Frauenkirche (Church of Our Lady), although many other buildings are thoroughly modern behind their period façades. The museums created to display August the Strong's fabulous collections have been refurbished and new ones are joining them every year.

Dresden is the city of the former German Democratic Republic that has adapted best to the new order and is now in many ways indistinguishable from the West, with its trendy restaurants, cycle tracks, articulated trams and modern cars (you'll only see a Trabant every three or four days, as a rule). It has little in common with most other East German cities with their high unemployment (even with the mass exodus of the young to western Germany) and derelict buildings. This is due partly to the intellectual base of its universities (with around 35,000 students livening the place up) and research facilities, and partly to tourism, which brings almost one and a half million overnight visitors to Dresden per year.

There are now direct flights from London and elsewhere to Dresden's modern airport, and the city is fully integrated into Germany's InterCity rail network, making for easy access to this previously obscure corner of Europe. However, there are no low-cost flights yet and no British stag parties, allowing visitors to appreciate this unique destination as it deserves.

FEEDBACK REQUEST

Dresden is on the move (especially the Aussere Neustadt, which often seems to pursue change and novelty for its own sake), so bars, restaurants and tourist attractions may open or close, businesses can change hands and go downhill or become a cult success, and new sights appear out of the blue. Any hot news can be posted on the Bradt website, never mind used for the next edition, so do feel free to drop me a line at e twburford@yahoo.co.uk or write c/o Bradt Travel Guides, 23 High Street, Chalfont St Peter, Bucks SL9 9QE.

DRESDEN AT A GLANCE

Location Eastern Germany (near the southern end of the former East Germany)

Size/area Saxony 20,443km², Dresden 328km² (32,830ha; 20,355ha green spaces including 5,000ha forest). Dresden is the fourth-largest city in Germany by area, but only the 15th largest by population.

Climate Continental European

Status Dresden is a democratically governed city and capital of Saxony, one of the constituent states of the Federal Republic of Germany

Population Saxony 4.6 million; Dresden 487,199 (Greater Dresden area 1.1 million)

Language German

Religion Mainly Lutheran 75,739; 15.5% (RC 20,460; 4.2%)

Currency Euro

Rate of exchange (September 2007) £1 = €1.48, US$1 = €0.73

International telephone code +49 351

Time CET (GMT + 1 hour; 6 hours ahead of New York City)

Electricity 220V 50Hz. Standard northern European twin-pin plug

Public holidays 1 January, Easter (March or April), 1 May, Ascension (40 days after Easter), Whit Monday (50 days after Easter), 3 October (Reunification Day), 31 October (Reformation Day), 22 November (Day of Prayer and Repentence), 25 December, 26 December

| Contexts

HISTORY

The first evidence of human habitation in Saxony dates from around 50,000 years ago when Neanderthal man was hunting mammoth and woolly rhino; the first farming settlements came in Neolithic times, between 7,500 and 4,200 years ago. There are also signs of settlement in the Bronze Age (2200–700BC), but the area was then largely uninhabited until close to the end of the 1st millennium of the Christian era.

Charlemagne extended his Frankish empire in 775–804 to include the Saxons, then to be found in western Germany, and crossed the Elbe River in 789 to temporarily subjugate the Sorbs, a Slavic tribe that had relatively recently arrived from central Asia. The area was still lightly populated when the Danes raided (up the Elbe) in 880, followed by the Magyars, also from central Asia, in 922. After 60 years of pillaging, the Magyars were finally repulsed in 955 when Otto of Saxony led a German alliance at the Battle of Lechfeld in Bavaria. His father, Heinrich der Vogler (Henry the Fowler), had resumed the campaign against the Sorbs in 929, and Otto finally established his sovereignty in 963. Otto also fought three campaigns in Italy between 951 and 972, being crowned Holy Roman Emperor by the Pope in 962; Heinrich II was the last of the Saxon line, dying in 1024, but in any case they'd never had that much to do with present-day Saxony.

In 929 Heinrich had established a castle in Meissen and set up Margrave (or Count) Heinrich von Eilenburg there to govern the area – he became the patriarch of the Wettin dynasty which was to rule Saxony until 1918. They became immensely wealthy due to the silver and tin of the Erzgebirge (Ore Mountains), first mined in around 1168. In 1423 the margraves became Electors, members of the body that elected the Holy Roman Emperor, a privilege granted to Friedrich the Warlike in return for supporting the Emperor against the Hussites.

Several times the Wettin lands were left jointly to brothers who soon fell out. Friedrich II the Humble ruled from 1428 with his younger brothers Wilhelm III, Heinrich and Sigismund; after Heinrich died and Sigismund became a bishop, the Division of Altenburg in 1445 gave Wilhelm the western part of their lands (Thuringia) and Friedrich the eastern part (Meissen), although the brothers were at war from 1446.

On Friedrich's death in 1464 his son Ernst became Elector, ruling jointly with his younger brother Albrecht the Brave, and in 1470 they began building a new castle in Meissen. Thuringia returned to Friedrich's side of the family in 1482 when Wilhelm III died. Ernst and Albrecht too fell out and in 1485 the Wettin lands were finally separated, with most (northern Thuringia and southern Meissen, including Dresden), going to Duke Albrecht and the Albertinische line he founded, and to the west northern Meissen, southern Thuringia (including Weimar, Jena, Eisenach and Coburg) and the Vogtland to Ernst, with his capital in Wittenberg.

The capital of (Albrechtine) Saxony also moved in 1485 from Meissen to Dresden, 25km to the east along the Elbe; there was probably a church here by around 1000, serving the surrounding Sorb villages (for many years it was the only one between Meissen and Pirna), and there was probably a bridge by 1200, with a castle at its southern end soon after. A town was first recorded in 1216, although at this time what was known as the old town of Altendresden was on the right/north bank, where the Neustadt now is, while the present Altstadt was thought of as the new town. However, in 1469–80 the castle was expanded into a princely residence and the south bank became more important, being the city centre ever since.

REFORMATION DRESDEN In Thuringia, Ernst died in 1486 and was succeeded by his son Friedrich III the Wise; with Leipzig University lost to the Albrechtine line, Friedrich founded a university in Wittenberg in 1502, where Martin Luther became a lecturer. Friedrich banned the friar Johann Tetzel from Saxony to prevent his subjects throwing away their money on his indulgences or extortionate promises of forgiveness for sins; Luther's *95 Theses*, supporting the Elector's policy, posted on the church door in Wittenberg in October 1517, triggered the Reformation. He defended Luther through the turbulent years in which Luther was excommunicated, summoned to the Diet of Worms (1521) and then given sanctuary by Friedrich in his Wartburg castle, where he began his translation of the Bible. On Friedrich's death in 1525 he was succeeded by his brother John the Steadfast who ruled until 1532, followed by his son Johann Friedrich I the Magnanimous, who became known as the Champion of the Reformation; in 1541 he introduced the Reformation to the Ernestine lands.

In Albrechtine Saxony Duke Georg the Bearded (who succeeded Albrecht in 1500) sympathised with the reformers but wanted change to occur within the existing

Church structures; however on his death in 1539 he was succeeded by his brother Heinrich IV the Pious, who swiftly brought the Reformation to Dresden, and then in 1541 by Moritz. He was a master tactician, forming the Schmalkald League of Protestant rulers against the Catholic Charles V, but when Charles attacked the League and captured Johann Friedrich at the Battle of Mühlberg in 1547 he handed Wittenberg and the Electoral title to Moritz and the Albrechtine line. The Ernestine lands fell apart into tiny states such as Saxe-Jena and Saxe-Coburg-Gotha, but their line led eventually to King George I of England and Queen Victoria's husband Prince Albert.

After the Reformation the external politics of Saxony became far simpler, while the development of Dresden gathered pace. In the 1530s Dresden's walls were extended to include the Frauenkirche area and in 1546 the wall between the old and new sections of the city was demolished, clearing the area which became the Neumarkt; Moritz also doubled the size of the castle, transforming it into a palace in 1548–56. Christian I, Elector from 1586 to 1591, extended it west, creating the Stable Court, Long Corridor and the armoury and stables (now the Johanneum). By the end of the century Dresden had the largest city walls in Germany and by 1678 a big moat.

Fortifications were needed due to the ravages of the Thirty Years War, a series of wars between 1618 and 1648 pitting the Habsburg rulers of the Holy Roman Empire and Spain against France, Sweden, Denmark and the Netherlands, which also became a civil war along religious lines between German principalities, and caused the deaths of a fifth of Europe's population. Saxony, under Elector Johann Georg (ruled 1611–56), was involved from 1620, first in alliance with the Emperor, then in the 1630s with Sweden against the Emperor; Dresden itself was never captured, but famine, plague, heavy taxation and economic dislocation caused immense damage. Nevertheless there was a swift recovery under Electors Johann Georg II to IV, ruling from 1656 to 1694, with the first industries established from 1670 in Friedrichstadt, the first Baroque buildings and gardens, as well as the music of Heinrich Schütz, master of the court's music from 1615 until his death in 1672.

THE AUGUSTAN AGE The years from 1694 to 1763 were Dresden's Augustan Age, a benevolent dictatorship fuelled by Saxony's silver mines. Johann Georg IV's brother became Friedrich August I, ruling from 1694 to 1733; he converted to Catholicism in 1697 and was elected King of Poland as August II. His wife remained a staunch Protestant and lived outside Dresden, while August fathered up to 365 illegitimate children (only the eight noble ones being acknowledged), becoming known as August the Strong as a result. In 1687 the 17-year-old August had met Louis XIV in the Hall of Mirrors at Versailles, and vowed to emulate the splendour of his court, and he succeeded so well that Voltaire was to declare his court second only to that of France. He spent huge amounts of money on building projects and on collecting works of art, incredible jewels and clocks, and above all on his particular obsession, porcelain. The Residenz's Georgenbau (built in 1535) and East Wing burnt down in 1701 and were rebuilt in 1717–19, when August began making plans for a Kunstkammer to display his collections. In 1717 he also bought the Japanese Palace across the river (see page 163) to show his porcelain collections. The old Frauenkirche was replaced by a fantastic new church in 1726–43; from 1720 new

5

building regulations led to a more open and symmetrical Neumarkt with houses of uniform height (many by Matthäus Daniel Pöppelmann) with clear sightlines to the massive stone bell of the Frauenkirche from all parts.

For Dresden this was a golden age, but August was not a success as King of Poland; the country was treated as a source of booty and a counterweight to the rising power of Prussia, while in the Northern Wars (1700–21) it was consistently ravaged by the Swedish armies. After the defeat of Poltava in 1709 August regained his throne only with the help of Russian troops and was seen thereafter as a Russian pawn; in 1717 Peter the Great banned the Saxon army from Poland, leaving August powerless against the chronically anarchic Polish aristocracy.

His son Friedrich August II the Corpulent succeeded as Elector in 1733, and in 1734 was imposed as King of Poland (as August III) by Russia and Austria in the War of the Polish Succession (1733–38). He had converted to Catholicism in 1712 and married Maria Josepha, daughter of Emperor Joseph I, in 1719, with immensely expensive festivities in the new Zwinger. However August III spent most of his time in Dresden and Poland's central government collapsed totally. During the Seven Years War (1756–63) Dresden suffered many attacks from the Prussians, being captured in 1756 and then bombarded in 1760, when the Kreuzkirche and much of the Neumarkt area was demolished; many early 18th-century buildings were rebuilt with little change.

THE 19TH CENTURY Again, in the Napoleonic period, Saxony, under Friedrich August III (Elector 1763–1827) continued fighting on the wrong side, joining Prussia against France but then switching to Napoleon's Confederation of the Rhine (with 16 other German states) just before he began losing. In 1806 Napoleon abolished the Holy Roman Empire and Friedrich August became King of Saxony. In 1813 Prussia, Russia and Austria drove Napoleon west from the Elbe after the failed invasion of Russia; he won the minor Battle of Dresden (or Südhohe) in August but suffered one of his worst defeats at the Battle of the Nations outside Leipzig in October 1813, leading to the invasion of France and his deposition. Dresden was occupied by Russian troops for a year; Prussia was keen to annex Saxony as a whole, but at the Congress of Vienna in 1815 Saxony lost only the northern half of its territory (the former Sachsen-Wittenberg, now the Land of Sachsen-Anhalt), and turned increasingly to industry rather than empire-building. The first long-distance railway in Germany opened in 1839 between Dresden and Leipzig, the first German steamship was used on the Elbe, the first illustrated newspaper was published in 1843 in Leipzig, and products as diverse as watches, calculators, mouth organs, artificial rubber and picture postcards were first manufactured in volume here (though not usually in or near Dresden itself). Condensed milk was invented in Dresden in 1886, followed by the beer mat (Bierdeckel) in 1892, the bra in 1895 (patented in 1899, well before the better-known French and US patents), toothpaste in 1907, the coffee filter in 1908 and the tea bag in 1929. In 1889 Heinrich Ernemann started manufacturing cameras in Dresden, being taken over by Zeiss Ikon in 1926; in 1932 they launched the Contax, the first camera using rolls of perforated 35mm film, which developed in 1936 into the first SLR camera, the Pentacon. The city's population, which had risen gently from around 3,000 in 1400 to 6,000 in 1530, 10,000 in 1575 and 55,000 in 1755, now more than doubled from 58,000 in 1813 to 130,000 in 1861 and then shot up to 220,000 in 1880 and 370,000 in 1900.

The waves of revolutions across Europe in 1830 and 1848–49 did not leave Dresden unscathed, with a constitution introduced by King Anton in 1831 (with a bicameral parliament meeting for the first time in 1833) and democrats flooding into Dresden for refuge in 1848. In April 1849 King Friedrich August II dissolved parliament and called on Prussian troops for support, provoking an uprising in May (in which Richard Wagner, Gottfried Semper and the Russian anarchist Mikhail Bakunin played leading roles), leading the royal family and ministers to flee to Königstein; however, the revolt was swiftly suppressed and Saxony, like the rest of Germany, came increasingly under Prussian domination. The Zollverein or Customs Union, introduced in 1834, grew into a union led by Prussia, especially after the Austro-Prussian war of 1866, in which Saxony once again backed the wrong side. In 1867 Saxony joined the North German Confederation, keeping nominally independent military units which were in fact under the command of the King of Prussia, now Kaiser (Emperor) of Germany. King Johann (ruled 1854–73) is known mainly for translating Dante's *Divine Comedy* into German. His son Albrecht commanded the Saxon forces with great credit in the Austro-Prussian and Franco-Prussian wars and even as king (1873–1902) took more interest in military affairs than in politics. The 1870s saw the start of large-scale suburbanisation, with a particular wealth of Jugendstil (German Art Nouveau) villas and apartment blocks at the end of the century. The liberal bourgeoisie did a remarkably good job of coping with the huge influx of workers to the city, developing a sort of municipal socialism similar to that of Vienna and Joseph Chamberlain's Birmingham.

THE 20TH CENTURY Saxony played a full role in World War I, with its military forces subsumed within the German army and Friedrich August III (king from 1904) no more than a figurehead; after Germany's defeat, a revolution broke out in November 1918 and he forbade the use of force before abdicating (telling the revolutionary leaders 'Do your dirty work alone') and leaving Dresden. Elections in 1919 produced Dresden's first city council elected by secret ballot on the basis of universal and equal suffrages; during the Weimar period Dresden was a centre of reformist politics, having been a hotbed of social democracy for a long time.

Dresden was thus a particular target for the Nazis; the first book-burning in Germany occurred here in March 1933, two months before breaking out nationwide, and an exhibition of *Entarte 'Kunst'* (Degenerate Art) was held in September 1933, almost four years before the more famous Munich show. During World War II Dresden's factories turned to war production, with around 300 Jews working as slave labour. Around half of the 5,000–6,000 Jews living in Dresden before the war died, and the deportation orders for the remaining ones were being delivered in February 1945 by, among others, Victor Klemperer, the great Jewish scholar of Romance languages and literature and diarist (and cousin of the conductor Otto Klemperer). However on the night of 13 February two waves each of over 500 RAF Lancasters dropped high explosive and incendiaries on the Altstadt, creating a firestorm within 45 minutes as the blaze sucked in oxygen from all around, producing immensely strong winds and temperatures up to 1,000°C (1,800°F). At midday on 14 February over 300 American Flying Fortresses came in to stoke the flames. Fifteen square kilometres of the city were reduced to 51 million tonnes of rubble, and 25,000–40,000 people were killed, with nearly 7,000 bodies cremated in the Altmarkt, by Kurt Vonnegut (see page 24) and other American POWs. On the other hand any Jews who survived, including Klemperer, were free and mostly able to see out the rest of the war, with all records destroyed. Trains were passing through Dresden again within two days, and crucial factories such as the Neusiedlitz electronics plant were unscathed.

Much has been written about Dresden's lack of preparedness for air raids; there had been three previous raids (killing around 800 people), but the population nevertheless felt secure, assuming Dresden would have the same kind of protected status as Hitler had given Oxford and Cambridge. Rather than surrendering, the Nazis sloganised, prolonging the war and costing hundreds of thousands more lives (and East Germany made similar use of the raids during the Cold War), but in fact the destruction of whole cities had been part of German strategy since the attack on Guernica in 1937. If anything, the lesson of the bombing of Dresden (and of Hiroshima and Nagasaki) is that in the end man will always do what technology permits. But Dresden also gave rise to a powerful peace movement, and it was in part responsible for finally killing off German militarism (after five wars in the 75 years from 1864).

The Red Army entered Dresden on 7 May 1945, the day Germany surrendered; in 1949 the communist Deutsche Demokratische Republik (DDR; German

Democratic Republic) took control of the Russian-controlled zone of East Germany while the pro-Western and genuinely democratic German Federal Republic was established in the American, British and French zones of the west. In 1952 Saxony was split into three regions, based on Dresden, Leipzig and Karl-Marx-Stadt (formerly – and now again – Chemnitz). In 1949 over 250,000 people came to the 'Das neue Dresden' exhibition and emphatically rejected plans for a Corbusier-esque new city; from this time on the policy was to rebuild the old city, recreating it as authentically as possible (in 1950 'Zwinger lotteries' were introduced to raise money for rebuilding); however, standard communist apartment blocks were built in the suburbs to solve the city's housing crisis, starting in 1951 on Grunauer Strasse.

In June 1953 an uprising began in Berlin, and up to 20,000 protestors gathered in Dresden squares; Soviet troops were ready to fire, but after warning shots the crowds dispersed peacefully and the uprising fizzled out. In the same year rebuilding began of the Altmarkt and Wilsdruffer Strasse (both widened, destroying the medieval street pattern), and in 1965 reconstruction of the Zwinger was completed. From the mid 1970s large areas of prefabricated apartment blocks were raised in the new suburbs of Prohlis and Gorbitz, and the Neustadt's Hauptstrasse was laid out in 1979; in 1977 work began on rebuilding the Semperoper (reopened in 1985) and from 1986 the Residenzschloss was rebuilt, being more or less finished by Dresden's 800th anniversary in 2006.

From 1982 there was an annual silent commemoration of the 1945 raids on 13 February, with citizens leaving candles at the ruins of the Frauenkirche, which became a forum for the peace and reunification movements (resisting government attempts to hijack them for political ends). The ecological movement also became important (in conjunction with the Church), a campaign against a silicon plant in Gittersee feeding into the protests against the communist regime that led to its demise in 1989.

THE END OF COMMUNISM Dresden had a higher proportion of its populace emigrating than anywhere else in the DDR, although the demonstrations that brought down communism were centred in Berlin and Leipzig. From September 1989 when the West German embassy in Prague started giving visas to all East Germans who wanted them, demonstrations greeted special trains through Dresden to Prague (supposedly expelling 'irresponsible antisocial traitors and criminals') and were forcibly dispersed. In October a second wave of trains brought those who had taken refuge in the Czech embassy in Berlin, until the border was closed. Gorbachev came to Berlin to urge the government to accept the need for reform, but was rebuffed; on 9 October a peaceful dialogue began in Dresden's Rathaus between the city authorities and the dissident Group of Twenty, with news relayed to 22,000 people waiting in churches. The Group of Twenty asked Dresdeners to signal support by depositing one mark each in a Postbank account, and collected 100,000 marks, symbolising 100,000 votes. Secretary-General Erich Honecker was deposed by his own politburo on 18 October, and the government as a whole resigned on 7 November; the new leadership at once withdrew restrictions on travel to the West and jubilant crowds began tearing down the Berlin Wall. Free multi-party elections were held in March 1990, producing a government with a mandate to negotiate union with West Germany and thus its own dissolution, which took place on 3 October 1990, when the three regions of Saxony were reunited as the Free State of Saxony.

In Dresden, local elections in May 1990 were won by parties oriented to the Christian Democrats (the ruling party in West Germany) and the ex-communist Party of Democratic Socialists, and Herbert Wagner of the Group of Twenty became mayor. Since then, although much heavy industry has closed down, Dresden has done better than many other cities in attracting new investment, in tourism and in silicon chip manufacturing among other things, and there has been a lot of investment in infrastructure, rapidly bringing the city into line with similar places in the West.

In August 2002 the Elbe reached a record 9m above its usual level, and floods caused considerable damage; in the spring of 2006 it was 8m above normal and flooding occurred again, though less damage was done.

Perhaps the most obvious controversy has been over the proposed Waldschlösschen bridge, east of the centre, which led UNESCO in 2006 to threaten the unprecedented withdrawal of the World Heritage status of the Elbe Meadows, an 18km-long stretch of riverside from the city centre to Pillnitz, including the rebuilt city centre, that was added to the World Heritage list in 2004.

POLITICS

Dresden is once again the capital of a unified Saxony, the Freistaat Sachsen (which was split into three under communism). The Landtag or state parliament is elected by proportional representation (with a 5% threshold); the state's chief executive is the Ministerpräsident, elected by a majority vote of the Landtag's members, who appoints a cabinet to run the Staatsregierung or state government.

The Ministerpräsident is also the leader of the state's delegation to the Bundesrat (the upper federal chamber); the size of the delegation and the number of votes is determined by the state's population (Saxony and six others have four votes while five have five or six votes and the five smallest have three). The other delegates would normally be members of the state cabinet, but in fact their presence is not necessary, as the leader can and often does cast all the state's votes himself. If a state is ruled by a coalition which cannot agree on a common position, they cannot use any of their votes. The presidency of the Bundesrat rotates annually among the ministers-president.

The lower federal chamber, the Bundestag, is directly elected for a four-year term, and elects the country's Chancellor or Prime Minister. Half its deputies are directly elected, and half are chosen from party lists on the basis of the number of votes each party receives in the direct election.

In the state elections of September 2004 the CDU (the centre-right Christian Democrats) took 855,203 of the just over two million votes cast (41%), winning 55 of the 124 seats. The PDS (the ex-communist Party of Democratic Socialism, now the Linkspartei or Left Party) won 31 seats, the centre-left SPD (Social Democratic Party) won 13, the far-right NPD (National Democratic Party) nine, the FDP (the liberal Free Democratic Party) seven, Alliance '90/The Greens six, and independents three. This is the strongest far-right representation anywhere in post-war Germany but, by the end of 2006, four of the NPD deputies had either resigned or been expelled. The net result of the election was that the CDU lost its absolute majority and had to form a coalition with the SPD.

There is also a city council, elected by proportional representation for a five-year term. This was also elected in 2004, the CDU winning 21 of its 70 seats; the Left Party won 17, Alliance '90/The Greens nine, the SPD eight, the FDP six, the Citizens' Group six (in fact two each for the Citizens' List, Free Citizens and Peoples' Solidarity) and allies of the NPD three. Thus no party has a majority. This doesn't much matter, as executive power is held by the mayor or Supreme Burgermeister, directly elected for a seven-year term. He has seven Burgermeisters under him, managing the seven arms of the city government. The current mayor has been suspended from office for embezzlement and deliberate bankruptcy, and has been succeeded by his deputy, the First Burgermeister. There are also advisory councils in the city's ten districts and in their subdivisions, the former boroughs.

In 2005 the largest neo-Nazi demonstration since World War II was held in Dresden, with between 5,000 and 8,000 marchers commemorating the so-called Allied bombing-holocaust (a pathetic attempt to devalue World War II's real Holocaust).

ECONOMY

Famous for its role in the camera industry in pre-war years, Dresden's economy is still strongest in the high-tech sphere, although tourism is increasingly important. However there was a rocky transition from the communist era, when many factories closed down, leading to an unemployment rate of 18% in the early

1990s, now reduced to 13.5%. There is still very high unemployment elsewhere in the former DDR, even though the population is shrinking, as the young and educated in particular move west. So far the federal republic has spent €1.5 trillion of 'solidarity funds' on its new eastern Länder, a programme which is to continue to 2019. Dresden's GDP per capita has risen to €31,100, not far below the West German level, which is often used as justification for the massive cost of restructuring the East German economy, but Dresden and Leipzig remain the exceptions rather than the rule. Other towns have been used simply as sources of cheap labour for subcontracted manufacturing, but Dresden and Leipzig, with their large pools of graduates and research centres, have developed primary industries of their own.

Robotron, based in Dresden, was the DDR's largest electronics manufacturer, with around 30,000 employees. Its success was built on a robust programme of industrial espionage, taking IBM and Amstrad computers apart and creating clones for use across the Soviet bloc. Where it failed to clone models it bought them from Japan and relabelled them. In 1969 the semiconductor company ZMD was established in Dresden; the government poured billions of marks into a vain attempt to produce a 1-megabit chip, although the DDR was barely able to produce 256KB chips. ZMD survives today, joined by newer companies such as AMD and Infineon Technologies and a Siemens–Motorola joint venture, employing around 20,000 workers in all, mostly near Dresden Airport; most recently Plastic Logic, of Cambridge, is setting up a manufacturing plant in Dresden. The Jena-Leipzig area is known as Silicon Saxony, with many more high-tech companies based there.

The pharmaceutical industry in Dresden dates from the late 19th century; the most interesting is the Sächsisches Serumwerk Dresden (Saxon Serum Plant, Dresden), founded in 1911. It was bought in 1992 by GlaxoSmithKline, which has invested over €65 million in a modern liquid influenza vaccine plant.

Engineering is also important, notably with Volkswagen's Transparent Factory (see page 175) making Phaeton cars and Elbe Flugzeugwerke (Elbe Aircraft Works) involved in Airbus manufacture.

In 2005 1,346,787 tourists visited Dresden for overnight stays, 11.8% more than in 2004; most were from Germany, but the proportion of foreign visitors increased to 15%.

PEOPLE

Almost uniquely in eastern Germany, the population of Dresden is increasing, with over a million people now resident in the Greater Dresden area. This is due both to young educated people moving from elsewhere for jobs, and to those people having a higher than average birth rate.

The largest ethnic minority are Turks, most visible in the kebab fast-food shops that are as omnipresent here as across Germany; there are also considerable numbers of Chinese, Vietnamese and Italians here. The main non-visible minority are the Sorbs, a Slavic people who settled to the east of Dresden (itself a Slav placename) in the 6th and 7th centuries. Today they number some 50,000–60,000. Although Sorbs in Dresden are to all intents and purposes assimilated with the German population, in their homeland their language and culture are still active.

BUSINESS

Germans are, as the cliché confirms, serious about their working lives and don't appreciate some of the more laidback and jokey Anglo-Saxon working practices. The Branson-esque seat-of-the-pants style won't fly here; careful research, analysis and planning are vital if you want a business idea to be taken up. A good supply of business cards (*Visitenkarten*) is also vital. In general the culture is risk-adverse, which is why there are few German Bransons, but equally fewer bankruptcies.

Be sure to arrive on time for meetings (arriving late is a clear indicator of a risky potential partner); the most senior member of a party should enter first, and greet the most senior counterpart first (German men will stand when a woman enters). Give a brief firm handshake when introduced, and remember people's correct names and titles (first names are not used in a business setting).

A meeting will usually have a clear structure with a set finishing time; don't expect an answer on the spot to your earth-shattering proposal, as it will need to be considered carefully before they get back to you.

Germans keep a clear divide between their working and private lives, with risk and humour largely kept for the private sphere; don't expect to be invited home for dinner, but you should gradually be able to break down some barriers over a beer or three after work.

Office hours are normally from 09.00 to 17.00, but you should avoid asking for a meeting on a Friday afternoon.

If you want to set up a business in the Dresden area, contact the Sächsisches Staatsministerium der Finanzen (Saxon State Finance Ministry) (*Carolaplatz 1, 01097 Dresden;* ☎ *0351 5640;* e *post@smf.sachsen.de*). German workers are productive and skilled, but labour costs are high, due largely to social security levies; they also have far more job security than in the Anglo-Saxon countries. Value added tax is 19% (7% on food), and corporate income tax is 25%.

RELIGION

Saxony is overwhelmingly Lutheran by culture (although only 15.5% of the population are active Lutherans), with a tiny Roman Catholic minority (3.4% in Saxony as a whole, and 4.2% in Dresden).

Nevertheless there is a fine Roman Catholic cathedral (the Hofkirche; see page 206), where you can attend services and concerts. There's an even smaller Jewish population (see page 157).

CULTURE

For many visitors, culture is what Dresden is about; in addition to the art galleries and museums, you can go to the opera, the Dresden Philharmonic or to theatres and many other groups and venues (see pages 129–38). Church music is also important, with J S Bach in particular featuring in many services and organ recitals also common; look at the noticeboards by the church doors and in the listings magazines.

MUSIC Above all, Dresden is a city of music, thanks to the Electors employing a series of great composers as Kapellmeister and then as director of the opera. The Sächsische Staatskapelle Dresden (Dresden State Orchestra of Saxony or SSKD) was founded by Elector Moritz in 1548; it's one of the world's oldest orchestras and has almost always been in the top rank. The first of the great Kapellmeisters was Heinrich Schütz (1585–1672), the leading composer of the 17th century along with Monteverdi (whom he may have met and even studied with in Venice). He was in charge in Dresden from 1615 until his death (although he did spend time in Venice and Copenhagen), writing what was probably the first German opera, *Dafne* (now lost), in 1627. However most of his work was liturgical, showing great sensitivity to the religious texts he set, and moving from elaborate settings to a more austere style as the Thirty Years War devastated Saxony's musical resources. His most famous successor was, of course, Johann Sebastian Bach (1685–1750), who did work for the Elector but remained based in the second city, Leipzig; his music is widely performed in Dresden too, especially in churches.

Jan Dismas Zelenka (1679–1745) was a Czech Baroque composer who was based in Dresden from 1710 until his death, although he was never appointed Kapellmeister. His music, mostly sacred works, is not widely known nowadays, but it does display remarkable imagination.

Carl Maria von Weber (1786–1826) was director of the Dresden Opera from 1817 and wrote the first authentically German opera, *Der Freischütz*, here, although it was in fact premiered in Berlin in 1821 before being performed in Dresden the next year. It's seen as the first Volksoper or national opera, in other words an opera in German about ordinary people. However, this ignores the black magic scene and the seriously weird village that Max, the Freischütz or Sharpshooter of the title, lives in. Still, it can be seen as paving the way for Wagner's dragons, dwarfs and giants (and the soundtracks of countless horror films), and magic is in any case much more part of German folk culture than in either Britain or France.

One of Weber's greatest admirers was Richard Wagner (1813–83), born in Leipzig, who grew up in Dresden from the age of one. After working in various opera houses across Europe, his third opera, *Rienzi*, was accepted by the Dresden Court Opera; it was premiered in the newly completed Semperoper in 1842 and was his first great success, despite its five-hour length, followed by *Der Fliegende Hollände* (The Flying Dutchman) in 1843, which led to his accepting (rather reluctantly) the post of director of the opera. He also put on *Tannhäuser* in 1845, as well as legendary performances of Beethoven's 9th Symphony. His involvement in the uprising of 1849 led to his fleeing from the city, although his operas remained in the repertory. In 1859, exiled in Paris, he struggled to find a theatre for the premiere of *Tristan und Isolde*; eventually, given the small cast and chorus and the three simple acts, it was taken by the Dresden Opera, but after 77 rehearsals and the near-collapse of the tenor, the opera was abandoned as unperformable. It was first performed in Munich in 1865 but the tenor did indeed collapse and die in Dresden three weeks after the final performance. There's now a Wagner Museum in his summer home at Graupa, not far from the Weber Museum in Hosterwitz.

Robert Schumann (1810–56) was a Saxon, born in Zwickau, who lived in Dresden in 1844–50; his wife Clara, one of the finest pianists of the time, gave the premiere of his piano concerto in Dresden in 1845. The years 1845–49 were his most productive, but also marked the onset of the bipolar disorder that eventually led to his suicide. He escaped the uprising of 1849 by moving to Kreischa, on the outskirts of Dresden, and writing music for Byron's *Manfred* and Goethe's *Faust*.

Richard Strauss (1864–1949) is the composer most closely associated with the Semperoper, where no fewer than nine of his operas were premiered, starting with *Feuersnot* (The Need for Fire; 1901). Heavily influenced initially by Wagner, the more Mozartian *Der Rosenkavalier* (1911) was his first great success, with special trains from Berlin bringing opera lovers who feared that because of its risqué nature it wouldn't be staged in the capital. He made his last visit to Dresden in June 1944; the wonderful *Metamorphosen* (1945), for 23 solo strings, was inspired by his grief at the destruction of the opera houses in Munich and Dresden by Allied bombing.

The Austrian tenor Richard Tauber (1891–1948) began his career in Chemnitz (where his father ran the opera) in 1913, but was very soon offered a contract with the Dresden Opera, staying until 1922. He gained a reputation as the 'SOS tenor' due to his ability to learn a role at short notice, most notably Calaf for the German premiere of Puccini's *Turandot*, in Dresden in 1926. He could have been the greatest Mozart tenor of his time, but turned more to operetta, for financial reasons.

Sergei Rachmaninov (1873–1943) resigned as music director of Moscow's Bolshoi Opera in 1906, after the turmoil of the 1905 revolution, and took his young family to Dresden, where he refused offers to conduct and concentrated on composing his second symphony and *Monna Vanna* (1907), his first piano sonata (1908), and *The Isle of the Dead* (1909). In 1917 he again left Russia, this time for good, stopping briefly in Dresden before moving to the USA; in 1925–26 he spent some months in Dresden, completing his fourth piano concerto. Dmitri Shostakovich (1906–75) visited Dresden in July 1960 to write the music to the film *Five Days and Five Nights*, about the destruction of the city; he also wrote (supposedly in three days) his eighth string quartet, dedicated 'to the victims of fascism and war'.

Many of the finest conductors of the 20th century were chief conductors of the Dresden Staatskapelle, notably Fritz Reiner (1914–21), Fritz Busch (1922–33), Karl Böhm (1934–43), Rudolf Kempe (1949–53), Kurt Sanderling (1964–67), Herbert Blomstedt (1975–85), Giuseppe Sinopoli (1992–2001) and Bernard Haitink (2002–04); the post of honorary conductor was created in 1990 for Sir Colin Davis, whose association with the Staatskapelle has led to many fine concerts and recordings. There's also the Dresdner Philharmonie (Dresden Philharmonic Orchestra), founded in 1870; after a relatively undistinguished start its recent principal conductors have included Kurt Masur (1967–72), Günther Herbig (1972–76), Michel Plasson (1984–2001), Marek Janowski (2001–04) and Rafael Frühbeck de Burgos (since 2004).

LITERATURE Dresden plays a far smaller role in the history of literature; the Romantic writer E T A Hoffman actually came to Dresden as a conductor in 1813, and made it the setting of his masterpiece *Der goldne Topf* (The Golden Pot; 1814), and of *Apparitions* (1817). There's also a musical connection to the poems by Wilhelm Müller (1794–1827) that were inspired by visits to the Plauenscher Grund, a dale in southwest Dresden long known for its mills that was also popular with the Romantic painters; he may have considered having the cycle of poems about a young man's hopeless love for a miller's daughter set to music by his friend Weber (dedicatee of his later *Winterreise*) but both died young in 1827 and *Die schöne Müllerin* was instead immortalised by Franz Schubert.

Other early Romantic writers passed through Dresden, as recorded in a museum in the Kügelgenhaus (see page 216), most notably Johann Wolfgang von Goethe (a frequent visitor from his student days in Leipzig until 1813), Friedrich Schiller (who lived in Loschwitz in 1785–87, writing his play *Don Carlos*) and the playwright Heinrich von Kleist, who fell in love with the city, especially its art and above all Raphael's *Sistine Madonna*, in 1802. On his way to Dresden in 1807 Kleist was arrested by the French military as a spy and imprisoned for six months; finally arriving in the autumn of 1807 he founded the journal *Phöbus*, moving to Berlin in 1809.

Dostoyevsky lived here in 1867–71, writing *The Idiot*, *The Devils* and *The Eternal Husband*, and mention must also be made of the American novelist Kurt Vonnegut (1922–2007), who was captured during the Battle of the Bulge and was a prisoner of war in Dresden at the time of its destruction. He was one of just seven Americans to survive the raids, in a cellar of *Schlachthof Funf*, immortalised in the title of his first great success, *Slaughterhouse-Five*. He was set to work collecting corpses for burial, but there were so many that they were simply incinerated with flame-throwers. He drew on his experiences in Dresden in half a dozen novels before being able to move on. Dresden was also home to Erich Kästner, author of *Emil and the Detectives* – see page 213.

ART The Dresden area also played a key role in the development of two of the most important movements in German painting, firstly Romanticism, the foundations for which were laid by two Swiss artists, Anton Graff (1736–1813), who was teaching in Dresden from 1766, and the less well-known Adrian Zingg (1734–1816). The great master of German Romantic painting was Caspar David Friedrich (1774–1840), who was drawn to Dresden by its art treasures in 1798 but became a landscapist here. Ludwig Richter (1803–84) was born in Dresden and became a designer for the Meissen porcelain factory and then a teacher of landscape painting at the Dresden Academy of Art; in addition to his landscapes, his illustrations shaped the classic image of the German fairy tale.

The other movement was known as Die Brücke (The Bridge), founded in Dresden in 1905 by a group of architecture students, including Erich Heckel, Ernst Ludwig Kirchner and Karl Schmidt-Rottluff, who aimed to create a bridge between neo-Romanticism and Expressionism. Otto Dix (1891–1969) was a full-blown Expressionist, who came to Dresden to study painting in 1910 and served in a machine-gun unit from 1915 to 1918. The war left him traumatised and affected all his later work; he painted Dresden in flames years before it actually happened. In 1919 he joined the Dresdner Sezession (the successor to Die Brücke, founded in

BELLOTTO AND CANALETTO

When Dresdeners speak of Canaletto they mean not the great Venetian painter but his nephew Bernardo Bellotto (1720–80), who studied under his uncle and was known by his name when working outside Italy. He was court painter to Elector Friedrich August from 1747 to 1766, painting 14 large-format town views by 1752, followed by etchings of the same subjects and other paintings of nearby towns such as Pirna. He visited Vienna in 1758 and Munich in 1761, and in 1767 went via St Petersburg to Warsaw, where he stayed as court painter until his death. His *vedute* or townscapes are highly detailed and accurate (partly due to the use of the camera obscura), although cooler and darker than his uncle's with heavier shadows, and have been invaluable historical documents in rebuilding Dresden and Warsaw.

1914) then flirted with Dada, collage and Neue Sachlichkeit (New Objectivity); the Nazis regarded him as a degenerate artist and soon had him sacked from his teaching post at the Dresden Academy.

Another Dresden-born artist who made a name for himself with the Dresdner Sezession was Conrad Felixmüller (1897–1977). Gerhard Richter (born 1932) was born in Dresden but moved to teach and paint in Hamburg, Düsseldorf and Köln; he is known for his photo-paintings and abstracts (and for his acerbic views on his fellow artists). Georg Baselitz (born 1938) grew up in the Sorb town of Kamenz, just north of Dresden, and was rejected by the Dresden Academy; however, he was accepted by the academy in East Berlin, later moving to the West and developing into perhaps the best-known German post-war artist.

FESTIVALS Like many European cities, Dresden, in addition to its traditional festivals, now has other cultural events to bring visitors in throughout the year – see pages 128–9 for more. The city's best festival is, in a way, the Striezelmarkt or Christmas Market, which takes over the Altmarkt from the end of November to Christmas Eve (see box, pages 146–7).

Every February the anniversary of the bombing of Dresden is commemorated, with the city's bells tolling in the evening of the 13th for the 20 minutes that the RAF's bombs fell on the city.

The Elbhangfest (Elbe Slope Festival; *www.elbhangfest.de*), on the last weekend of June, takes over the 7km-long stretch of riverbank from Loschwitz to Pillnitz with concerts, drama, art exhibitions, craft markets, fairs and children's events. This is followed in July by the Vogelwiese or Dresden Stadtfest (City Festival), a funfair which is over 400 years old.

The Dresdner Musikfestspiele (Dresden Music Festival; *www.musikfestspiele.com*), held every year in late May and early June, is one of Germany's most important music festivals. In early October there's the Dresden Festival of Contemporary Music (*www.zeitmusik.de*), and in mid May the Dixieland Festival (*www.dixieland.de*), the world's second largest, with half a million people listening to bands on Prager Strasse and on river steamers as well as in concert halls.

27

The 'White Fleet' or Sächsische Dampfschiffahrt (Saxon Steamship Company) turn out their nine historic paddle-steamers for a parade on May Day, and also on 19 August.

GEOGRAPHY AND CLIMATE

Dresden lies in the relatively small hillier part of Germany between the Alps and the great North German Plain; the surrounding countryside is pleasantly rolling, with some vineyards. The city lies on the Elbe, one of central Europe's principal rivers, flowing for 1,091km (678 miles) from the Czech Republic (where it's known as the Labe) and entering Germany through a gap in the Elbsandsteingebirge (Elbe Sandstone Mountains), also known as the Sächsische Schweiz (Saxon Switzerland; see pages 266–77). From here it flows through Dresden, Meissen, Magdeburg and Hamburg, reaching the North Sea at Cuxhaven; there's a great cycle route following pretty much its whole length.

Dresden lies 110m (360ft) above sea level, with its airport at 230m and its highest point, the Triebenburg, at 383m.

The climate is continental, without the moderating effect of the sea, so that summers are warmer and, particularly, winters are colder than in western Europe (and most of Germany), occasionally reaching –20°C. Temperatures in December and January are regularly freezing and may reach only 2°C (36°F), while summers are warm and damp, with average temperatures in July and August around 25°C (77°F). Official temperatures are recorded up at the airport, which is a degree or two colder than the city centre; what's more, temperatures currently seem to be 3–4°C above the 20th-century average. However even summer evenings can be cool, so be sure to have a spare layer to put on.

Precipitation is highest in July and August, with an average 23cm (9.1 inches) in each month, and lowest in January, with an average 9cm (3.5 inches); nevertheless, there are between eight and 11 days with rain every month on average.

NATURAL HISTORY

The river Elbe was for many years regarded as Europe's longest sewer, thanks mainly to the lack of interest of communist governments in controlling pollution. Much of the worst industrial plants were rapidly closed down (for mainly economic reasons) in the 1990s, and over 200 sewage plants were built along the Elbe. Heavy metals and toxic hydrocarbons are now more or less absent. There are now 94 species of fish in the Elbe (64 at Dresden), including lampreys, loach, sea trout, and most significantly, salmon. Beavers, the only ones in central Europe, have survived in the Elbe wetlands, near its mouth.

In Dresden, the Elbe meadows, a floodplain that is frequently under water and has been largely undeveloped, is home to many kinds of invertebrates and birds, including corncrakes, kingfishers, black kites, herons, cormorants, swans, mallards and other ducks such as goldeneye. You'll also see hooded and common crows and in summer storks, nesting on chimneys and utility poles.

2 Planning

THE CITY – A PRACTICAL OVERVIEW

Dresden is split in two by the river Elbe, with the historic Altstadt (Old Town) on the left/south bank and the more arty Neustadt (New Town) on the right/north bank. Each has a mainline railway station and they are linked by four bridges and an extensive tram system. Most of the museums, churches and other sights are in the Altstadt, while the more interesting bars and restaurants are in the Neustadt. The cheapest accommodation is on the Neustadt side, but there are also some upmarket places to stay on this side of the river.

Most of the city's suburbs are on the south side; to the north the city abuts what used to be a huge military preserve, with low hills and forest beyond.

On the river 25km to the west is Meissen, an older city than Dresden that's now known mainly for its porcelain factory but which also has a fine cathedral and castle (see pages 241–54). In the other direction, on the Czech border, is Saxon Switzerland, a beautiful area of sandstone hills that have been carved over the centuries into gorges and table mountains; they are not particularly high, but the cliffs offer some of the finest rock climbing in Germany. There's also an excellent cycle route that follows the river for virtually its whole length.

WHEN TO VISIT (AND WHY)

Dresden is a year-round city, with the Christmas market making December a good time to visit. Many of its attractions are indoors, but nevertheless the warmer weather from May to October makes this the busiest and most obvious season for tourism.

HIGHLIGHTS

The heart of Dresden is the Altstadt or Old Town, on the left/south bank of the Elbe; almost totally flattened in 1945, rebuilding is now nearing completion, and it's been very well done. Strolling through the largely car-free streets it's possible to imagine that the bombing didn't happen, although the remaining communist intrusions take a bit of explaining away. The Baroque jewel of the Zwinger and the Residenzschloss or royal castle are home to most parts of the State Museums, an amazing trove of great art and other treasures, notably porcelain, both from Asia and from Meissen. There are many other museums and art treasures throughout the city, and also some beautiful churches, above all the Catholic cathedral, the Frauenkirche and the Kreuzkirche, all in the Altstadt.

Across the river, the Neustadt or New Town was largely built in the 18th century (and rebuilt after 1945) and is still a classic Baroque streetscape; immediately to its north the Aussere Neustadt or Outer New Town, built in the 19th century, is the bohemian/student quarter and home to the city's liveliest nightlife and an array of interesting ethnic restaurants.

Between the Altstadt and the Neustadt, and stretching a long way beyond, are the Elbe Meadows, flood plains along the river that have been placed on UNESCO's World Heritage list for their historical and scenic value, above all as the setting for Dresden's Altstadt and its marvellous skyline. You can take delightful short walks by the river, or extend them as far as you want – the Elberadweg is a cycle route that follows the whole length of the river to the North Sea.

SUGGESTED ITINERARIES

A **one-day** visit will necessarily concentrate on the Altstadt or Old Town [maps 2 & 3], on the south bank of the Elbe; the reconstructed Frauenkirche (Church of our Lady) is unmissable, as are the Zwinger and some of the museums there and in the Residenzschloss (Royal Palace). Don't forget to stroll along the Brühl Terrace, once known as the Balcony of Europe, overlooking the Elbe Meadows. The Semperoper (opera house), synagogue and two other churches, the Hofkirche (Roman Catholic cathedral) and Kreuzkirche (Church of the Cross), are also well worth a visit. Try to cross the river to the Neustadt or New Town [map 4] if only for the stunning views of the Altstadt skyline. Here there is a fine spacious Baroque streetscape and, if you have an evening in Dresden, the ethnic restaurants, bars and nightlife of the Aussere (Outer) Neustadt.

If you have **two days**, you should spend more time visiting the museums (see *Chapter 10*, page 192), see more of the Neustadt, and walk along the Elbe Meadows; you could also go out to Loschwitz and Pillnitz (see pages 183 and 186) but I'd probably prefer to save that for a three-day visit. With **three or more days** you can also go to Meissen or Saxon Switzerland (see *Chapter 11*, pages 241–54 and 266–77 respectively), both pleasant day trips, although there are plenty of places to stop overnight too.

TOUR OPERATORS (WORLDWIDE)

UK
ACE Study Tours Babraham, Cambridge CB22 3AP; ☎ 01223 835055; e enquiries@acestudytours.co.uk; www.acestudytours.co.uk. Offer slightly less grand tours, including Leipzig, Weimar & Dresden (10 nights for £1,490, or a week for £1,190), Christmas in Dresden (a week for £1,390), 1 side-trip from Bach tours of Leipzig.

DER Travel 18 Conduit St, London W1S 2XN; ☎ 0870 142 0960; e tours@dertour.co.uk; www.dertravel.net, www.dertour.co.uk. Can book hotels, cruises & tours anywhere in Germany.

Great Rail Journeys Saviour Hse, 9 St Saviourgate, York YO1 8NL; ☎ 01904 521936; e grj@greatrail.com; www.greatrail.com. Offer a Colditz & the Great Escape tour (11 days for £1,350–1,450) every 2 weeks in summer, taking the train (first class) from London to Berlin then a bus via Zagan in Poland (to visit the Stalag Luft III prison camp) & Moritzburg before spending 3 nights in Dresden & returning by train via Nürnberg. They will also combine rail travel with a cruise on the Elbe from Prague to Potsdam via Dresden (10 days for £1,795–1,850). Their subsidiary, Rail Select (☎ 01904 527891; www.railselect.com), puts together flexible packages, including Dresden.

Martin Randall Travel Voysey Hse, Barley Mow Passage, London W4 4GF; ☎ 020 8742 3355; e info@martinrandall.co.uk; www.martinrandall.com. Offer a high-powered cultural tour of Dresden & Berlin (£1,690–1,720 for 8 days), as well as extensions to Bach-oriented tours to Leipzig.

Noble Caledonia 2 Chester Cl, London SW1X 7BE; ☎ 020 7752 0000; ℮ info@noble-caledonia.co.uk; www.noble-caledonia.co.uk. Offer excellent cruises, including 7 nights from Prague to Berlin for £995–1,495 pp, based on dbl occupancy (£1,395–1,545 sgl occupancy) including flights & transfers (but not tours of Prague, Pillnitz, Dresden, Meissen, Wittenburg, Magdeburg, Potsdam & Berlin, which cost £195 as an additional package).

Peter Deilmann River & Ocean Cruise, Albany Hse, Suite 101, 324 Regent St, London W1B 3BL; ☎ 0845 310 4400; ℮ info@deilmann.co.uk; www.deilmann.co.uk. Classy operation offering 7 days, Hamburg to Dresden, from €720–1,050 each in a 3-bed cabin to €1,790–2,820 in a suite; 7 days Prague to Potsdam €940–1,490 in a twin cabin to €1,590–2,570 in a sgl.

USA

Great Performance Tours 1 Lincoln Plaza, Suite 32V, New York, NY 10023; ☎ +1 212 580 1400; www.greatperformancetours.com. Offer almost customised trips in pursuit of great music across Europe, including of course Dresden.

Peter Deilmann Europamerica Cruises, 1800 Diagonal Rd, Suite 170, Alexandria, VA 22314; ☎ +1 800 348 8287, +1 703 549 1741; ℮ pdcmail@deilmann-cruises.com; www.deilmann-cruises.com (see above under *UK*)

GERMANY

Peter Deilmann Peter Deilmann Reederei GmbH, Am Holm 25, 23730 Neustadt in Holstein; ☎ +49 4561 3960; ℮ info@deilmann.de; www.deilmann-kreuzfahrten.de (see above under *UK*)

AUSTRIA

Oberösterreich Touristik Freistädter Str 119, A-4041 Linz; ☎ +43 732 727 7200; ℮ info@touristik.at; www.radurlaub.com. Cycle holidays along the Elbe. Will book you a 9-day trip from Dresden to Magdeburg, cycling independently but with your luggage transferred between pre-booked hotels (from €429 pp).

CITY TOURS

BY BUS Several companies offer city tours by bus, with the ability to get on and off as you choose. The most visible is the **Stadtrundfahrt Dresden** (*Königstr 6;* ✆ *899 5650/60;* e *info@stadtrundfahrt.de; www.stadtrundfahrt.de*), which offers a 22-stop tour (covering the Altstadt and Neustadt, the Transparent Factory, the Blue Wonder Bridge and the Elbe castles), as well as a longer excursion to Pillnitz and a nine-stop evening tour (both €12). The city tour costs €18, plus €8 to cover a second day; accompanying children under 14 go free and those aged 15–17 pay €9. With a ticket for the city tour you can also have a free walking tour (guided in English) of the Zwinger, the Fürstenzug and the Frauenkirche (otherwise priced at €5 each). The city tour leaves from Theaterplatz every 15–30 minutes from 09.30 to 17.00 (every 30–60 minutes 10.00–15.00 Nov–Mar, although they're more frequent during Striezelmarkt) and lasts 90 minutes if you don't get off. The Pillnitz tour leaves every three hours from 09.45 to 15.45 (only at 12.45 Nov–Mar), and evening tours leave hourly from 18.00 to 22.00 (16.00 to 19.00 in winter). Tours are on red-and-white double-decker buses (open-topped in summer), with recorded commentaries in major languages. They also put on excursions to Meissen, Saxon Switzerland and Prague.

There's also the smaller **Hummelbahn** operation using red buses (*Feldschlösschenstr 8;* ✆ *494 0404;* e *hummelbahn-dd@web.de; www.stadtrundfahrt-dresden.de*), whose 90-minute tour, including the Zwinger, leaves eight times daily from April to October (with two extra Fri evening trips), and three a day in winter. A similar tour with a visit to Pfunds Molkerei instead leaves four times a day in summer and only at 11.00 from January to March, and both cost €15, free for accompanying children under 12. A longer trip to Pillnitz leaves four times a day (twice in winter) and costs €21, and another including a tour of the Semperoper runs daily all year (€23). A tour to Loschwitz, returning by paddle-steamer, runs only on summer weekends and costs €31.

The **DVB** (which runs Dresden's public transport) also runs tours in white-and-yellow buses, leaving from outside the Kulturpalast (opposite their information centre). A 90-minute Altstadt tour (at 11.00 & 15.30 in summer, 12.30 in winter) costs €10, a one-hour culture tour including a day ticket for the state museums (eight a day in summer, three in winter) costs €15, a two-hour tour including a ride on the Loschwitz funicular runs three times a day (only at 11.15 in winter) and costs €19, and a summer-only 2³/₄-hour tour including funicular and paddle-steamer costs €21 (on all these tours children ride for €3).

ON FOOT There are also historic walking tours of the Altstadt, notably the tour put on by **Barokkokko** (*Trachenberger Str 66;* ℘ *479 8184;* e *barokkoko@web.de; www.erlebnisrundgang.de*), in which a fully wigged and costumed Count Brühl and a lady companion give a champagne reception and take you on a tour of their Baroque haunts; this leaves from the Zwinger's Kronentur at 11.00 and 14.00 and lasts 2¹/₂ hours from April to October (€14) and 1¹/₂ hours in winter (€15.50; €9 all year for ages 7–14).

Others include **Touristic Service Dresden Natalie Blau** (*Baumzeile 13;* ℘ *252 6158;* e *rundgangdresden@hotmail.com; www.dresden-stadtrundgang.de*), with 90-minute tours daily at 10.15, 12.15, 14.15 and 16.15 from Schlossstrasse (€10, free to age 15;

or with a tour of the Semperoper €17); and **Touristischer Extra Service Dresden** (*Am Niedergarten 6, Bannewitz;* ℡ *472 6260;* e *tesdmueller@t-online.de; www.tesd-dd.de*), also with 90-minute tours daily at 10.00, 11.00 and 13.00 from in front of the Schinkelwache (€10). There's also **igeltour** (*Pulsnitzer Str 10;* ℡ *804 4557;* e *igeltour-dresden@t-online.de; www.igeltour-dresden.de*), who offer an excellent range of tours, from an €8 city tour (including the Baroque inner Neustadt) and all kinds of specialised cultural themes (Semper, Schiller, Erlwein, communist architecture, Jehmlich organs, Plauensche Grund, you name it) to tours of Saxon Switzerland (€69).

The **Nightwalk**, a tour of the culture and *Kneipen* (pubs) of the Aussere Neustadt is also good fun, starting at 21.00 at the artesian well on Albertplatz; reserve through the Boofe hostel (*Hechtstr 10;* ℡ *801 3361;* e *info@nightwalk-dresden.de; www.nightwalk-dresden.de*); €10.

OTHER TOURS Perhaps the most entertaining option is the **Trabi Safari** (℡ *899 0066;* e *dresden@trabi-safari.de; www.trabi-safari.de*), a 90-minute tour in a Trabant (open-top if you're lucky, or maybe even the customised Stretch-trabi), costing €25 each for a group of four (€30 each for three or €35 each for two). **Cycling tours** are also available.

BOAT TRIPS

Dresden is home to the famed **White Fleet**, founded in 1836 as the Elbdampfschiffahrtsgesellechaft and offering excursions to Meissen, Saxon

Switzerland and intermediate points more or less continuously since then. Owned since 1992 by a Munich company, the Sächsische Dampfschiffahrt (Saxon Steamship Line) still has nine active historic paddle-steamers, built between 1879 and 1929, as well as two modern salon ships, and carries over 700,000 passengers a year.

In addition to its head office at Hertha-Lindner-Strasse 10 (✆ 866090; e info@saechsische-dampfschiffahrt.de; www.saechsische-dampfschiffahrt.de), the booking office is on the embankment just west of Münzergasse (immediately below the Brühl Terrace). In season (late April to mid October) there's one sailing a day to Pirna and Děčín (in the Czech Republic) and two to Bad Schandau (these and a couple of others calling at Königstein), one to Meissen and four to Pillnitz.

Closer to home, there are four 90-minute tours (the last leaving at 17.00; €11.50), going east to the Blue Wonder Bridge at Loschwitz, and two three-hour World Heritage tours (€18), going east to Pillnitz and west to Übigau. These do not make intermediate stops, but on the longer trips it's possible to board and disembark along the way, with fares from €2.80 (€5.50 return) from Heidenau to Pirna or Pillnitz, €4.80 (€9 return) from Blasewitz to Pillnitz or Dresden, up to €20 from Dresden to Bad Schandau or from Pirna to Děčín (single or return). Children aged six to 14 are charged half price (except where catering is included). A Kombiticket costs €27 (children 6–14 €16.50, a family of two adults with five children €43), allowing travel by the steamers and local transport.

In the shoulder seasons (April and October) some are cancelled or sail only Thursday to Saturday; in winter the vintage paddle-steamers are rested but the two large modern boats keep working, with sailings at 10.30 to Pillnitz (€11) and at 14.00 to the Blue Wonder (€9), both without stops and sailing daily (Thu–Sat during Striezelmarkt); from 29 November to 23 December there's an Advent Cruise to Pillnitz and back from 11.00 to 14.00 daily (€21, or €24 on Sat, with two-course lunch), a Stollen cruise to the Blue Wonder and back from 15.00 to 17.00 (€11, or €13 on Sat, with cake and hot drinks), and a Christmas Lights cruise to Pillnitz and back from 18.30 to 21.30 (€26 Tue–Thu, €30 Fri/Sat, with three-course dinner).

i TOURIST INFORMATION

Plenty of information can be had in advance from both the Dresden Tourism Promotion Board and the German National Tourist Board, which has 11 offices around the world, as well as partnerships with Lufthansa airline offices and the like.

GERMAN NATIONAL TOURIST BOARD

Head office Deutsche Zentrale für Tourismus, Beethovenstraße 69, 60325 Frankfurt am Main; ☎ +49 60 974640; e info@d-z-t.com; www.germany-tourism.de

UK office PO Box 2695, London W1A 3TN; ☎ +44 20 7317 0908, brochures ☎ 09001 600100 (£0.60/min); e gntolon@d-z-t.com; www.germany-tourism.co.uk; ⏲ 10.00–16.00 Mon–Fri

US Office 122 East 42nd St, 20th Floor, Suite 2000, New York, NY 10168-0072; ☎ +1 212 661 7200; e gntonyc@d-z-t.com; www.cometogermany.com

DRESDEN TOURISM PROMOTION BOARD

Dresden-Werbung und Tourismus GmbH Ostra-Allee 11, 01067 Dresden; ☎ +49 351 4919 2100 (room reservations ☎ 4919 2222, advance ticket sales ☎ 2233, guides ☎ 2140); e info@dresden-tourist.de; www.dresden-tourist.de

If you're planning to wander further afield in Saxony, contact the Tourismus Marketing Gesellschaft Sachsen mbH (Saxony Tourism Marketing Corporation) (*Bautzner Str 45, 01099 Dresden;* ☎ *+49 351 49700;* f *496 9306;* e *info@sachsen-tour.de; www.visitsaxony.com*). For information on the city see www.dresden.de; and for the Free State of Saxony www.sachsen.de.

Once in Dresden you'll find two tourist offices, in the Schinkelwache (on Theaterplatz – see page 155) and at Prager Strasse 10 (both ☎ *0351 4919 2233*).

Recommended incoming tourism agencies (offering city and wine tours and walking and cycling holidays) include:

AugustusTours Bischofsweg 64, 01099 Dresden; ☎ +49 351 563480; e info@augustustours.de; www@augustustours.de

Compact Tours GmbH Georgenstr 2A, 01097 Dresden; ☎ +49 351 808090; e service@compact-tours.com; www.compact-tours.com

RED TAPE

Most nationalities will require nothing more than a passport to visit Germany; if you think you might need a visa, contact a German embassy or consulate. Once in Germany you should carry your passport (or national ID card) on you at all times.

If you lose a British passport, the nearest consulate is at the embassy in Berlin (*Wilhelmstr 70, 10117 Berlin;* ☎ *030 204570;* e *consular@british-embassy.de; www.britischbotschaft.de*), which can issue an emergency passport to get you home. However, full British passports are issued only by the consulate in Düsseldorf (*Yorckstr 9, 40476 Düsseldorf;* ☎ *211 94480, 0900 170 0661 (premium rate);* e *consular.section@duesseldorf.mail.fco.gov.uk*).

Hotels will register your details and pass them to the authorities; if you plan to stay in Germany for three months or more you must register with the Residency Registration Office (Einwohnermeldeamt) within seven days of entering Germany. In Dresden this is in the Rathaus (City Hall) at Dr-Kulz-Ring 19 (☎ *0351 4880*).

🇪 GERMAN EMBASSIES

UK 23 Belgrave Sq, London SW1X 8PZ; ☎ 020 7824 1300, 09065 508922. Visa Information Service:
e info@german-embassy.org.uk; www.london.diplo.de; ◷08.30–17.00 Mon–Thu, 08.30–15.30 Fri; passport/visa section: ◷09.00–12.00 Mon–Fri

USA 4645 Reservoir Rd NW, Washington, DC, 20007-1998; ☎ 202 298 4000; www.germany.info;
◷08.30–17.00 Mon–Thu, 08.30–15.30 Fri; visa applications: ◷08.30–11.30

Australia 119 Empire Circuit, Yarralumla ACT 2600; ☎ 02 6270 1911; e info1@germanembassy.org.au;
www.germanembassy.org.au; ◷08.00–17.00 Mon–Thu, 08.00–14.00 Fri; passport & visa section:
◷09.00–12.00 Mon–Fri

One of the best things about Dresden, to my mind, is that there are no low-cost flights from Britain, and thus no weekend stag parties or drunken youths in the gutters. Yet it is easy to get here, with direct flights with British Airways (BA) from early 2007 to Dresden Airport (see page 68), 15–25 minutes by train from the city-centre stations. There are also easy connections at Frankfurt am Main or Munich airports, and it's possible to fly in to various other airports and continue to Dresden. My preference is to come by train, an easy day's travel from London, while driving is also a possibility, in a longer harder day.

✈ **BY AIR** Since March 2007 **British Airways** have flown daily from London Gatwick to Dresden, with fares from £44 each way or £78 return including TFCs (taxes, fees and charges). You can book on www.ba.com, or at a price by ✆ 01805 266522 (€0.14/min; ⏰09.00–18.00 Mon–Sat).

You might prefer the German flag-carrier **Lufthansa** (often code-sharing with its partners in the Star alliance, such as Austrian Airlines, BMI, United and SAS), which has flights to Dresden from Frankfurt, Munich, Düsseldorf and Vienna, with worldwide connections. Cirrus Airlines also flies daily, on behalf of Lufthansa and Swiss, to Zurich, also with worldwide connections. Flying from London, with Lufthansa or BMI, the basic return fare is £259 including taxes; however the best fare from New York is just £268.

Easily the best of the low-fare airlines flying between Britain and Germany is **Air Berlin** (www.airberlin.com), who fly two to four times a day from London Stansted to

Berlin-Tegel, Düsseldorf and Leipzig/Halle, with fares starting from just £20 each way including taxes. From Leipzig/Halle and Berlin it's not far by train to Dresden (see below), while from Düsseldorf Air Berlin fly to Dresden three times a day, with fares from € 32 each way including taxes. There are also connecting flights from Manchester, Glasgow and Belfast via Stansted, costing from £34 each way to Düsseldorf or £55 to Leipzig. Note however that flights currently arrive at Leipzig at 23.00, returning at 06.00. Air Berlin also has many flights from Dresden to holiday destinations in Spain (and north Africa, although these are only available for journeys starting in Germany). Air Berlin has also taken over dba (formerly Deutsche BA), which has flights from Dresden to Düsseldorf and to Munich, the latter connecting to Nice four days a week.

A similar operator is **Germanwings** (*www.germanwings.com*), which flies from London Stansted and Edinburgh to Köln-Bonn (and from Stansted to Stuttgart), with fares from just £12 each way including taxes. From Köln-Bonn (Cologne) they have two flights a day to Dresden, from € 19 each way including taxes; through ticketing from Stansted to Dresden should be possible from mid 2007. **EasyJet** (*www.easyjet.com*) also fly to Köln-Bonn from London Gatwick, from £20 each way including taxes. EasyJet and other low-cost airlines also fly from various British airports to Prague, from where it's 2 hours 45 minutes by train to Dresden. The Slovak low-cost airline **SkyEurope** flies from Prague to Paris, Brussels, Amsterdam, Copenhagen, Barcelona, six Italian cities, and five in the Balkans.

If you must, **Ryanair** flies from Stansted to Altenburg-Nobitz Airport, 75km south of Leipzig. Buses are provided from the airport, costing € 3.50 to the town of Altenburg (12km and 15mins from the airport) and € 12 to Leipzig (1hr 15mins).

From Altenburg you can take a train to Leipzig (€7; 30mins), connecting to Dresden (€26–33; 2hrs 10mins–2hrs 35mins from Altenburg).

Other flights, for German sun-seekers, are operated by the German holiday airline Condor, the Turkish airlines Atlasjet, Inter Airlines, Onur Air, Sky Airlines and SunExpress, and Tunis Air.

⊞ BY RAIL
Airport transfer There are hourly trains **from Leipzig-Halle Flughafen** (airport) to Leipzig for connections to Dresden, taking 90 minutes in all; the fare is between €22.30 and €30.

From Köln-Bonn Flughafen it's possible to reach Dresden in 6½ hours, generally with two changes of train, with regular fares from €102 each way and Sparpreis advance fares from €29; you can also do this with an overnight sleeper train (Nachtzug) and one change of train.

In **Berlin**, easyJet, Ryanair and Jet2 all fly from Britain to Schönefeld Airport, on the south side of the city; from here the **Airport Express** bus runs twice an hour to the new Hauptbahnhof (Central Station) in 27 minutes. Most other airlines use Tegel Airport, linked by bus with the Hauptbahnhof, from where **EuroCity** trains currently leave at 46 minutes past the even hours and take just under two hours to Dresden-Neustadt and seven minutes more to Dresden-Hauptbahnhof. Fares start at €32 each way.

From Schönefeld it is also possible to change at Treptower Park or Ostkreuz to take the ring S-Bahn to the new Sudkreuz interchange and catch the EuroCity train here. Other options (taking up to 4hrs) include **InterCity Express** trains (from Berlin-Hauptbahnhof or Sudkreuz) to Leipzig, costing from €55, or a regional train every two hours to Senftenberg, with connections to Dresden.

In 2011 the new Berlin-Brandenburg International Airport (BBI) will open at Schönefeld, and Tegel and Tempelhof airports will close. There will be a new mainline railway station and an extension of the U7 metro line from Rudow to the new airport. It will be possible to take the U7 to Neukölln and then the ring S-Bahn to Sudkreuz for trains south.

International trains It's perfectly possible to travel overland (and under-Channel) to Dresden, an 06.00 **Eurostar** from London Waterloo to Brussels getting you there at 19.00, the 08.30 at 21.00, and the 10.40 at 23.00. Returning, you can leave at 09.00 (or 10.00 with a tight connection) and reach London at 20.18. For cheaper Eurostar fares you may have to leave later and break your journey overnight; however from November 2007 the Eurostar trains will run from London St Pancras, knocking 24 minutes off the journey to Brussels, and about the same amount of time will also be cut from the Brussels–Köln leg at the same time. Between Frankfurt and Leipzig it's also worth considering a stopover at one or more of the delightful historic towns of Weimar, Erfurt and Eisenach.

Tickets from London to Brussels and as far as Köln, with Eurostar and Thalys trains, can be booked online (*www.eurostar.com*), or for £5 extra plus premium phone charges (✆ *0870 518 6186*). Eurostar fares to Brussels, currently costing from £59 to £89 return, are valid to any Belgian station; Liège–Dresden fares start from

Planning GETTING THERE

2

€129 or £84 (for a Sparpreis 50 ticket, booked well in advance and preferably online) plus reservations and supplements. Certain fares are valid in Belgium only on German trains, but it is possible to book a Eurostar ticket to Köln and then a separate ticket to Dresden. Tickets on German trains, including a couple a day from Brussels, can be booked on www.bahn.de. The night trains can be booked on www.nachtzug.de (and printed by you) – all offer English-language options. German train fares are reasonable in any case, but for long-distance travel you can pay either 25% or 50% less by booking the Sparpreis 25 or Sparpreis 50 fares in advance. You can also make savings by buying the BahnCard 25 (€51.50), which gives a 25% discount and pays for itself if you'll be spending more than €200; for €15 you can add on RailPlus, which gives a 25% discount in Belgium and 19 other countries (but not France or Britain). There are also tickets allowing very cheap long-distance travel on evenings and weekends, and for groups of five or more.

It's also possible to travel in the afternoon via Brussels to Köln (from £69 from London) and continue to Dresden by **Nachtzug** (overnight sleeper train, with a reclining seat costing from €29, a Liegewagen or couchette from €49, or a sleeper from €69), or indeed to leave London after 19.00 and take the Nachtzug from Brussels to Berlin (from £159 return from London in a couchette). You can also have a seat, which is a false economy, or a full sleeper compartment, with one, two or three berths (and breakfast and a shower). You will also have to buy Berlin–Dresden tickets (as above), which can be booked online, unlike the combined Eurostar/sleeper tickets; for these you should call Deutsche Bahn's UK office (℡ 0870 243 5363; e sales@bahn.co.uk; www.bahn.co.uk; ⏱09.00–17.00 Mon–Fri).

You can also buy tickets from European Rail (☏ *020 7387 0444*; *www.europeanrail.com*); don't confuse this with Rail Europe (*178 Piccadilly, London W1*; ☏ *08708 371371*; e *reservations@raileurope.co.uk*; *www.raileurope.co.uk*), which is owned by French Railways and would only be useful for routings via Paris. This might involve the Nachtzug from Paris Est to Stuttgart (from €40 each way with Prems advance online fares), and then an ICE via Fulda to Dresden, arriving at 13.00.

Other agencies in Britain that specialise in European rail bookings include:

Ffestiniog Travel Harbour Station, Porthmadog, Gwynedd LL49 9NF; ☏ 01766 512400;
e info@ffestiniogtravel.co.uk; www.festtravel.co.uk/index.php?ffestiniog=tickets
International Rail Chase Hse, Gilbert St, Ropley, Hants SO24 0BY; ☏ 0870 084 1410;
e sales@internationalrail.com; www.international-rail.com
Trainseurope 4 Station Approach, March, Cambs PE15 8SJ; ☏ 0871 700 7722;
e enquiries@trainseurope.co.uk; www.trainseurope.co.uk

The bible for information about rail travel in Europe is www.seat61.com.

There are also sleeper trains to Dresden from Basle, Wiesbaden and Frankfurt, Stuttgart and Munich, arriving at 07.00 and continuing to Prague (09.20). Another leaves Dresden eastbound at 21.00 (and Bad Schandau at 21.30) and splits into three portions, for Vienna (06.00); Brno, Bratislava (06.00) and Budapest (10.00); and Ostrava, Poprad-Tatry (08.30) and Košice (10.00). To Vienna and Košice there are only sleeper cars, from €30 and €20 respectively, but to Budapest you can also travel in a seat (€3.50 reservation fee) or couchette (from €13.40).

EuroCity trains (from Hamburg and Berlin) leave from Dresden to Prague every two hours (09.00 to 19.00), taking 2 hours 15 minutes; two of these continue to Brno, Bratislava and Budapest (9hrs) and two to Vienna (7hrs). Although Dresden is not far from the Polish border, links are surprisingly poor, with regional trains every two hours to Görlitz for connections to Wrocław (still better known to Germans as Breslau), taking between four and 4$^{1}/_{2}$ hours in all. There's a similar service to Cottbus, further north, but for Warsaw and northern Poland you'd be better off going via Berlin.

ICE (InterCity Express) trains run hourly from Dresden west to Leipzig, Weimar, Erfurt, Eisenach, Frankfurt and Frankfurt-Flughafen (often the best place to make connections for western Germany), many continuing to Wiesbaden and elsewhere. Eastern Germany's main north–south line, from Berlin to Munich, runs through Leipzig, so for many destinations you'll find yourself changing trains there. There are direct trains to Nürnberg every two hours, but they take a little longer, due to extremely curvaceous terrain. There is also a fairly dense network of local railways, with linking bus services filling the gaps.

Saxony is famed for its narrow-gauge steam railways, still filling a role as public transport and indeed operated by the Deutsches Bundesbahn (German Federal Railways); just outside Dresden, one of these links Radebeul, Moritzburg and Radeburg – see page 236.

The private operator InterConnex (❧ 03581 76760, 01805 101617 (€0.14/min); www.interconnex.com, www.connex-sachsen.de) has a contract to run the branch line from Leipzig to Geithain and also operates a couple of open-access services, with a daily train from Görlitz to Leipzig, calling at Dresden Neustadt at 07.56 (returning from Leipzig at 13.20 and from Dresden at 15.00), and a Saturday-only train from Dresden (at 07.11) to Berlin and Stralsund, returning on Sunday. These offer cheap fares but are of course of interest only if you want to travel at those precise times. Tickets are sold on the train, and the Dresden–Leipzig fare is just €12 (€8.40 for those under 26, or €9 for all on Sat), versus €19.40 on the hourly DB service or €27 by ICE.

Information on German Railways services is available on ☎ 0800 150 7090 (free); or www.bahn.de/sachsen.

In 2007 the InterRail and EuroDomino passes, allowing respectively unlimited travel across Europe and within specific countries, were combined into one single InterRail Pass (*www.interrailnet.com*). The InterRail Global Pass is valid for travel in all 31 InterRail countries and the InterRail One Country Pass for travel within a single country. Morocco has dropped out, but just about every European country is involved (as well as the 'Attica' ferries between Greece and Italy), although it's not possible to buy a pass for the country in which you are resident.

There's a range of options for both passes, with first- and second-class adult and second-class youth (ages 12–25) tickets available for any five days' travel within a ten-day period (£237/179/114), ten days within a 22-day period (£352/258/172), 22 days continuous validity (£453/431/222) and one month's continuous validity (£582/431/287) for the Global Pass. The One Country Pass for Germany is valid for any three days within a month (£184/136/114), four days (£205/150/100), six days (£261/193/126) and eight days (£291/215/140); passes for many other countries are considerably cheaper than this. You'll also have to pay for some high-speed supplements and for night trains.

For those resident outside Europe (and Russia, Turkey, Morocco, Algeria and Tunisia) there's the Eurail range of passes, covering 18 countries: the Global Pass gives first-class travel for all or second class for under-26s (US$635/415 for 15 days' continuous travel, US$1,025/655 for a month, US$1,445/940 for two months or US$1,785/1,160 for three months). The Global Pass Flexi gives either ten days within two months (US$749/448) or 15 days (US$987/639); the Select Pass gives travel in a group of countries for between US$404/263 for five days within two months in three countries, to US$891/581 for 15 days within two months in five countries. There are also passes covering Germany with any one of France, Switzerland, Benelux, Denmark or Austria, but there's no single-country pass for Germany. Passes also give reductions on travel with various private railways, buses and ferries.

When you reach Dresden InterCity and InterCity Express trains from elsewhere in Germany call first at Dresden Neustadt (handy for hostels and budget accommodation) and then cross the Elbe to the Hauptbahnhof or main station. The Neustädterbahnhof, as it's also known, was built in 1901 and refurbished in 1997–98, with a Pei-esque glass pyramid added over the main hall; this has a beautiful ceiling and the world's second-largest porcelain mosaic (a 90m^2 montage of Saxon palaces, castles and gardens), added in 2001. There are ATMs, a biggish bookshop with lots of foreign newspapers, a restaurant (⏲ *from 07.00 Mon–Fri, 10.00 Sat/Sun*), snack counters, and the Point supermarket, as well as a Lidl (the

Ryanair of supermarkets, not even providing baskets) outside at its southern end. Buses to Moritzburg and Radeburg (see page 231) leave from outside. Just south of platform 10 is the very dilapidated old Leipziger Bahnhof, the city's second railway station, dating from 1847.

The Hauptbahnhof (where trains from Prague and Nürnberg also arrive; see page 161) is still being rebuilt in parts, but is entirely functional. Lockers are available for €2.50 for 24 hours, and with extra payment to a maximum 72 hours. There's an excellent restaurant, Le Marché (↘ 4389 9010; www.marche-restaurants.com), with buffet service and a bakery/coffee bar and kids' area; it's actually worth coming early for the brunch on Sundays and holidays (⏱10.00–14.00; €10).

BY BUS In general buses are kept for local traffic in Germany, with trains used for longer distances, but even so **Bayern Express** (Bahnhofplatz 5, 95028 Hof; ↘ 09281 2252, 0180 123 9287) does operate a daily service (05.30 Mon–Sat, 15.15 Sun) from Bayrische Strasse, on the south side of Dresden Hauptbahnhof, to Chemnitz, Hof, Bayreuth, Nürnberg, Ingoldstadt and Munich, arriving at the Hauptbahnhof at 12.30 (22.15 on Sun). Fares are €27 to Bayreuth, €35 to Nürnberg and €53 to Munich, €38/49/74 return (or €19/24/35 and €34/44/66 if bought in advance). Bohemia Express (↘ 01802 443443, €0.06/call; www.rvd.de) has a service to Prague at 06.25 daily, charging €15 single/€26 return. **Taeter Tours** (www.taeter-tours.de) has a service to Wrocław (Breslau) in Poland at 05.30 daily (also picking up at the Neustadt station, Dresden Airport and Görlitz), returning at 18.30; fares are €19 single/€35 return (€13.30/25 for those under 26).

Touring (*www.touring.de*), the Eurolines partner in Germany, does have a network of international coach services operated by Berlin Linien Bus (*www.berlinlinienbus.de*), mainly for the benefit of eastern Europeans coming to work in Germany. Many of those starting from Berlin call in Dresden (Bayrische Str), including overnight services to Budapest (at 19.30, except Mon and Tue) and Vienna (23.30 except Mon and Wed). Longer slogs include those to Kiev (19.15 Tue, Thu & Sat); Sofia, Plovdiv and Varna in Bulgaria (13.30 Mon & Fri, with two nights on the move). There are also services to Sarajevo, Košice, Minsk, Vilnius and other remoter locations. Sample fares are €29 single/€52 return to Prague (€27/47 for ages 13–26, over 60s & students), €40/71 and €36/64 to Vienna, €53/96 and €49/87 to Budapest, and €83/140 and €75–126 to Sofia. A new service (Mon & Fri) connects into the Berlin–London bus, arriving at Victoria Bus Station at noon the next day, with departures from London on Tuesday and Sunday; fares are €88 single/155 return (reduced rate €70/124).

BY CAR Dresden lies immediately south of the A4 autobahn from Köln (Cologne), Eisenach and Chemnitz in the west to Görlitz and the Polish border to the east; it's joined at Chemnitz by the A9 from Munich and Nürnberg and just west of Dresden by the A14 from Hannover, Magdeburg and Leipzig. The A13 from Berlin joins the A4 just to the north of Dresden, right by the airport, and continues around the southeast of the city as the A17 to the Czech border and Prague. From the Channel Tunnel you should head for Dunkerque then take the A25 to Lille and cut through southern Belgium (past Mons, Cherleroi, Namur and Liège) to Köln.

Dresden is 108km by road from Leipzig, 205km from Berlin, 314km from Nürnberg, 572km from Köln,152km from Prague and 461km from Vienna.

As you probably know, there is no overall speed limit on German autobahns, but there is a 'recommended speed' of 130km/h (80mph). In fact about half their length is in any case subject to local or temporary limits, and buses, trucks and vans over 3.5 tonnes and cars hauling trailers are limited to 80km/h, with the exception of buses and trailers certified for 100km/h. The A4 between Chemnitz and Dresden, where traffic levels are still low by the standards of western Germany, is, alas, known as a racing stretch for those keen to see how fast their car will go.

You must be 18 years old to drive in Germany, and must carry a valid driving licence (not necessarily a photo-licence), insurance certificate and car registration documents in the car. If the owner is not present you should have his/her written permission to use the vehicle. For informaton on hiring a car, see page 76.

✚ HEALTH *with Dr Felicity Nicholson*

Visitors from European Union member states should carry the credit card-style European Health Insurance Card (EHIC), as the paper E111 form is no longer valid. This can be obtained from the post office using form T7 or online at www.ehic.org.uk. This entitles you to any medical treatment that becomes necessary during your trip because of either illness or an accident. This may not include all the things you get under the NHS, though, and sometimes 'co-payments'

Gordon Rattray www.able-travel.com

Although Dresden's cobbled Old Town can mean a bumpy ride for wheelchair users, most disabled travellers should be able to enjoy this city as much as anyone. Germany's current campaign 'Tourism without Barriers' encourages accessible accommodation and transport, and even boasts personal guides who can communicate in sign language.

GETTING THERE AND AROUND

Air At Dresden Airport all levels are accessible by lift, including the underground S-Bahn station. There are accessible toilets and telephones in the building and non-ambulant visitors can expect to be carried by trained staff to and from the plane using an aisle chair.

Road and rail Many buses and trams are 'low-floored', allowing easier access, and by 2010 the whole of Dresden's fleet should be of this type.

Rail travellers must call ☎ 01805 512512 to book assistance at stations, and it is sometimes possible for the disabled person or their assistant to travel free of charge or at a reduced rate. As well as booking, it is important to follow routine and announce to the platform manager in good time that you will need assistance; in Germany I have been pointedly ignored by staff (and have subsequently seen my train depart without me) for not doing this.

Taxis Several taxi companies in the city run wheelchair-accessible vehicles. Rates are on a par with standard cars and you must call ☎ +49 (0) 351 211211 one day in advance to book.

TRAVEL INSURANCE Travel insurance can be purchased from Age Concern (☎ 0845 601 2234; www.ageconcern.org.uk), who have no upper age limit, and Free Spirit (☎ 0845 230 5000; www.free-spirit.com), who cater for people with pre-existing medical conditions. Most insurance companies will insure disabled travellers, but it is essential that they are made aware of your disability.

FURTHER INFORMATION Both www.germany-tourism.de and www.dresden.de carry information (in English) for disabled visitors, and specific queries can be posed to the Dresden Tourist Office (see page 40).

An information booklet *Dresden – für Gäste mit Handicap* (*Dresden – for Disabled Visitors*) can be obtained by calling ☎ +49 (0) 351 4919 2100 or emailing e prospekt@dresden-tourist.de, but is available in German only.

Natko (National Tourism Co-ordination Agency for All People) is the central organising body on the subject, although again, its website – www.natko.de – is in German only.

are necessary. The EHIC also covers any treatment you need for chronic disease or pre-existing illness. However, you will need to make arrangements in advance for kidney dialysis and oxygen treatment. Even if you are carrying an EHIC card you are strongly advised to have separate and comprehensive travel insurance.

Bird flu (avian influenza) was found in domestic poultry in Saxony in April 2006, as well as in dead cats and wild birds. The risk to humans is minimal, but do ensure that egg and poultry dishes are properly cooked.

TRAVEL CLINICS AND HEALTH INFORMATION A full list of current travel clinic websites worldwide is available on www.istm.org. For other journey preparation information, consult www.tripprep.com. Information about various medications can be found at www.emedicine.com/wild/topiclist.htm.

SAFETY

Dresden is very safe to visit and crime levels are low. Tourists may occasionally be the victims of pickpockets, but this is less of a problem here than in many European cities. As anywhere, take the basic precautions of not leaving bags unattended and keeping your valuables hidden – indeed, don't leave anything on display in an unattended car. There's an efficient police force, often seen patrolling on foot, and many officers speak some English. If you are guilty of some misdemeanour you'll have little choice but to accept your punishment – attempting to bribe the police will only make things much worse. You should carry identification at all times, in the form of a passport or ID card, although a photocopy of the key pages of your passport should usually suffice.

The European emergency phone number is ☏ 112.

WHAT TO TAKE/ELECTRICITY/PLUGS

There's little need to bring anything more than you'd need to visit any other northern European city. You should be ready for a bit of cold or rain, or a bit of heat, but nothing excessive. You might want a camera, sunglasses, a travel alarm, a corkscrew, or good walking shoes, but nothing more exotic.

The electric supply is 220 Volts 50 Hertz, using the standard northern European twin-pin plug. If you did not bring an adaptor many hotels will be able to lend you one, and they can be bought in larger supermarkets and department stores.

$ MONEY AND BUDGETING

MONEY The currency of Germany is the euro, comprising 100 cents. There are seven different banknote denominations, each with a distinctive colour and size (the larger the denomination, the larger the note) to aid identification for the visually impaired. The denominations, with colour, are: €5 (grey), €10 (red), €20 (blue), €50 (orange), €100 (green), €200 (yellow-brown) and €500 (purple).

The most useful notes to carry are 10, 20 and 50 euros, which are accepted by most automated ticket machines.

Coins also increase in size, and therefore weight, with increasing value. The denominations are 1, 2, 5, 10, 20 and 50 cents, €1 and €2. For information on banks, exchanging currency, credit cards, ATMs and travellers' cheques, see *Chapter 3*, page 61.

BUDGETING Dresden is surprisingly affordable for a tourist hotspot – no doubt prices will rise, but for the time being they are considerably lower than in Berlin or western Germany. Of course it's possible to spend a small fortune, but it's equally possible to find bargains and have a good time without breaking the bank.

The breakdown below lists daily costs per person, based on two people sharing average-priced accommodation during summer. Solo travellers might pay more for a bed, but probably less on swish restaurant and bar bills, which is where real damage can be done. If a breakfast buffet is on offer, as it often is, make the most of it!

Shoestring You can just about live on €25–30 per day if you sleep in a hostel dorm, travel everywhere on foot, look from the outside but don't pay to go in, self-cater at the supermarket, grab a cheap coffee and drink a couple of beers in the park.

Modest If you want a private room and a just a little indulgence, you'll get by on €40 per day by taking a room in a hostel and buying a Dresden City-Card for free public transport and entry to museums and galleries. You could also eat a simple lunch and dinner and have a couple of drinks in a local pub.

Comfortable For around €60 per day you can get a good weekend rate at a tourist hotel or rented apartment. See a few more sights, stop for coffee and cakes, buy some souvenirs, take a modest meal in a mid-price restaurant and finish up with drinks on a stylish summer terrace.

Indulgent With an allowance of €100 per day you can really mix it with the bourgeoisie. Book a swish four-star hotel, take a boat tour on the Elbe, browse the Neustadt's boutiques, stop for coffee and cakes whenever you fancy it, dine in a top-class restaurant, go to the Semperoper and drink cocktails in one of the city's most stylish bars.

Ouch! If money is no object, check into the best room at the Hotel Taschenberg Palais, wine and dine at the Michelin-starred Carousel restaurant, get top seats at the opera, and buy the most grandiose Meissen porcelain. I'm not going to put a budget on this because, like all life's luxuries, if you need to know the price you probably can't afford it.

TIPPING A service charge is included in café and restaurant bills, but it's still customary to leave a tip of about 10% (as also for a taxi). If you have rounded up the bill and don't want change, say *Stimmt so*.

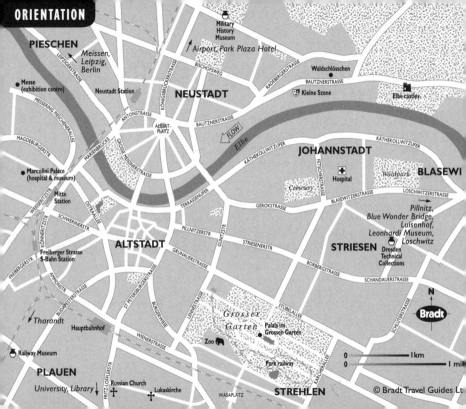

ORIENTATION

PIESCHEN

Meissen,
Leipzig,
Berlin

Messe
(exhibition centre)

Military
History
Museum

Airport, Park Plaza Hotel

BISCHOFSWEG

Waldschlösschen

BAUTZNERSTRASSE

Kleine Szene

Elbe castles

Neustadt Station

NEUSTADT

ALBERT-
PLATZ

BAUTZNERSTRASSE

FLOW

Elbe

KÄTHEKOLLWITZUFER

JOHANNSTADT

BLASEWI

Marcolini Palace
(hospital & museum)

Hospital

Waldpark

Mitte
Station

GEROKSTRASSE

BLASEWITZERSTRASSE

LOSCHWITZERSTRASSE

Cemetery

Pillnitz,
Blue Wonder Bridge,
Luisenhof,
Leonhardi Museum,
Loschwitz

Freiberger Strasse
S-Bahn Station

ALTSTADT

PILLNITZERSTR

STRIESENERSTR

STRIESEN

BORBERGSTRASSE

Dresden
Technical
Collections

GRUNAERSTRASSE

SCHANDAUERSTRASSE

Tharandt

Hauptbahnhof

WIENERSTRASSE

Grosser
Garten

STÜBELALLEE

N

Zoo

Palais im
Grossen Garten

Bradt

Railway Museum

Park railway

0   1 km
0   1 mi

PLAUEN

University, Library

Russian Church

Lukaskirche

WASAPLATZ

STREHLEN

© Bradt Travel Guides Lt

3 Practicalities

$ BANKS

There's no shortage of banks in Dresden, and a wider choice of ATMs (Geldautomat or Bankomat) – these are often inside lobbies, rather than on the street, with an EC symbol displayed outside. Most recognise foreign cards and offer the option of instructions in English or other languages. Debit cards and credit cards are widely accepted; travellers' cheques can be changed at banks, although they're an expensive way to carry money, and they can't generally be used to pay for hotels, meals or fuel, as in the US.

The only American bank is CitiBank, with branches at St-Petersburger-Strasse 18B (*just off Prager Str;* ↘ *494203* [map 2]) and Schillerplatz 6 (*Blasewitz;* ↘ *316840* [map 1]).

Banks are mostly open 09.00–12.00 and 15.00–18.00 Monday–Friday; outside these hours the only place to change cash is the ReiseBank Dresden at the Hauptbahnhof (🕐 *08.00–19.30 Mon–Fri, 09.00–12.00 & 12.30–16.00 Sat, 09.00–13.00 Sun*).

By the way, the Dresdner Bank, founded here in 1872, moved to Frankfurt am Main after World War II, becoming one of Germany's largest banks. In 1995 it bought the merchant bankers Kleinwort Benson (now Dresdner Kleinwort), and in 2002 was itself bought by the insurance company Allianz.

61

MEDIA

Dresden's main newspapers are the *Sächsische Zeitung* and *Dresdner Neueste Nachrichtungen*; the *Sächsische Zeitung* is still based in the Haus der Presse on Ostra Allee, built by the communists to keep the media under tight control.

The best range of foreign newspapers (*The Independent*, *The Guardian*, *Daily Mail*, *Financial Times* and *The Sun* from Britain; the *International Herald Tribune*, *Wall Street Journal* and *USA Today* from the USA; Spain's *El País* and Italy's *Corriere della Sera*, for instance) can be found at the Ludwig shop at the Neustadt station. The luxury hotels also sell a few of these, for instance the *FT* and the *Herald Tribune* at the Kempinski Taschenberg Palais, and the *Herald Tribune*, *USA Today* and *The Guardian* at the Hilton.

There are a couple of free listings magazines, *Dresdner Kulturmagazin* (*www.dresden.nu*) and the monthly *Frizz* (*www.frizz-dresden.de*), as well as *SAX* (*www.cybersax.de*), which costs € 1.30. All are very much youth- and party-oriented, with coverage of the clubbing scene dominant.

COMMUNICATIONS

✉ **POST** The main **post office** is at Webergasse 1 in the Altstadt (⏱09.30–20.00 Mon–Sat), with other branches nearby at Prager Strasse 12 (same hours) and Annenstrasse 10 (⏱09.00–12.30 & 13.30–18.00 Mon–Fri, 09.30–12.00 Sat) with stamp machine, DHL, ATM available 24 hours a day; across the river the Neustadt branch is at Königsbrücker Strasse 21 (🕒 *09.00–19.00 Mon–Fri, 10.00–13.00 Sat*), with stamp machine and ATM available 24 hours a day.

(**TELEPHONE** The German **telephone** system is very efficient, but note that numbers can have any number of digits, as subsidiary numbers can just get added on as required (especially for faxes). The same sort of thing applies to local codes – a major city will have a short simple code (followed by a long number), while a village will have a long code, but then a shorter number.

To make an international call, dial 00 then the country code (eg: 1 for the USA and Canada, 44 for the UK), then the town code and number. Calling Germany from abroad, the code is 49. In Germany, toll-free numbers mostly begin with 0800, but you may still come across some old 0130 numbers. Public phones mostly use phonecards, available from post offices and newsagents; these are for a fixed sum, with value deducted as you use them. There are also some credit-card phones, in airports, major railway stations and some tourist sights.

Germans love their mobile phones (*Handis*), which work on the GSM system, so that almost no US cellphone will work here. In any case remember that using your own mobile here (unless you buy a German SIM card) will be expensive, as you'll be paying international rates to call home, and the same again if in fact you're calling a number here, as it's charged as a call home and back again.

Directory information is online at www.teleauskunft.de (with English, French and Spanish options) or by calling ☎ 11880.

ⓔ INTERNET Most Germans who want it have **internet access** at home, but there are some internet centres catering for travellers, especially in the backpacker area of the Aussere Neustadt. In addition to those in hostels, these include the Internet Telecafé at Böhmische Strasse 3, just off Alaun Strasse (€2/hr); and the Spielothek (video games arcade) at Friedrich-Wolf-Strasse 2, opposite the Neustadt station. In the Altstadt, there are four terminals upstairs in the Joker Spielothek at the east end of Webergasse (€3/hr).

There are far more places offering Wi-Fi (known here as 'wireless LAN'), if you have a laptop with you; these include all the top hotels, some backpacker hostels and the Materni Strasse youth hostel, and many of the Neustadt bars and restaurants.

German web addresses are very simple – generally all you have to do is add '-dresden.de' to an establishment's name (using 'ae', 'ue' etc instead of letters with umlauts).

ⓔ EMBASSIES

All embassies in Germany are now in Berlin, a couple of hours from Dresden, rather than the former capital Bonn.

Australia Friedrichstr 200, 10117 Berlin Mitte; ☎ 880 0880; e info@australian-embassy.de; www.australian-embassy.de
Canada Friedrichstr 95, 10117 Berlin Mitte; ☎ 203120; e brlin-cs@dfait-maeci.gc.ca; www.kanada-info.de
France Kochstr 6/7, 10969 Berlin Mitte; ☎ 2063 9000; e info@botschaft-frankreich.de; www.botschaft-frankreich.de

Ireland Friedrichstr 200, 10117 Berlin Mitte; ☎ 220720
New Zealand Friedrichstr 60, 10117 Berlin Mitte; ☎ 206210; e nzemb@t-online.de
UK Wilhelmstr 70-71, 10117 Berlin Mitte; ☎ 204570; e info@britischebotschaft.de; www.britischebotschaft.de
USA Neustädtische Kirchstr 4-5, 10117 Berlin Mitte (moving to Pariser Platz in early 2008); ☎ 83050;
e (consular) consberlin@state.gov; www.usembassy.de

✚ HOSPITALS AND PHARMACIES

Dresden's main hospital is the Universitätsklinikum Carl Gustav Carus at Fetscherstrasse 74 (☎ 4580; e info@uniklinikum-dresden.de; www.uniklinikum-dresden.de [map1]); it's to the east of the centre, reached by tram 12 from the Altstadt and tram 6 from the Neustadt. Call ☎ 112 for an ambulance.

Pharmacies (*Apotheken*) are marked by a distinctive red 'A' sign and are generally open roughly 08.30–12.30 and 15.00–19.30 Monday to Saturday. There will be always at least one open outside these hours – details are posted outside the pharmacies and in local papers, or at www2.dastelefonbuch.de/apotheken.html. Citizens of EU countries should travel with an EHIC (European Health Insurance Card), which has replaced the British E111 form (see page 53).

The Verband der Körperbehinderten (Physically Handicapped Society) (☎ 472 4942; www.kompass-dresden.de) has an advice centre at Michelangelostrasse 2 (🕒 09.00–15.00 Mon–Thu, 09.00–14.00 Fri). There's also the Notdienst für Rollstuhlnutzer, a 24-hour repair service for wheelchairs (☎ 44300, 0172 350 3012; www.ord.de).

LOCAL TOUR OPERATORS AND TOURIST INFORMATION

See pages 35–7 and 39–40.

RELIGIOUS SERVICES

The main churches in the Altstadt are the Hofkirche (Roman Catholic cathedral; see page 206) and the Lutheran Frauenkirche and Kreuzkirche (see pages 193 and 228); the main church in the Neustadt is the Dreikönigskirche (Church of the Three Kings; see page 227).

Services in the cathedral are at 08.30 and 18.00 Monday to Friday, 18.00 Saturdays, and 07.30, 09.00, 10.30 and (in Polish) 16.30 on Sundays. At the Frauenkirche services are at noon Monday to Saturday, 18.00 Monday to Friday and 11.00 and 18.00 on Sunday. At the Kreuzkirche services are at 09.30 on Sundays, with prayers and organ music at 17.00 on Wednesdays.

The synagogue, with services on Saturdays, is on the eastern edge of the Altstadt (see page 157).

LAUNDRY

The Eco-Express SB-Waschsalon chain of laundromats (*www.waschsalon.de*) has branches at Rudolf-Leonhardt-Strasse 16 and Königsbrücker Strasse 2, both in the Aussere Neustadt, and Grossenhainer Strasse 135, just southeast of Trachenberger

Platz; all are open 06.00–23.00 Monday to Saturday. The Rudolf-Leonhardt-Strasse charges €1.50 for a 5kg load until 11.00, and then €2; the others charge €1.90 until 11.00 and then €2.40. A load of up to 14kg costs €5, and drying costs €0.50 per ten minutes. There's also Waschladen at Louisenstrasse 6 (⏰ 07.00–23.00 Mon–Sat).

Frauenkirche

4 Local Transport

AIRPORT TRANSFER

Dresden Airport (international code DRS, although shown as DD-Flughafen on trains and buses) is 9km north of the city and linked to it by train twice hourly. It's a modern terminal, opened in 2001, and a new runway is now being added to handle the double-decker A380 from 2008. Arriving on Level 0, you'll find an ATM, change machine and a café; the railway station is below on Level −1, while there's a restaurant on Level 2 and a viewing platform on Level 3. **Taxis** are available in front of the terminal on Level 0 (requiring about 15–30 minutes and €15 to reach the city centre), together with a bus stop, although buses run only to local destinations such as Klotzsche and Radebeul. If you want to get into town you should take the **train** (see *Chapter 2*, pages 44–5); the airport is in the central Dresden tariff zone so that a single ticket allows you to ride trams and buses for an hour to reach your destination (see below for more). Trains currently leave at 15 and 46 minutes past the hour on S-Bahn line 2, reaching Neustadt in 13 minutes and Hauptbahnhof in 23 minutes, and continuing to Heidenau or Pirna.

The **airport information** phone number is ☎ 0351 881 3360 (*www.dresden-airport.de*) and for baggage enquiries ☎ 881 4050. It's worth mentioning the amazing number of last-minute flight/holiday outlets here (such as Bucher Last Minute,

EuroSun, Holiday Express, LMTS, Neckermann Last Minute Specials and Reiseland) – if you're in Dresden and suddenly need a break in the sun, it's well worth the trip out to the airport. There are also regular offices of the holiday companies TUI (✆ 881 4720; www.tui.com), Thomas Cook (✆ 881 4710; www.thomascook.de) and Neckermann (✆ 881 5120; www.neckermann-reisen.de).

TRAMS, TRAINS AND BUSES [map 6]

TRAMS As you might expect almost anywhere in northern continental Europe, Dresden has a comprehensive and thoroughly integrated public transport system. Its backbone is a 200km tram network that is being upgraded from a communist rollercoaster into a modern mass-transit system. This means that there are always sections of track that are closed for rebuilding, with replacement buses, but there's plenty of information provided, in *Achtung! Orange* leaflets, by calling ✆ 857 1011, or online at www.dvbag.de, clicking on *Linienänderungen*.

Tram lines 3, 4, 9 and 11 and buses 61 and 82 now run every ten minutes Monday to Saturday. Many of Dresden's trams are modern articulated beasts, and some are the longest trams in the world at 45m from end to end; they are also very high-tech inside, with screens giving details of the next three stops.

MOUNTAIN RAILWAYS The city also boasts two vintage Bergbahnen or mountain railways, both running from Loschwitz to the villa quarter above. One is the Standseilbahn or funicular, opened in 1895 from Körnerplatz to Weisser Hirsch and running every 10–15 minutes daily from 08.10 to 20.23; the other, just to the east, is the Schwebebahn, the world's only mountain monorail, opened in 1901. This runs every 10–15 minutes from 10.00 to 17.45 (to 19.50 Apr–Oct) and has viewing galleries at its upper terminal. Both close for maintenance in November and March, though not at the same time. They are not covered by normal city tickets, each costing an extra €3 (children and bikes €2) single, €4/2.50 for a day return, or €10 for a family.

S-BAHN TRAINS Like any self-respecting German city, Dresden also has S-Bahn trains, but it's a pretty rudimentary network. The main route is the 78km line S1, from Meissen in the west, running along the main line through the city to Pirna and Schöna on the Czech border. There's also line S2, using a short branch from the airport and running through the city to Heidenau or Pirna, and S3, from the Hauptbahnhof to Tharandt in the southwest. All lines run twice an hour, with lines S1 and S2 giving a combined service of four trains an hour between Dresden-Neustadt and Pirna (although not quite at a regular 15-minute interval); regional trains from the Hauptbahnhof (Central Station) to Leipzig and the north give a more frequent service between Hauptbahnhof, Mitte and Neustadt. There are also now two trains an hour on the line west through Friedrichstadt and Cossebaude to Coswig, although this is not an S-Bahn route. In addition to zonal tickets covering Dresden and the Upper Elbe region (see opposite) you can also buy a Sachsen-Ticket, allowing up to five people together (and any number of children) to travel for a day (09.00–03.00 Mon–Fri, from midnight Sat/Sun) on local trains only throughout Saxony, Saxony-Anhalt and Thuringia; it's available from machines and online for €26. There's also the Schönes-Wochenede-Ticket (Happy Weekend Ticket) which allows travel for a group of up to five people on local trains anywhere in Germany on Saturday or Sunday from midnight until 03.00 the next day, and costs €33 from a machine or online; both tickets cost €2 more at a sales desk.

BUSES Buses connect with trams in the suburbs, and some buses also run to the city centre, using the tram trackways and platforms. Regional buses don't quite penetrate the centre but run from places like the Neustadt station and Ammonstrasse, just west of the Hauptbahnhof.

FARES The DVB (Dresdner Verkehrsbetriebe), which runs the city's buses and trams, the RVD (Regionalverkehr Dresden), which runs regional buses, the DB (German Railways) and many local bus companies are members of the VVO (Verkehrsverbund Oberelbe or Upper Elbe Transport Alliance), which sets zonal **fares** for the whole region. A single ticket within one zone (such as the whole of Dresden, stretching out to the airport, Plauen, Loschwitz and Pillnitz) currently costs €1.80 for an hour, or €1.30 for those aged 6–14). You can also buy four single tickets for €6.50 (€4.50 for a child) or four short-trip tickets (also valid for an hour) for €4.50 (€3.50 for a child). A day ticket (to 04.00 the next day) also costs €4.50 for one zone, or €3.50 for those aged six to 14 or over 60.

For two zones a single ticket (valid for 90 mins) costs €3.50 (€2.50 for a child) and a day ticket costs €7.50/€6.20; a single for three zones (extending from

Dresden to Meissen or Bad Schandau and lasting 2hrs) costs €5.10/3.60 and for four or more €6.80/€4.80 (for 4hrs). A day ticket for three or more zones costs €11/9.20. Family day tickets (for up to two adults and four children) costs €6 for one zone, €10 for two, or €14 for three or more. There are also seven-day, monthly and annual season tickets available.

You can also buy an all-zone Nachtticket (Night Ticket) for €6, valid from 18.00 to 06.00. A basic network of night trams and connecting buses run roughly hourly to soon after 04.00; the last S-Bahn trains leave between 23.30 and midnight, after which bus 411 to Coswig and Meissen, bus 308 to Radeberg and bus 457 to Radeburg all leave from Postplatz at 01.15 and 02.25, with bus H/S at 02.25 only to Pirna.

There are ticket machines at tram stops, railway stations and other central locations, and you should buy a ticket before boarding. There are machines on trams and a few regional trains, intended for use only by those boarding in remoter locations. Machines take both coins and cards, and give change; some also offer instructions in English as well as German.

Bikes can be carried on trains, trams and buses as long as they don't inconvenience other passengers; you'll need to pay a child fare (as also for a dog); there's also a one-month bike ticket at €12.

Dresden City-Card

Visitors should definitely consider investing in a Dresden City-Card or Regio-Card, giving free travel within the city or the Upper Elbe region, respectively, plus free or reduced entry to museums and other sights. They are available from tourist information centres, DVB service centres, by telephone, email or online (4919 2281; e souvenir@dresden-tourist.de; www.dresden.de/dresden-cards) be sure to sign and to enter the date and time of first use.

The City-Card costs €21 for 48 hours (for an adult and any children under six, or two under-15s in the State Art Collection museums); it allows free tram, bus, train and ferry travel within the Dresden zone (not the Loschwitz funicular and monorail) and also tram 4 west to Weinböhla. The Regio-Card costs €32 for 72 hours and allows free travel on the whole Upper Elbe Transport Network (excluding the private Rathen, Riesa-Grossenhain and Schöna-Hrensko ferries); a single ticket for the Loschwitz funicular and monorail, the Kirnitzchtal tram line, the Lössnitzgrund steam railway and the Meissen City-Bus is valid for a return journey. Both give free admission to the Dresden State Art Collections (the Zwinger and Residenz museums, the Museum of Saxon Folk Art and the Museum of Decorative Arts at Pillnitz – but not the Historisches Grüne Gewolbe) and reduced-price access to the City Museum and Municipal Art Gallery, German Hygiene Museum, the Dresden Transport Museum, the Museum of Ethnology, the State Museum for Prehistory, the Festung, the Grosser Garten Palace, the Zoo, the Dresden Panometer, the City Technical Collections, the Kügelgenhaus, the Karl-May-Museum, as well as the Schiller, Weber and Kraszewski houses and four viewing towers, plus reductions on city tours and cruises, many concerts and plays, and in some restaurants at the Schloss Wackerbarth winery. The reductions range from €1 or 5% off to a full 50% off at the Museum of Ethnology. New for 2007 is a City-Card for families, costing €42 for two adults and up to four children up to the age of 14; this gives similar benefits, although not to the Dresden City Museum and Municipal Art Gallery.

The Regio-Card gives all these benefits plus reductions at Moritzburg, the Käthe Kollwitz House, the Meissen Porcelain Museum, the Albrechtsburg, the Hoflössnitz Winery Museum, the DDR 'Time Travel' Museum, Pirna Museum, Gross-Sedlitz, the castles of Königstein, Stolpen and Weesenstein, the Robert-Sterl-Haus, the Felsenbühne Rathen open-air theatre, and tours of Meissen and Pirna.

Information on city transport is available from the DVB (↘ 857 1011; e dvbinfo@ dvbag.de; www.dvbag.de); for regional transport contact the VVO's 24-hour InfoHotline (↘ 0180 2266 2266, €0.06 per call from a landline; e info@vvo-online.de; www.vvo-online.de/en/index.aspx).

The DVB Mobilitätszentrum is at Wilsdruffer Strasse 25 (↘ 857 1011; ⊕09.30–19.00 Mon–Fri, 09.00–16.00 Sat), with information and ticket desks on the ground floor and offices upstairs handling car-sharing and city tours and special trips; you can also book bus tickets to Poland with Taeter Tours, who have two services a day to Wrocław (see page 51). There are also DVB service centres at the Hauptbahnhof, Wallstrasse and Pirnaisches Tor interchanges.

TAXIS

As everywhere in Germany there is a plentiful supply of comfortable Mercedes taxis driven by comfortable middle-aged Germans. There are close to a hundred taxi ranks across the city, most obviously at the main railway stations, but it's often easier to phone for a cab, which will usually turn up within five minutes. Taxis are also available for courier deliveries and tours.

The main operator is Funktaxi (Radiotaxi) (☏ *211211*; e *funktaxi211211@t-online.de; www.taxi-dresden.com*), and you can also try Taxi-Ruf Dresden (☏ *811911*).

PORT TRANSFER AND FERRIES

Cruises along the Elbe dock on the embankment immediately below the Altstadt's Brühl Terrace, within minutes of the cathedral, the Zwinger, and other sights. This is also the starting point for the White Fleet's day cruises (see page 37).

There are still not a lot of bridges over the Elbe (although new bridges have been built for the Meissen and Pirna bypasses), which may be why Dresdeners feel so attached to the ugly Blue Wonder Bridge at Loschwitz, as well as to their ferries. The DVB operates three ferries, all to the east of the city centre including the 'Palace Ferry' from Kleinzschachwitz to Pillnitz (05.30–midnight daily), which takes cars. The others, which carry only pedestrians and bikes, run between Johannstadt and Neustadt (06.30–22.00 Mon–Fri, from 09.30 Sat/Sun; to 18.30 in winter), and Laubegast and Niederpoyritz (06.00–20.00 Mon–Fri, from 10.00 Sat/Sun).

There are other ferries outside the city, especially in Saxon Switzerland – heading east from the city these are at Heidenau/Birkwitz (04.30–22.50 Mon–Fri, from 07.00 Sat/Sun), Wehlen (04.40–23.50 Mon–Fri, from 05.40 Sat/Sun), Rathen (05.30–23.58 daily), Königstein (05.30–22.55 daily); Bad Schandau (04.30–22.00 Mon–Fri, from 06.55 Sat/Sun); Bad Schandau-Krippen (08.22–21.30 daily), Krippen-Postelwitz (06.10–21.44 daily); and Schmilka (05.45–22.05 daily). Finally, from April to September there's an international ferry from Schöna to Hrensko in the Czech

Republic (07.45–21.45 daily). These are all for pedestrians, most linking towns with their rail station (hence the early crossings on weekdays, for commuters to Dresden); they are also very popular with cyclists on the Elberadweg. Apart from the Rathen ferry, these all charge standard VVO rates of €0.90 (child/bike/dog €0.60), €1.50/1 return; the Pillnitz ferry charges €1.50 for a car less than 2.5m in length or €2.90 for one less than 5m (and including driver).

To the west, between Dresden and Meissen, there are ferries at Gauernitz-Kötitz (near Coswig) and Brockwitz-Scharfenberg; and beyond Meissen at Zehren, Seusslitz-Niederlommatzsch and Promnitz (near Riesa).

🚌 LONG-DISTANCE BUSES

There are few long-distance buses in Germany, but those that serve Dresden (stopping outside the Hauptbahnhof) are detailed on page 51.

🚗 DRIVING

See page 52 for information on reaching Dresden by car; to rent a car in Dresden you can contact any international firm. Arriving at the airport you'll find the following all vying for your custom:

Avis ✆ 881 4600/1; www.avis.de; ⊕07.00–23.00 Mon–Sat, from 08.00 Sun
Budget ✆ 881 4640; www.budget.de; ⊕07.00–23.00 Mon–Fri, 08.00–15.00 Sat

Europcar ☎ 881 4590/1; www.europcar.de; ⏰09.00–00.30 Mon–Sun
Hertz ☎ 881 4580–4; www.hertz.de; ⏰07.00–23.00 Mon–Fri, 07.30–21.00 Sat, 08.00–23.00 Sun
National/Alamo ☎ 01805 462526; e AlamoReservierung@emea.vanguardcar.com; www.alamo.de;
⏰07.00–21.00 Mon–Fri, 08.00–16.00 Sat
Sixt ☎ 01805 252525; www.e-sixt.com; ⏰07.00–23.30 Mon–Fri, 07.00–23.30 Sat, 08.00–23.30 Sun

Elsewhere you'll find:

Avis Friedrich Str 24 (just west of the Mitte station); tram 10; ⏰07.00–18.30 Mon–Fri, 07.30–12.00 Sat,
08.30–11.00 Sun, closed holidays
Europcar Neustadt Bahnhof; ☎ 01805 8000; Strehlener Str 5 (east of the Hauptbahnhof); ☎ 877320; ⏰24hrs
daily
Hertz Anton Str 39 (south of the Neustadt Bahnhof at Robert-Blum Str; ⏰07.00–19.00 Mon–Fri, 08.00–14.00
Sat, 09.00–12.00 Sun
National/Alamo Kotzschenbroder Str 193; ☎ 01805 462526; ⏰07.00–19.00 Mon–Fri, 08.00–12.00 Sat
Sixt Hauptbahnhof (by the ticket office); ☎ 01805 252525; ⏰05.45–21.00 Mon–Fri, 07.00–21.00 Sat/Sun; &
at the Hilton; ☎ 01805 252525; ⏰07.00–19.00 Mon–Fri, 08.00–12.00 Sat–Sun

It's well worth looking at a **car-sharing scheme** such as TeilAuto, partners with
German Railways (DB) (*Schützengasse 16;* ☎ *494 3371, 01801 494949;*
e *dresden@teilauto.net; www.teilauto.net*), which has 13 locations across Dresden, or
Green Wheels (☎ *01803 332332;* e *info@greenwheels.de; www.greenwheels.de*) which
has 29 locations. For occasional users prices for a compact car start at €2.28/hour

(7–10hrs), €23 for 24 hours to €137 for a week, plus €0.20–0.28/km. Green Wheels charge from €1/hour (€3 from 08.00–20.00) plus €0.15/km.

Parking in Dresden is not expensive (the modern Parkhaus Mitte, immediately south of the Yenidze building, charges just €1 a day). Parkschein (pay and display) machines, mostly solar-powered, take credit cards or coins. Real-time information on available space in Dresden's car parks is available at www.dresden.de/apps/lhdd_parkinformationssytem/index.php.

Fixed green arrows by traffic lights indicate where it is permitted to turn right on a red light, while a flashing yellow light means that you should beware pedestrians crossing. Many streets are one-way for cars but not for bikes (and in some cases trams too); otherwise traffic rules are much as you'd expect, and they are complied with better than in most places.

🚲 CYCLING

Cycling is part of German culture, although there's not the same level of facilities as in western Germany; however, the routes along the Elbe Meadows in particular make it a great way to get around Dresden. Streets that are one-way for cars are all assumed to be open for contraflow cycling, and some cyclists also ride on the pavement (sidewalk) at all times, even when the road is virtually unused – pedestrians have to pay attention at all times. Lots of people carry children on their bikes, especially in the Aussere Neustadt, where there are also fewer bike lights than elsewhere. There's lots of parking, including semi-permanent sponsored racks outside shops and businesses, and covered racks at some tram stops; these are not cluttered with abandoned bikes because there's almost no vandalism. Bikes can be taken on trams as long as they don't inconvenience anyone; for DB trains a bike ticket costs €3.50 per day. You should be careful crossing tramlines; some streets are cobbled, which is uncomfortable on many bikes.

There's information on the VVO website (*www.vvo-online.de/ en/auto_und_verkehr/fahrrad/index.aspx*), including details of Germany's only **bicycle library**, at the Bürgertreff Leubnitz-Neuostra, Heydenreichweg 4 (*www.fahrradbibliothek.de;* ⊕*19.00–21.00 Tue and by appointment*), where you can find maps, books and leaflets, get personal advice or see slide shows. The Allgemeiner Deutscher Fahrrad-Club (General German Bicycle Club) is at the Umweltzentrum (Environment Centre), Schützengasse 16 (↘ 494 3321; e info@ adfc-dresden.de; www.adfc-dresden.de). You can buy a **cycling map** of Dresden (1:20,000; €3) at either of these locations, at the DVB Mobilitätszentrum or at some cycle and book shops, and the Städtisches Vermessungsamt, Room 1080 of the Technisches Rathaus, Hamburger Strasse 19.

There are several reasonably signed cycle routes, the most obvious following the Elbe east to Pillnitz (11km from the Altmarkt) and Saxon Switzerland, and west to Meissen (23km).

A very nice touch is the provision of **DIY bike-repair shops** such as:

Omsewitzer Ring 61, Gorbitz; ⊕16.00–20.00 Thu, closed Dec & Jan
Radi.O The University, Wundtstr 9; ⊕16.30–19.00 Wed/Thu

Radschlag Katharinenstr 11, Neustadt; ✆ 656 7515; www.radschlag.de.vu; ⏰ 11.00–19.00 Mon/Thu, 11.00–17.00 Sat. Unfortunately it's not likely to actually be open when you have a puncture.

A couple of shops have dispensers outside selling inner tubes (€26 for a Schwalbe 26/28in tube, and no, they're not metric), such as:

BikeLand 262 Rothenburger Str 36; ✆ 858 6695; www.bikeland.de
Radsport Tietz Meixstr 15, Pillnitz

There are plenty of other **bike shops** including, in the Neustadt:

Alpha Bikes Louisenstr 73; www.alphabikes-dresden.de
Fahrrad Schwarzer Cnr Bischofsweg & Königsbruckes Str
Generator Radsport Louisenstr 19, at Försterei Str; www.generator-radsport.de
Rons Customs Tannenstr 22, at Königsbrücker Platz; www.rons-customs.com
Zweirad Steffen Grossenhainer Str 184; www.zweirad-steffen.de. Has branches across the region.

There's not much on the south side of the river, but you could try the following:

Antrieb der Fahrradladen Könneritzstr 7 (by the Mitte station); www.antrieb.com
Müllers Fahrradladen Werkstatt Altstrehlen 13, Strehlen
Räder Reichelt Leutewitzer Ring 17, Gorbitz; www.raeder-reichelt.de

Rental bikes are easily available at hotels such as the Hilton, the main railway stations and the places listed below. You'll pay around €8–12 per day or €20 for a weekend, including lock and helmet (if you want – not many people use them here, especially on the riverside routes). German bikes are comfortable rather than sporty, with kickstands and handlebar extensions to give a variety of riding positions.

Antrieb der Fahrradladen Könneritzstr 7; ☎ 858 2059; www.antrieb.com; ⏰08.00–20.00 Mon–Fri, 08.00–18.00 Sat
Engel Reisen Wiesentorstr 3; ☎ 281 9206
Radsport Päperer Veilchenweg 2; ☎ 264 1240; e info@radsport-paeperer.de; ⏰09.00–19.00 Mon–Fri, 09.00–13.00 Sat
Roll-On Dresden Königsbrucker Str 2; ☎ 810 7255, m 0177 461 9148; www.rollon-dresden.de; ⏰09.00–18.00 Mon–Fri, 09.00–13.00 Sat. For bikes & roller-blades.

Outside Dresden you can rent bikes in:

Coswig: Campingplatz Am Badesee Coswig-Kötitz, Feldweg 40; ☎ 03523 700220; e camping@tw-coswig.de; www.campingplatz-coswig.de; ⏰09.00–18.00 daily
Meissen Tourismusverein Meissen, Markt 3; ☎ 03521 41940; e service@touristinfo-meissen.de; www.touristinfo-meissen.de; ⏰10.00–18.00 Mon–Fri, 10.00–16.00 Sat/Sun & holidays
Moritzburg: Bike & Fun Fahrradpool; ☎ 0172 790 2480; ⏰Apr–Oct
Radebeul: Meissner Str 152; ☎ 0351 19433; e tourismus@radebeul.de; ⏰Mar–Oct 09.00–18.00 Mon–Fri, 10.00–15,00 Sat; Nov–Apr 10.00–16.00 Mon–Fri; & Verleihstation Reich, Kötzschenbrodaer Str 127; ☎ 0351 656 3651; ⏰08.00–18.00 daily
Weinböhla: Zentralgasthof Weinböhla, Kirchplatz 2; ☎ 035243 56000; www.zentralgasthof.com

There are also plenty of **bike shops, for spares and repairs**, along the Elberadweg (Elbe Cycle Way), including (from east to west):

Fahrrad Bässler Hauptstr 4, Pirna-Copitz; ☎ 03501 523268
Fahrradhaus Bieberstein Clara-Zetkin-Str Str 14, Pirna; ☎ 03501 781574
Radsport Päperer Veilchenweg, Loschwitz; ☎ 264 1240
Radsport Tietz Meixstr 15, Pillnitz; ☎ 261 0909; www.radsport-tietz.de
Rund ums Fahrrad Sebnitzer Str 6, Bad Schandau; ☎ 035022 42883

To the west of Dresden:

Radsport Kotyrba Cossebauder Str 34, Cotta; ☎ 421 4064

And beyond Meissen:

Bikes and More Fischerstr 1, Torgau; ☎ 03421 704981
Fahrrad Herfurth Bahnhof Str 2, Nünchritz-Weissig; ☎ 035267 50777
Fahrräder Busch Mühlberger Str 50, Belgern; ☎ 03422 40260
Fahrräder Redel Leipziger Str 8, Torgau; ☎ 03421 714685
Fahrradservice Lommatscher Str 6, Zehren; ☎ 0178 614 5623
Zweiradservice Seifert Grossenhainer Str 21, Riesa; ☎ 0162 916 3440

HITCHHIKING

Rather than heading for an autobahn intersection and sticking their thumb out, German hitchhikers often use a Mitfahrzentral or ride-sharing agency, now almost entirely online, such as Mitfahrgelegenheit (*www.mitfahrgelegenheit.de*) and Mitfahrzentrale (*www.mitfahrzentrale.de*).

In Dresden you'll find ADM Mitffahrbüro at Dr Friedrich-Wolf-Strasse 2 (↻ *19440*); Nürnberger Strasse 57 (↻ *4636060*); and Bischofsweg 66 (↻ *53439*).

If you do find yourself by the roadside, remember that almost every town in Germany has a two-letter number-plate code that will tell drivers where you want to go if you have a sheet of card and a marker pen – Dresden's is DD.

5 Accommodation

As you might expect, there is a wide choice of accommodation in all ranges in Dresden, and all are decent at the very least. At the budget end there are hostels with shared dormitories and bathrooms; the private backpacker places are in the bohemian Aussere Neustadt, north of the Elbe, while the official youth hostels are to the south. Virtually all hotel rooms have private bathrooms, plus television and other comforts; however breakfast almost always costs extra, as do car parking and, usually, internet access.

Early in 2008 a new luxury hotel is to open in the Haus am Zwinger at the rear of the Taschenberg Palais; it's being built by Octavian Hotels to a design by Norman Foster and costing €50 million.

If phoning from elsewhere to book, Dresden's code is 0351 (+49 351 from abroad); there are also many attractive places to stay in Radebeul (see below, page 96), Meissen, Pirna, Bad Schandau and elsewhere (see *Chapter 11*, page 231).

For longer stays it's worth renting an apartment, from:

Der Immo-Tip Semperstr 1; ☎ 433130; www.der-immo-tip.de
EMV Dresden Niedersedlitzer Platz 7; ☎ 207400; www.emvdresden.de
Home Company Rothenburger Str 21; ☎ 19445; www.homecompany.de
M2 Servicezentrum Immobilien Waldschlössenstr 12; ☎ 899350; www.m2-servicezentrum.de

PRICE CODES

THE CHEAPEST DOUBLE ROOM PER NIGHT

Exclusive	$$$$$	€140+
Upmarket	$$$$	€105–140
Mid range	$$$	€70–105
Budget	$$	€35–70
Shoestring	$	up to €35

ALTSTADT [map 2]

EXCLUSIVE HOTELS $$$$$

🏠 **Art'otel** (155 rooms, 19 suites) Ostra Allee 33; ☏ 49220, free 0800 814 7000; e aodrinfo@artotels.de; www.artotel.de/dresden/dresden.html

Decorated throughout with works by Dresden artist A R Penck, this achingly cool place is excellently located just 300m from the Semperoper & Zwinger, & 200m from the Mitte Station. Rooms (some non-smoking & disabled-accessible) are spacious & well equipped, with dataports & Wi-Fi, & a fairly small TV – but there's a pointless gimmick, a transparent bathroom door, which can be made opaque with what seems to be a light switch. Reception staff speak perfect English & are very helpful, but b/fast is poor & expensive, & the internet terminal in the lobby is also extortionate. The Factory restaurant (not at all industrial) is pretty good, & there's a gym, sauna & solarium.

⌂ **Hotel Kempinski Taschenberg Palais** (182 rooms, 32 suites) Taschenberg 3; ☎ 49120;
e reservations.taschenbergpalais@kempinski.com; www.kempinski-dresden.com
Perhaps the most luxurious & prestigious of the city's 5-star hotels, the Taschenberg Palais (see page 154) has
been beautifully recreated, from the lovely front courtyard, with its Baroque fountains, to the inner court &
Pöppelmann's grand main stairs (a surprisingly long way from the foyer). Even so, there are hiccups, with
curtains that can't easily be drawn & TV porn channels that are inadequately protected. There's a pool, sauna,
solarium & gym on the fifth floor (🕐06.30–22.00), underground parking, & a range of excellent restaurants.

⌂ **Maritim Congress** (328 rooms) Ostra Ufer 2; ☎ 2160; e info.dre@maritim.de;
www.dresden-congresscenter.de
Opened in 2006, this is a conversion of one of the first reinforced-concrete buildings in Germany, built in
1914 by Hans Erlwein as a tobacco warehouse. In a great riverside location, it's linked by a tunnel to the
International Congress Centre, but it's a good base for tourists too. Rooms are huge (as is the underground
car park), there's a great b/fast buffet looking out over the river, but the lifts can be annoying (you need
your electronic keycard, so make sure everyone has one) & the pool & sauna aren't too big.

UPMARKET HOTELS $$$$
⌂ **Hilton** (157 rooms, 19 suites) An der Frauenkirche 5; ☎ 864 2120, free 0800 4445 8667;
e info.dresden@hilton.com; www.hilton.de/dresden
With possibly the best location of any hotel in Dresden, in the shadow of the Frauenkirche, this is however a
thoroughly modern building, with big comfortable rooms, no fewer than 12 restaurants, cafés & bars (inc some
of Dresden's best Italian & Japanese food), a Living Well health club, swimming pool, dry saunas, steam bath,
gym & beauty salon.

🏠 **Steinberger Hotel de Saxe** (178 rooms, 7 suites) Neumarkt 9; ✆ 43860;
e desaxe-dresden@steigenberger.de; www.desaxe-dresden.steigenberger.de
Also a rebuilt Baroque palace in a great location, but without the pretensions of the Taschenberg Palais (see previous page), this offers remarkable value for money, with non-smoking floors, underground parking, Wi-Fi & a gym available. Opened in early 2006, its Modernist furniture still seems new & the staff are helpful; but there can be a long wait for a lift at busy times (& there's a spa but no swimming pool). B/fast is good, but restaurant service can be slow for lunch & dinner.

MID-RANGE HOTELS $$$
🏠 **Elbflorenz** (212 rooms, 15 suites) Rosenstr 36; ✆ 86400, free 0800 183 8780;
e info@hotel-elbflorenz.de; www.hotel-elbflorenz.de
In the World Trade Center, next to Freiberger Str S-Bahn station, this is not just a business hotel, but a tastefully designed haven (a 10min walk from the Zwinger) with sauna, gym, Italian restaurant, piano bar & library. Rooms (some non-smoking) have a safe, hairdryer, fax & internet connections plus Wi-Fi, & you can rent bikes.

🏠 **Four Points Hotel Königshof** (93 rooms/suites) Kreischaer Str 2 (on Wasaplatz, Strehlen); ✆ 87310, free 24hrs 0800 3253 5353; e fourpoints.koenigshof@arabellasheraton.com; www.fourpoints.de/koenigshof [map 1]
In the attractive suburb of Strehlen, with plenty of Jugendstil villas, the Königshof is just 5mins from the Altstadt by frequent trams, & a few mins from the S-Bahn. However streetside rooms can be noisy, due to those very trams. There are Greek & Chinese restaurants, bakers & ATMs nearby. It's a fine old building but very modern inside, with a very grand Ballsaal that's used for concerts. Rooms (some smoke-free) are elegant & service is good; the ample b/fast buffet is usually including in weekend rates. There's a fairly basic spa & sauna.

🏠 **Dorint Novotel** (244 rooms, 1 suite) Grunauer Str 14; ☎ 49150; e h5370@accor.com; www.novotel.com
Immediately east of the Altstadt (at the Deutsches-Hygiene-Museum tram stop), this is a fairly modern place that's been taken over by the French chain & now belies its slightly drab exterior with modern facilities including swimming pool & sauna, & a nice pub & Mediterranean-style restaurant. No fewer than 155 rooms are smoke-free (but there's only one with facilities for the disabled, & not all have Wi-Fi).

🏠 **Hotel Am Terrassenufer** (189 rooms) Terrassenufer 12; ☎ 440 9500; e hat@hotel-terrassenufer.de; www.hotel-terrassenufer.de
In a great location across the road from the synagogue, & with good views from the upper floors, this is nevertheless still a communist block (built as student housing), without bath tubs or AC (not that that is vital in Dresden). However the staff are friendly, b/fast is ample, & there's Wi-Fi in public areas & some rooms.

🏠 **Mercure Hotel Newa Dresden** (319 rooms) St Petersburger Str 34; ☎ 48140, reservations 481 4109; e h1577@accor.com; www.mercure.com
Slightly more upmarket than its sister Ibis hotels across the pedestrian Prager Str, this is a modern & very affordable hotel a short distance from the main railway station. Although obviously a monolithic communist block it has been very well modernised with some stylish design features. Rooms (169 of which are non-smoking) have full-height windows & showers are all-glass attention-catchers too. There's a good b/fast buffet & sauna/solarium, but internet access is very expensive & staff can be unfriendly.

🏠 **Radisson SAS Gewandhaus** (94 rooms, 3 suites) Ringstr 1; ☎ 49490, free 0800 3333 3333; e info.dresden@radissonsas.com; www.radisson.com/dresdende
Built in 1768–70 as the New Cloth Hall & destroyed in 1945, it opened as a hotel in 1966 & became a

5-star Radisson in 1997. The inner court is now a glass-roofed atrium surrounded by restaurant, bar & conference rooms; the Biedermeier-style bedrooms have a safe, espresso machine & kettle, fax line & free Wi-Fi. There's a lovely swimming pool (though it's not huge) in the basement, as well as sauna, solarium & gym. The b/fast buffet is good, but it's quite a pricey option.

BUDGET HOTELS $$

🏠 **City-Herberge** (200 beds) Lingnerallee 3; ☎ 4859900; e info@city-herberge.de; www.city-herberge.de/index_english.php [map 1]
In the former Robotron computer plant (1968–74), just east of the Altstadt, this is little known to foreigners but does provide a clean, convenient & low-cost place to stay. En-suite dbls cost €63 while rooms with shared bathrooms range from 4-bed rooms at €128 to dbls at €56 & sgls at €38; all including a buffet b/fast (until noon) & parking.

🏠 **Ibis Bastei, Königstein & Lilienstein** (306 rooms each) Prager Str 5/9/13; ☎ 4856 2000; e reservierung@ibis-dresden.de; www.ibis-dresden.de
If you want rooms, Ibis has them, & at a fair price too – 3 identical blocks on the pedestrian boulevard just 300m from the Hauptbahnhof. Now run &, like so many of the ex-communist hotels, thoroughly overhauled by the French, the rooms are now clean & light, with the usual facilities (inc modem ports & Wi-Fi) & modern bathrooms. There's a decent b/fast buffet (€9) & staff are helpful.

🏠 **Hotel-restaurant Café Friedrichstadt** (11 rooms) Friedrichstr 38; ☎ 4927 8810; www.café-friedrichstadt.de; ⊕ 11.00–18.00 Sun/Mon, 11.00–22.00 Tue–Thu, 11.00–midnight Fri/Sat, closed holidays [map 1]
In a Baroque building in an untouristed area just across the tracks from the Altstadt, this is a classy little

restaurant with tasteful rooms as well as a sauna & pool. There's a good & relatively inexpensive b/fast, as well as other meals. The downside is that you can check in only when the café is open.

PRIVATE APARTMENTS

See page 84 for information on renting apartments for longer stays.

⌂ **Pension am Zwinger** (18 rooms) Ostra Allee 27 (Innenhof); ✆ 899 0030: e post@pension-zwinger.de; www.pension-zwinger.de
Very tasteful private apts right on the edge of the Old Town, for 2–4 & 4–6 people. B/fast can be provided, & there's parking too.

HOSTELS

⌂ **Jugendgästehaus Dresden** (480 beds) Maternistr 22; ✆ 492620; e jhdresden@djh.de; www.djh-sachsen.de
Dresden's main official youth hostel is a 7-storey block with 1- to 4-bed rooms, more than half en suite & the others with a basin (& huge clean shared bathrooms). A few rooms have disabled facilities, & a good buffet b/fast is included. It's reached by tram 12 & is near the Freiberger Str S-Bahn station. *Beds cost €19 in rooms with shared bathroom or €23.50 with private bathroom.*

⌂ **Jugendgästehaus Rudi Arndt** (77 beds) Hübnerstr 11; ✆ 471 0667; e jhdresden.rudiarndt@djh.de; www.djh-sachsen.de [map 1]
Dresden's smaller official youth hostel is near the university, 1km south of the Hauptbahnhof (tram 3 or 8 to Nürnberger Platz). There are rooms for up to 11 people, including 3 rooms with bunks, & shared bathrooms. *A bed costs €16, including b/fast.*

There are also official DJH hostels in Radebeul (12km west), Pirna-Copitz (25km east) and Bad Schandau (30km east).

NEUSTADT [map 4]

EXCLUSIVE HOTELS $$$$$

🏠 **Hotel Bülow Residenz** (25 rooms, 5 suites) Rähnitzgasse 19; ✆ 80030; e info@buelow-residenz.de; www.buelow-residenz.de

A member of the Relais & Châteaux group, this is easily the most luxurious place to stay north of the river, & perhaps in the whole city. A very chic boutique hotel in a rebuilt Baroque townhouse, it offers excellent service, free internet, minibar & newspapers & flat-screen TVs, & there's the great Caroussel restaurant (see page 112).

🏠 **Westin Bellevue** (326 rooms, 14 suites) Grosse Meissner Str 15; ✆ 8050; e hotelinfo@westin-bellevue.com; www.westin.com/dresden

Built in 1982–85 around a Baroque townhouse by Pöppelmann, this was renovated in 2004 & is no longer exclusively aimed at business clients. There's now a glass-roofed patio & a heated garden terrace where you can drink & eat simple food looking out over the Elbe Meadows. Rooms looking over the meadows have marvellous views of the Altstadt, but those on the other side are noisy. Some rooms are non-smoking & disabled-accessible, & all have AC, satellite TV, Wi-Fi, minibar & safe; there's also a spa with 2 swimming pools, saunas, gym & a hairdresser. In addition to wine & beer cellars, the Canaletto is an excellent Mediterranean-inspired restaurant (which also has the Altstadt view that inspired the painter, properly known as Bernardo Bellotto — see page 26).

MID-RANGE HOTELS $$$

🏠 **Hotel Martha Hospiz** (50 rooms) Nieritzer Str 11; ☎ 81760, reservations ☎ 817 6333;
e marthahospiz.dresden@t-online.de; www.vch.de/marthahospiz.dresden
Somehow this has acquired a reputation as the best value for money in the Neustadt, & while it is more than adequate there are newer more stylish places that actually charge less. This is a nicely restored 1890s' building with Biedermeier-style rooms & a pleasant garden on a very quiet street, just 5mins from the Neustadt station & close to good restaurants.

🏠 **Hotel Rothenburger Hof** (26 rooms, 13 apts) Rothenburger Str 15; ☎ 81260;
e kontakt@rothenburger-hof.de; www.rothenburger-hof.de
In a typically Aussere Neustadt building dating from 1865, this was refurbished in 2003 & now offers comfortable en-suite rooms with TV & minibar, as well as apts with kitchens (& a sauna & solarium). Some have balconies, but the street can be noisy at night & there's no AC. There's a good b/fast plus a garden terrace & indoor pool. The exterior & reception still seem a bit tired, but this is the best hotel in the heart of the nightlife area.

BUDGET HOTELS $$

🏠 **Best Western Macrander Hotel** (84 rooms) Buchenstr 10; ☎ 815 1500;
www.macrander-dresden.bestwestern.de
This is a functional modern place that's handily placed between the city & the airport, on the edge of the Aussere Neustadt (not far from trams 7 & 8). There's a swimming pool, gym & spa with sauna & massages, plus free bicycle loan. Rooms (some of which are non-smoking) have dataports & Wi-Fi, satellite TV, hairdryers & tea- & coffee-making facilities. Next door, for some reason, there's a display of DDR-vintage ambulances & the like behind plate-glass windows. 10% discount for seniors.

🏠 **Guest House Mezcalero** (23 rooms) Königsbrücker Str 64; 📞 810770; e info@mezcalero.de; www.mezcalero.de
At the back of a courtyard (immediately north of the Nahkauf supermarket), this is remarkably quiet for its Aussere Neustadt location. Decorated in a funky Mexican style, there are rooms for 1–6 people, with sgl beds in a shared room costing from €17. It's clean & friendly & a great base for the party area in particular.

🏠 **Holiday Inn** (120 rooms) Stauffenbergallee 25A; 📞 81510, free (Germany) 0800 181 5131, (UK) 0800 89712; e info@holiday-inn-dresden.de; www.holiday-inn-dresden.de
Just north of the Aussere Neustadt (at the top of Königsbrücker Platz, 10mins to the Altstadt by trams 7 & 8), this is a fairly bland but very efficient modern place. Rooms are large with AC, coffee-/tea-maker, minibar, modem & Wi-Fi, hairdryer & cable TV, & there's a good pool & spa, plus free use of bicycles & free parking. There's a fine b/fast buffet which is included in some deals (but pricey otherwise); Americans in particular can benefit from special rates for AAA & AARP members, & it's said to be gay-friendly too.

🏠 **Hotel NH** (269 rooms) Hansastr 43; 📞 84240; e nhdresden@nh-hotels.com; www.nh-hotels.com [map 1]
A little way from the centre (10mins by tram 13), but handy for the autobahn (& buses to Moritzburg & Radeburg), this is a stylish modern building that offers great value for money, with satellite TV, fax & internet connections, solarium & free sauna & gym. Staff are helpful, although not all speak English.

🏠 **Mercure Albertbrücke** (126 rooms, 6 suites) Melanchthonstr 2; 📞 80610; e h2824@accor.com; www.mercure.com
A slightly more upmarket version of the Ibis hotels, this is a modern business hotel in a duller part of the Neustadt, but close to trams & within easy walking distance of both Altstadt & Neustadt. Everything is

competent but unmemorable, with disabled & non-smoking rooms, underground parking; there are no health/sports facilities & no restaurant, but a decent b/fast is served.

🏠 **Park Plaza Hotel** (146 rooms, 2 suites) Königsbrücker Str 121A; ✆ 80630; e ppdres@parkplazahotels.de; www.parkplaza.com/webExtra.do?hotelCode=GERDRESD [map 1]
On the main road to the airport, opposite the Alaun Platz park, this is 10mins from the Altstadt (trams 7 & 8). It's a clean modern place that offers great value for money; the gym is free for guests & open 24hrs, & some deals include free sauna & Wi-Fi; however there are steep charges to use their internet terminal & for parking. Half the rooms are non-smoking, & all have dataport & Wi-Fi, cable TV & minibar; executive rooms have tea- & coffee-making facilities & free mineral water & newspaper.

HOSTELS

🏠 **Die Boofe** (95 beds) Hechtstr 10; ✆ 801 3361; email; info@boofe.de; www.boofe.de
Slightly out of the liveliest zone of the Aussere Neustadt (10mins walk north of the Neustadt railway station), this is a relatively quiet hostel with rooms for up to 4 people (& 1 5-bed room) over 4 storeys (with no lift), plus a nice bar/restaurant & garden. There's also a sauna, table football & 2 internet terminals (€0.50 per 15mins) plus Wi-Fi & there's a kitchen on each floor. *Beds cost €16 with a basin or €18.50 en suite in a 4-bed room, €20.50/25 in a dbl, or €29/34 sgl. B/fast is available for €5.50, or €7.50 for Sun brunch.*

🏠 **Hostel Louise 20** (14 rooms, 4 apts) Louisenstr 20; ✆ 8894 894; e info@louise20.de; www.louise20.de
Above the Planwirtschaft pub (where there's a b/fast buffet for €8), this is right where the action is in the Aussere Neustadt. It's a friendly place with dorms for up to 5, with pine bunks & a nice clean design, plus sgls & dbls, all with a basin, & lovely apts. There's a kitchen, internet access, a safe, games & TV, & car

parking nearby. Beds cost from €16 in a shared room, €19.50 in a dbl or €29 in a sgl; apts cost from €96 for 3 persons.

⌂ **Lollis Homestay** (56 beds) Görlitzer Str 34 (around the corner on Sebnitzer Str); ☎ 810 8458; e lolli@lollishome.de; www.lollishome.de

This is a relatively small hostel & very arty, with each room decorated by a different artist (all friends of the owners), including the Trabizimmer, with a dbl bed in the back of a Trabant. There's a great communal area with kitchen & free tea & coffee (& a fridge stocking 3 types of beer from the world's smallest brewery). There's free use of some old bikes, games, 1:1 book exchange, & a self-service b/fast for €3. There are rooms (all sharing bathrooms) for 2–5 people plus dorms for up to 8. *Winter prices range from €13 in a dorm to €27 for a sgl, & summer prices from €14 to €38.*

IN THE SUBURBS

⌂ **Schloss Eckberg** (82 rooms, 2 suites) Bautzner Str 136; ☎ 80990; e info@ www.schloss-eckberg.de; www.schloss-eckberg.de/english/home.htm [map 1]

One of the 3 Elbe castles (see page 183), this has been beautifully restored in a rather twee traditional style & opened as a 17-room luxury hotel in 1997, along with the new Kavaliershaus (Knights' House) & spa in the park. $$$$

⌂ **Schloss-Hotel Pillnitz** (42 rooms, 3 suites) August-Böckstiegel-Str 10, Pillnitz; ☎ 0351 26140; e reservierung@schlosshotel-pillnitz.de; www.schlosshotel-pillnitz.de

Within the grounds of Pillnitz Castle, this 4-star hotel combines the attractions of a country-house hotel (especially walking in the park once the tour groups have gone) with those of the city, a 20min drive west (or a riverside bike ride). The rooms are spacious & recently refurbished, with modem connections & minibar, & there's a gourmet restaurant with very friendly staff. $$$$

⌂ **Hotelpension Fliegerhorst** (10 rooms) Moritzburger Weg 24, Hellerau; ＼ 0351 880 825; e info@pension-dresden.de; www.pension-dresden.de
In the garden suburb of Hellerau, handy for the airport, high-tech industry, Moritzburg & Radeberg, this is also close to the Festspielhaus (see page 189) & easily reached from the city centre by tram 8. Rooms are clean & simple, with bathroom & TV, & there's a decent restaurant serving fondues, fish, grills & spaghetti. $$

RADEBEUL

There's a good range of accommodation in Radebeul, on the way to Meissen, with plenty of pensions and small bed and breakfasts, as well as some delightful country-house hotels. Near the Radebeul-Ost S-Bahn station and the Zinzendorfstrasse tram stop there are rooms at **Pension Trauschke** (*Eduard-Bilz-Str 18;* ＼ *830 2757;* $$), **Pension Moritzhof** (*Eduard-Bilz-Str 51;* ＼ *830 3466;* $$), **Pension-Gästhaus zu den Linden** (*Meissner Str 64;* ＼ *836 2226;* $$) and with **Birgit Oehmichen** (*Meissner Strasse 309;* ＼ *830 2162;* $). A block north of Meissner Strasse between the Radebeul-West and Radebeul-Weintraube S-Bahn stations, there's a convenient group of pensions: **Restaurant-Pension Adria 'Die blaue Lagune'** (*Heinrich-Zille-Str 27;* ＼ *830 8261;* $$), **Pension Elchlepp** (*Dr-Rudolf-Friedrichs-Str 15;* ＼ *830 9078;* $$) and **Pension Villa Marie** (*Dr-Rudolf-Friedrichs-Str 17;* ＼ *830 7140;* $$).

🏠 **Hotel-Restaurant Villa Sorgenfrei** (14 rooms) Augustusweg 48; ☎ 0351 795 6660;
✉ info@hotel-villa-sorgenfrei.de; www.hotel-villa-sorgenfrei.de
In a delightful Baroque mansion (1783–89) with a French-style park, this is perhaps the classiest place to stay in the region. Rooms are classically decorated in subtle pastel colours & have all amenities including satellite TV, Wi-Fi, modem & fax ports, free newspapers & hairdryers. You can stroll in the perfectly manicured gardens or have a drink on the terrace before dining in the traditional French restaurant (with Saxon wines a feature). $$$$$

🏠 **Steigenberger Parkhotel** (189 rooms, 11 suites, 216 apts) Nizzastr 55; ☎ 0351 83210;
✉ parkhotel-dresden@steigenberger.de; www.parkhotel-dresden.steigenberger.de
Spread across a hillside above the Elbe is an array of low modern buildings housing accommodation, a fine restaurant, & a spa offering Ayurvedic treatments & massage, saunas, hammam, solariums, gym & a 25m pool with pool-bar & whirlpool. There are wide lawns, art by local artists including Georg Baselitz, & large rooms (some non-smoking, with TV, radio, Wi-Fi, modem & fax ports, safe & minibar) & apts (with kitchen); bikes can be rented to enjoy the local vineyards & the Elbe path. $$$

🏠 **Goldener Anker** (60 rooms) Altkötzschenbroda 61; ☎ 0351 839 99010;
✉ goldener-anker-radebeul@t-online.de; www.goldener-anker-radebeul.de
In Altkötzschenbroda, the oldest & most charming part of Radebeul (first recorded in 1271), this is a pretty standard hotel, which is to say that it offers good spacious rooms with TV & internet access, & a restaurant with b/fast buffet included in room rates. It's 200m from the Radebeul-West S-Bahn station & the Moritzburger Str stop of tram 4, for easy access to the city. $$

PILLNITZER LANDSTRASSE

Along the riverside road from Loschwitz to Pillnitz (served by bus 83) are many attractive inns and guesthouses, including (from west to east):

⌂ **Pension Landhaus Maria am Blauen Wunder** (4 rooms) Körnerweg 4, Loschwitz; ✆ 264 0497;
e landhaus.maria@gmx.de; www.landhaus.maria.info $

⌂ **Pension Arends** (4 rooms) Pillnitzer Landstr 112 (Josef-Herrmann-Str stop); ✆ 268 8974;
e mail@urlaub-dresden.de; www.urlaub-dresden.de $$

⌂ **Pension Im Grünen an der Elbe** Pillnitzer Landstr 174 (Moosleite stop); ✆ 2150 0421;
e post@im-gruenen-an-der-elbe.de; www.im-gruenen-an-der-elbe.de $$

⌂ **Pension zur Königlichen Ausspanne** Eugen-Dieterich-Str 5, Niederpoyritz (Staffelsteinstr stop); ✆ 268 9502;
www.koenigliche-ausspanne.de $$

⛺ CAMPING

For tents, the only campsite in the city is near the Pillnitz ferry, although there are others in the countryside. Campervans have the option of stopping in a guarded compound on the north embankment (on Grosse Meissner Strasse between the Japanese Palais and the Augustusbrücke (€14/day) or at the City-Herberge (see page 89), immediately east of the Altstadt. You can also rent campervans or caravans at Schaffermobil Wohnmobile, Kötzschenbroder Strasse 125 (*Kaditz;* ✆ *837480;* e *schaffer@schaffer-mobil.de; www.schaffer-mobil.de*). This is just west of the city close to the Kaditz terminal of trams 9 and 13.

Ⅹ Campingplatz Am Badesee Coswig-Kötitz Feldweg 40; 📞 03523 700220; e camping@tw-coswig.de; www.campingplatz-coswig.de

Near the Elbe cycle route west of Radebeul (a half-hour's walk from Coswig S-Bahn station), this is mainly a swimming lake & caravan site, but tents are also welcome. It costs €2.70/4.80 for a tent, €6.20 for a caravan or campervan, plus €4.70 per adult & €2.70 for children aged 6–14, €1.70 for a car or €1 for a motorbike. There are also a few rooms ($$).

Ⅹ Campingplatz Wostra An der Wostra 7; 📞 201 3254; e cp.wostra@freenet.de; www.dresden.de/de/05/20/03/01/c_03.php

Open from mid Apr to late Oct, this is an attractive leafy site 6km east (bus 86 to Wostra, from the Heidenau S-Bahn station or the Laubegast terminal of trams 4 & 6). It costs €3–6 for a tent (depending on size), €5.50 for a caravan or €6.50 for a campervan, plus €3.50 per adult & €2.50 for under 12s, €2.50 for a car or €1.50 for a motorbike.

6 Eating and Drinking

Breakfast is important to Germans and usually consists of bread or rolls (*Brötchen* or *Semmeln*) with tea or coffee, jam, cheese and cold meats, as well as meat spreads such as *Leberwurst*; cereals and muesli are also popular. Traditionally lunch was the main meal of the day, but with more industrious modern working practices lunch has become shorter and most Germans now eat their main meal in the evening.

Pork is the most popular meat, with beef and chicken also widely available; pot-roasting is the most common cooking technique, while sausages are also very popular, of course. Trout, pike, char, carp and perch are the most popular fish, usually being grilled. Vegetables such as carrots, cabbage, beans, peas, spinach and root vegetables are eaten as side dishes or in stews; potatoes or egg noodles are almost compulsory. *Hefeklösse* are yeast dumplings served with meat or stewed fruit compote. The most commonly used herbs are parsley, thyme, bay and chive, with pepper, caraway and juniper berries. *Waldmeister* (sweet woodruff) is used in sorbets and ice creams, and also in sausages.

Bread is one of the highlights of the German table, and there are plenty of excellent bakeries. Most breads are made with sourdough and a mix of wheat and rye flour, and also seeds and wholegrains; *Schwarzbrot* (black bread) is a dark-brown rye bread, and *Pumpernickel* is a steamed black bread from Westphalia.

Kurbiskernbrot (pumpkin seed bread) is a speciality, and you'll also find *Zwiebelbrot* or onion bread. Several traditional seasonal specialities are made in Saxony, in particular for religious festivals. At Easter a bread is made of sweet yeast dough with raisins, candied lemon peel and almonds and shaped like a mitre.

Saxon menus often include potato soup (with cumin and thin slices of sausage, alas), grilled *Bratwurst* (a grilled or fried sausage served with mustard either in a bread roll or on a cardboard plate), *Sauerbraten* (braised beef in a red wine sauce with red cabbage, apple sauce and potato dumplings), and for dessert *Quarkkeulchen* (potato-flour pancakes with curd cheese filling and cinnamon sprinkled on top), served with *Apfelmus* (apple sauce). *Himmel und Erde* (heaven and earth) is a mix of mashed potatoes and stewed apples topped with sautéed onion and ham; Leipzig is famous for its *Allerlei* or vegetable hotpot of carrots, peas, mushrooms and asparagus with a butter sauce. In Dresden restaurants you'll often find venison from Moritzburg (often with local mushrooms) and seasonal specialities such as asparagus from Meissen in spring and goose in autumn and winter.

Fruit tarts and cakes are very popular as desserts, together with cheesecakes (made with *Quark* or sweet curd cheese) and *Pfannkuchen* or pancakes. *Eierscheke* is a soft cake with an egg-flan base and a topping of Quark with raisins. Gingerbread is popular all over Germany, but Saxons claim that the best is from Pulsnitz.

Since World War II Turkish, Greek, Italian and Spanish cuisines have also become established in Germany, with many good restaurants in Dresden.

The most popular snack has traditionally been Bratwurst with *Sauerkraut* (pickled cabbage) or potato salad. Recently *Currywurst*, with a curry sauce, has become more

Dresden's main claim to gastronomic fame is *Stollen*, also associated with the Erzgebirge (Ore Mountains). It's a fruit cake made from a yeast dough with butter, almonds, raisins and orange, and relatively little sugar, and is associated with the Advent Striezelmarkt (also known as Stollenmarkt), for which a three-tonne *Stollen* is baked each year. It's now in the shops from October to December and no doubt the season is slowly getting longer. Traditionally every family had its own recipe for *Stollen*, needing at least three parts of butter and six of dried fruit to every two parts of flour, and took it to the local bakery to be cooked.

popular, but in fact the most common fast food is *Dürüm Kebab*, roast lamb (as a rule) in pitta bread with rice and salad. This was invented in Berlin in the 1970s to suit European tastes, and is now available in almost every German town, the many Turkish kebab shops being easily recognised by their green and yellow colour scheme. They also sell *Pide*, a sort of flatbread pizza, and *Borek*, like a large soft pasty with a filling of either meat or spinach and haloumi cheese. They'll all give you a free glass of chemical-green apple tea, even while waiting for a take-away.

It's equally traditional, especially on Sundays and special occasions, to snack on *Kaffee und Küchen* (coffee and cake). German coffee is usually filtered, rather stronger than usual in the Anglo-Saxon nations though weaker than espresso.

Beer is of course associated with Germans (and Meissner Schwerter and

Radeberger Pils are very fine – see pages 254 and 244), but in Saxony wine is perhaps of more interest. The hills above the north bank of the Elbe, especially around Pillnitz and between Radebeul and Meissen, expose vines to just the right amount of sun to make this one of Europe's northernmost wine-making regions. There are records of wine-growing here from 1161, the industry peaking in the 16th century when around 10,000ha were cultivated; now that area is just 360ha. The main grape is the Müller-Thurgau, with Weissburgunder (White Burgundy, ie: Pinot Blanc), Traminer, Grauburgunder (Pinot Gris) and Riesling, producing dry white wines with a character full of fruity acidity. Some *Sekt* (sparkling) wines are also made, as well as a few soft reds, from Spätburgunder (Pinot Noir) and Dornfelder grapes.

Several estates offer wine tastings and wine tourism; there's a Saxon Wine Road (*www.saechsische-weinstrasse.de*) and even a Saxon Wine Hiking Trail (*www.saechsischer-weinwanderweg.de*).

RESTAURANTS

AVERAGE PRICE OF MAIN COURSE

Expensive	$$$$$	€30+
Above average	$$$$	€15–30
Mid range	$$$	€9–15
Cheap and cheerful	$$	€6–9
Rock bottom	$	<€6

✘ RESTAURANTS AND CAFÉS

ALTSTADT There are some gourmet restaurants in the Altstadt [map 2], mainly in hotels, but most are over-priced touristy places, mentioned here for the sake of convenience.

In addition to the restaurants and cafés listed below (covering the Altstadt and nearby areas south of the Elbe), there are two main concentrations of fairly glitzy chain-style establishments. Those on Münzgasse, between the Frauenkirche and the Elbe embankment, include the Australian-themed Ayers Rock and the Spanish Las Tapas; on Weisse Gasse, a car-free square behind the Kreuzkirche, you'll find another tapas place, Capetown Seafood, the Dutch Fliegende Holländer, the Vietnamese Kinh Do, the Eiscafé Venezia and the Cuchi Lounge, in fact a sushi place.

✘ **Alte Meister** Theaterplatz 1A; ☏ 481 0426; e info@altemeister.net; www.altemeister.net; ⏲ 10.00–01.00 daily
Tucked away at the end of the Semper Gallery on the north side of the Zwinger (behind the statue of Weber), so remarkably few tourists find this bright modern place that acts as a café until 18.00, with a lovely terrace, & then a good international restaurant that's busy before & after opera performances. **$$$$**

✘ **Alte Schankwirtschaft am Schiesshaus** Am Schiesshaus 19; ☏ 484 5990; e schuetze@zum-schiesshaus.de; www.zum-schiesshaus.de; ⏲ 11.00–01.00 daily
Just west of the Old Town & not far from the Semperoper (& the Environment Centre) this Baroque inn (dating from 1554) is now in an area of new lofts. It has a large & attractive garden, with good simple food & fair prices. **$$$**

✗ **Altmarktkeller Sächsisch-Böhmisches Bierhaus** Altmarkt 4; ☎ 481 8130; e info@altmarktkeller.de;
www.altmarktkeller.de; ⏰from 11.00 daily
On the northeastern corner of the Altmarkt, this cavernous AC cellar now serves rib-sticking Saxon & Czech
food plus draught Radeberger & Krušovice beers, with a beer terrace & a Dixie/Bohemian brass band on
Fri/Sat evenings. $$$

✗ **Balduccis** Am Altmarkt 16–17; ☎ 495 1179, 495 5095; ⏰11.00–midnight daily
In a big hall above the Café Prag, you can still see traces of communist design in what is now a lively
classical Italian restaurant, serving pizza, pasta & *musica* (Signor Balducci may be singing Italian love songs, if
you're lucky). Service is friendly & prompt, & there's wine by the glass, pitcher or bottle. $$$

✗ **Bistro am Zwingerteich** Theaterplatz 2; ☎ 491 1521; ⏰from 12.00 daily
The Bistro by the Zwinger Pond is tucked away behind the Semperoper in its modern extension; it's a very
pleasant spot to take a break from the Zwinger's art, & there's also a restaurant with an unadventurous
choice of Saxon food, although the menu is also in English. $$

✗ **Brenn Nessel** Schützengasse 18; ☎ 494 3319; e info@brennnessel-dresden.de; www.brennnessel-dresden.de;
⏰11.00–midnight daily
Dresden's main vegetarian restaurant, the Stinging Nettle shares a Baroque house (built in 1650) with the
Umweltzentrum (Environment Centre). Food ranges from soups & baguettes to baked dishes & pasta, as well as
desserts. $$

💻 **Café Friedrichstadt** Friedrichstr 38; ☎ 4927 8810; www.cafe-friedrichstadt.de; ⏰11.00–18.00 Sun/Mon,
11.00–22.00 Tue–Thu, 11.00–midnight Fri/Sat, closed holidays [map 1]

Just west of the Altstadt, with a pleasant garden, this is the best place for a drink or light meal on this side of town. $$

⌨ **Café Schinkelwache** Theaterplatz 2; ☏ 498 9803; e info@rank-buettig.de; ⏰ 10.00–midnight daily
Cramped inside but with plenty of space outside in summer, a pricey but perfectly sited spot for coffee, cakes & ice creams, as well as more filling snacks. $$

✗ **Chiaveri** Bernhard-v-Lindenau-Platz; ☏ 496 0399; e prima@chiaveri.de; www.chiaveri.de; ⏰ from 11.00 daily
In the modern Landtag (state parliament) this gourmet restaurant (named after the builder of the cathedral) serves light meals, such as soups, pasta & *picatta milanese*, until 17.00, & thereafter is very popular for pre-opera dinners, with dishes including Argentine steak & fillet of monkfish or seabass. $$$$

✗ **Festungsmauern am Brühlschen Garten** Am Brülschen Garten 4; ☏ 262 6032; e info@bruehlscher-garten.de; www.bruehlscher-garten.de; ⏰ from 09.30 daily
A stylishly designed café-restaurant in the city wall near the synagogue that offers good food (such as ragout, schnitzel & pasta) for rather less than some more central establishments. $$$

✗ **Fischhaus Alberthafen** Magdeburger Str 69; ☏ 498 2110; www.fischhaus-alberthafen.de; ⏰ 12.00–15.00 & 18.00–23.00 Mon–Fri, 12.00–23.30 Sat, 12.00–22.00 Sun [map 1]
Perhaps the most authentic place in town for fish, on the edge of the docks west of the Altstadt (see page 168) & easily reached by bus 75. They also have a Hafencasino (Port Canteen, ⏰ 07.00–14.00) & rooms. $$$

✗ **Gänsedieb** Weisse Gasse 1; ✆ 850905; e email@gaensedieb.de; www.gaensedieb.de; ⏰ from 11.00 daily
The Goose Thief is the pick of a group of restaurants on a square behind the Kreuzkirche; it naturally specialises in roast goose as well as Saxon staples, such as potato soup & *Sauerbraten* & desserts such as *Eierschecke* & *Quarkkeulchen*. It also serves a dozen beers by the Bavarian Paulaner brewery. **$$$**

✗ **Intermezzo** Am Taschenberg 3; ✆ 491 2712; e reservations.taschenbergpalais@kempinski.com; www.kempinski-dresden.de; ⏰ 06.30–10.30 (to 11.00 Sat/Sun & hols), 12.00–14.30 & 18.00–23.30 daily
In the Hotel Kempinski Taschenberg Palais, this offers gourmet food but at absurd prices. You can also have lighter Mediterranean meals at the Palais Bistro & Kaffee und Küchen in the Café Vestibul, with drinks also served in the inner courtyard in summer. **$$$$$**

✗ **Italienisches Dörfchen** Theaterplatz 3; ✆ 498160; e gastro.theaterplatz@t-online.de; www.italienisches-doerfchen.de; ⏰ from 12.00 daily; Piccolo from 17.00 Tue–Thu, from 11.00 Fri–Sun
A delightful setting but usually overrun by tourist groups (the main coach pick-up point in the Altstadt is outside), this is a Baroque pavilion with period furnishings; the Ristorante Bellotto serves good Italian food & cocktails, & there's also a café, beer hall & wine room. Across the road by the river there's the similar Basteischlosschen, housing the Piccolo restaurant (✆ 498 1688), also Italian & run by the same management. **$$$$**

✗ **Kahnaletto** Terrassenufer (by the Augustusbrücke); ✆ 495 3037; www.kahnaletto.de; ⏰ 12.00–15.00 & 18.00–midnight daily
On board the Theaterkahn floating theatre, this offers a lunch menu that's great value at €10 (with a salad, pasta, meat or fish & a non-alcoholic drink), & a fine place for a break on a chilly day. There's also à la carte dining, mainly on Italian & fish dishes. **$$$**

✕ **Kakas** Krenkelstr 12; ✆ 652 8423; e info@restaurant-kakas.de; www.restaurant-kakas.de; ⏰ 11.30–14.00 & 17.00–23.00 Tue–Sun [map 1]
To the north of the Grosser Garten, this is a Hungarian restaurant with suitably rustic furnishings, serving mainly beef, chicken & fish. $$$

⛉ **Konditorei Kreutzkamm** Seestr 6; ✆ 4954172; www.kreutzkamm.de; ⏰ 08.30–19.00 Mon–Sat, 12.00–18.00 Sun & hols
Founded in 1825, this was Dresden's classic location for coffee & cakes & especially *Stollen*; the Kreutzkamm family relocated to Munich in 1950 but have now opened a Dresden branch again, not far from the original Altmarkt site. It's pricey but worth it. $$

✕ **Kunst-café Antik** Terrassengasse; ✆ 496 5217; ⏰ 09.00–midnight daily
In a modern cellar behind the Hilton, this is a rather touristy café serving the usual light meals, but it does have interesting décor, with antique furniture strewn around & hanging from the ceiling. $$$

✕ **La Osteria** Kreuzstr 1; ✆ 497 6230; e mail@laosteria.de; www.laosteria.de; ⏰ 11.00–01.00 Mon–Thu, to 02.30 Fri/Sat (pasta to 23.00/midnight, pizza to midnight/02.00, happy hours 17.00–18.00 & 23.00–midnight)
A decent Italian place, though far slicker & less atmospheric than those in the Neustadt. $$

✕ **Las Tapas** Münzgasse 4; ✆ 496 0108; e info@las-tapas.de; www.las-tapas.de; ⏰ from 11.00 daily
More touristy (predictably) than its Neustadt rivals, this still provides good tapas & other Spanish dishes, as you'd expect. $$

✕ Lesage Lennéstr 1; ☏ 420 4250; e restaurant.lesage@kempinski.com; www.kempinski-dresden.de; ⏰12.00–14.30 & 18.00–22.00 (bar to midnight); 11.00–15.00 Sun brunch
Fine dining in the ultra-cool setting of VW's Transparent Factory, provided by the chefs of Kempinski's Taschenberg Palais Hotel. Daytime snacks include Saxon potato soup (€4), burgers or penne rigate (both €7), while the gourmet evening menu includes gazpacho soup, halibut fillet with basmati rice, coconut & pine nuts or duck tortellini with cabbage & mushroom sauce. $$$$

✕ Lingner Lingnerplatz 1; ☏ 484 6600; e info@restaurant-lingner.de; www.restaurant-lingner.de; ⏰10.30–midnight Mon–Sat
In the unexpected setting of the German Hygiene Museum, this is a good restaurant that also acts during the day as the museum café, serving soups, salads, baguettes & desserts till 18.00, & for dinner dishes ranging from enchiladas to Chateaubriand. Live jazz on Mon at 21.00. $$$$

✕ Ogura An der Frauenkirche 5, Dresden Hilton; ☏ 864 2855; e info.dresden@hilton.com; www.hilton.de/dresden; ⏰12.00–22.30 Tue–Sun
This offers Dresden's best sushi, sashimi & teppan (hot iron plate) food; it's one of several good restaurants in the Hilton Hotel, including the Applaus steakhouse (⏰11.00–midnight daily) & Rossini (see below). $$$$$

✕ Pulverturm An der Frauenkirche 12; ☏ 262 600; e info@pulverturm-dresden.de; www.pulverturm-dresden.de; ⏰11.00–01.00 daily
One of a group of Altstadt cellars with staff in 18th-century costume & musicians or other performers wandering about, not to mention the Condemned Man's Last Meal, served in a dungeon. In summer there's also seating outside. Food & prices are fair for a tourist restaurant in this location. $$$

✕ Radeberger Spezialausschank Terrassenufer 1; ✆ 484 8660; e spezialausschank@radeberger.de; ⏰11.00–01.00 daily
With tables on the Brühl Terrace, this is the best place to drink Radeberger Pilsner (see page 254), especially the unfiltered Zwickel, available only here & in Radeberg. Potato soup & sausages are the obvious accompanying foods, although in season dishes such as goose are also available. **$$**

✕ Restaurant & Grand Café Coselpalais An der Frauenkirche 12; ✆ 496 2444; e info@rank-buettig.de; www.restaurant-dresden.de; ⏰10.00–01.00 daily
In one of the most prestigious locations in Dresden, right up against the Frauenkirche, the ground floor of the Baroque Coselpalais now serves French & German food as well as Kaffee und Küchen; the non-smoking Vogelzimmer (Bird Room) is furnished with porcelain birds. **$$$**

✕ Rossini An der Frauenkirche 5; ✆ 864 2860; e info.dresden@hilton.com; www.hilton.de/dresden; ⏰18.00–23.30 daily
An excellent Italian restaurant (with 14 Gault-Millau points), serving regional specialities from all over Italy, such as monkfish in pesto, saffron gnocchi or fish carpaccio, with an extensive list of Italian wines. **$$$$$**

✕ Sala Thai Sushi Kleine Brüdergasse 3; ✆ 862 1919; ⏰11.30–23.30 daily
More relaxed than Ogura, this serves an uncomplicated mix of Thai & Japanese food, with 8 fixed menus as well as à la carte choices. **$$$**

✕ Sophienkeller Taschenberg 3; ✆ 497260; e info@sophienkeller-dresden.de; www.sophienkeller-dresden.de; ⏰11.00–01.00 daily

A cellar restaurant under the Taschenberg Palais that's very popular with tourist groups, with its long wooden tables, buxom maids & waiters in 18th-century costume & occasional visits from August the Strong & Countess Cosel. Food is mainly Saxon, including potato soup, *Sauerbraten* & *Dresdner Quarkkeulchen*. **$$$**

✗ **Wettiner Keller** Terrassengasse; ☏ 864 2860; e info.dresden@hilton.com; www.hilton.de/dresden; ⏱ 18.00–midnight Tue–Sat
In the crypts under the Brühl Terrace, entered by a lovely Renaissance door at the rear of the Hilton, this is a cosy wine cellar serving hearty food such as carpaccio of veal, fried zander (pike-perch), *Dresdner Sauerbraten*, goulash or meats on a hot stone slab. **$$$**

✗ **Yenidze Cupola Restaurant** Weisseritzerstr 3; ☏ 490 5990; e info@kuppelrestaurant.de; www.kuppelrestaurant.de; ⏱ 11.00–midnight daily
In the glass cupola on top of the mosque-like former cigarette factory (see page 167) is a restaurant with fairly standard offerings plus a few vegetarian & Asian dishes. There are readings most nights of the *Arabian Nights* & other fairy tales, which are remarkably popular here (*www.1001maerchen.de*). One floor below (take the lift to level 6) there's a roof terrace with fantastic views of Dresden; absolutely the best place for a sunset Kronbacher. **$$$**

NEUSTADT [map 4]
✗ **Bauernstuben** Hauptstr 13; ☏ 8042791; http://bauernstuben-kuegelgenhaus.de; ⏱ from 11.00 daily
In the Baroque Kügelgenhaus (see page 216), this cheerful informal place offers excellent value; with simple Saxon meals & farm-style tables & chairs. **$$$**

🍽 **Café Der Löwe** Hauptstr 48; ✆ 804 1138; ⏱from 11.00 daily
A smallish café serving the usual grills & steak, as well as goose breast & venison, & Augustiner beer from Munich; its chief attraction may be the free Wi-Fi. **$$$**

✗ **Canaletto** Grosse Meissner Str 15; ✆ 805 1658; e restaurant@canaletto-dresden.de; www.canaletto-dresden.de; ⏱06.30–10.30, 12.00–14.30 & 17.30–22.30 daily
The restaurant of the Westin Bellevue Hotel serves fine Italian food & nouvelle cuisine versions of classics such as tournedos but the great attraction is the stunning view across the river to the Altstadt. **$$$$$**

✗ **Caroussel** Rähnitzgasse 19; ✆ 80030; e info@buelow-residenz.de; www.buelow-residenz.de; ⏱12.00–14.00 & from 18.30 Tue–Sat (& a limited choice for hotel guests on Sun/Mon)
In the boutique Hotel Bülow Residenz, this is Dresden's only Michelin-starred restaurant (it also has 17 points from Gault-Millau & 4 Bertelsmann toques), with an exquisite setting & service for its flawless light modern cuisine, emphasising the use of fresh seasonal produce, locally grown as far as possible (& with Saxon wines). A new chef has recently taken over, but there's no reason to suppose standards will slip. **$$$$$**

🍽 **Eiscafé Venezia** Hauptstr 2A; ✆ 804 5458; ⏱09.00–midnight daily
A classic ice cream café with a large terrace facing the Golden Rider statue & the Altstadt; there's a great range of homemade ices, fruit salads, cakes & pastries. **$**

✗ **El Español** An der Dreikönigskirche 7; ✆ 804 8670; e mail@elespanol.de; www.elespanol.de; ⏱11.00–01.00 Sun–Wed, 11.00–02.00 Thu–Sat
The better of the pair of tapas bars to the west of the Three Kings church, with a range of more substantial Spanish dishes too; Mon is paella night. **$$$**

✕ Kartoffelkeller Nieritz Str 11; ☎ 817 6358; ⏱from 17.00 daily
A Dresden institution, doing anything you could possibly imagine with the noble spud — potato soup, potato bread, potato goulash, potato pancakes, & potato strudel to finish with. **$$**

✕ Kö5a Königstr 5A; ☎ 802 4088; e info@koe5.de; www.koe5.de; ⏱from 11.30 daily
In the cellar & courtyard of a beautifully restored Baroque townhouse (built in 1776), this is unpretentious but classy dining, with filling Saxon dishes such as goose breast or venison goulash. **$$$**

✕ Le Maréchal de Saxe Königstr 15; ☎ 810 5880; ⏱from 11.00 daily
Opposite the Dreikönigskirche in the same Baroque townhouse as the Kulturrathaus, the 'Marshal of Saxony' (named after Count Moritz, August the Strong's illegitimate son who led the French army) is similar to Kö5a, but with French cuisine, wine & décor. **$$$**

✕ Pfunds Café-Restaurant Pfunds Molkerei, Bautzner Str 79; ☎ 810 5948; e info@pfunds.de; www.pfunds.de; ⏱10.00–20.00 daily
Above the world's loveliest cheese shop (see page 166), the relatively plain restaurant is also heavy on dairy products, with fondue, raclette & cheese plates available, as well as steaks. **$$$**

✕ Rähnitz Café-Bar Rähnitzgasse 7; ☎ 652 4868; e info@raehnitz.de; www.raehnitz.de; ⏱from 11.00 Mon–Sat
A stylish place to relax, serving brunch & a small range of Italian dishes. **$$**

💻 Schwarzmarkt Café & Bistro Hauptstr 36; ☎ 801 0833; ⏱from 08.00 daily
Opposite the Dreikönigskirche, this is a stylish little café that also has Wi-Fi. **$**

6

✘ **The Red Rooster** Rähnitzgasse 10; ☎ 272 1850; e info@redrooster-pub.de; www.redrooster-pub.de; ⏲ 17.00–03.00 daily

Dresden's oldest pub, with over 100 Scottish single malts as well as Irish whiskeys, & food such as Irish stew, trout, schnitzel & steak. There's a garden, & live jazz & blues music at times. $$$

✘ **Watzke Café & Speisehaus** Hauptstr 1; ☎ 810 6820; e hauptstrasse@watzke.de; ⏲ 09.30–midnight daily

The city-centre outlet of the Brauhaus Watzke (see page 126), this is more a restaurant than a bar, with a range of food from beer pastry & vegetarian dishes to rumpsteak to soak up their fine unfiltered beers (€ 2 for half a litre on Mon, Tue & Wed). $$$

✘ **Wenzel-Prager Bierstuben** Königstr 1; ☎ 804 2010; e dresden@wenzel-prager-bierstuben.de; www.wenzel-prager-bierstuben.de; ⏲ 11.00–midnight daily

A Czech tavern in a Baroque townhouse, with rib-sticking Bohemian & Moravian food (heavy on the stodgy dumplings) to accompany the *Staropramen*; their dark beer is cheap on Tue. There's a livelier scene in the covered courtyard than in the restaurant. $$

AUSSERE NEUSTADT [map 5] There's a great range of ethnic cuisines available here, from Indian to Portuguese and Thai, as well as *Kneipen* or pubs which offer Saxon food to accompany their beer.

✘ **Am Fass** Kamenzer Str 28; ☎ 0172 353 294094

At Bischofsweg, a Hungarian bar, with food such as goulash & chicken paprika. $$

✗ **Babos Dönerpoint** Katharinenstr 20; ☎ 804 0666; www.babos-dresden.com; ⏰09.00–04.00 daily
At the corner of Alaunstr, this is one of the best kebab places in Dresden. Also at Wallstr 11 (*near the Altmarkt;* ☎ 654 04 76; ⏰09.00–22.00 Mon–Sat, 10.00–22.00 Sun*) & Anton Str 18 (*near the Bahnhof Neustadt;* ⏰10.00–23.00 daily*). $

✗ **Bamiyan** Bischofsweg 38; ☎ 210 5774; ⏰11.00–14.30 & 17.00–23.00 Mon–Sat, 12.30–22.30 Sun
At the corner of Alaunstr, an Afghan restaurant (also serving pasta etc). $$

✗ **Beirut** Rothenburger Str 1
A Lebanese restaurant – a bit like the local doner places but with a better ambience. $

✗ **Bierstube Bischof 72** Bischofsweg 72; ⏰11.30–15.00 & from 18.00 Mon–Fri, from 18.00 Sat, 12.00–15.00 & 18.00–midnight Sun & hols
Despite the name, this is definitely more of a restaurant than a pub, with relatively pricey food for this area, including goose, carp & steaks, as well as *Stollen* parfait. $$$

⊡ **Café Neustadt** Bautzner Str 63; ☎ 899 6649; www.neustadt-cafe.de; ⏰07.30–01.00 Mon–Fri, 09.00–01.00 Sat/Sun
At the corner of Pulsnitzer Str, a nice clean modern place serving b/fast to 16.00, dinner to 22.00, & with jazz on Thu at 21.00. $

✗ **Come-In Bistro** Rudolf-Leonhardt-Str 16; ☎ 646 5859
Handy for the Boofe hostel (& the laundromat), serving panini, steaks, Schnitzel, beer & wine. $$

✗ **Cous-Cous Haus** Louisenstr 28; ⏱11.00–01.00 daily
Algerian & Arab food. $$

✗ **Cuba Bar-restaurant Martínez** Rudolf-Leonhardt-Str 31
Cuban food, including snacks such as empanadas & yuca frita, & fish & steak, plus a selection (*plato de todo un poco*, including a vegetarian option), & cocktails (€4–5). $$$

✗ **Curry & Co** Louisenstr 62; ☎ 0152 0708 5402; e essen@curryundco.com; www.curryundco.com; ⏱11.00–22.00 Sun–Wed, 11.00–02.00 Thu–Sat
A fast-food place, serving Currywurst, not Indian curry. $$$

✗ **Da Michele** Louisenstr 33; ☎ 810 8680; ⏱17.00–23.00 Mon–Sat
Pizza. $$

✗ **Da Rosa** Pulsnitzer Str 1; ⏱from 11.00 daily
On the northeast corner of Martin-Luther-Platz, a friendly local place serving pizza, pasta, salads etc. $$

✗ **Dürüm Kebab Haus** Rothenburger Str 41; www.durum-kebab-haus.de; ⏱till the early hours
A recommended kebab joint. $

🍵 **Eiscafé Lloyds** Martin-Luther-Platz 17; ☎ 803 6790
A coffee house serving ices & light snacks, with good music nightly. $

✖ **El Perro Boracho** Alaunstr 70; ☎ 803 6723; e info@elperro.de; www.elperro.de; ⏰ from 16.00 Mon, from 11.30 Tue–Fri, from 10.00 Sat/Sun & hols
In the delightfully arty Kunsthof, a Spanish restaurant serving food such as tortillas, paella & tapas, as well as b/fast at w/ends. **$$**

✖ **Espitas** Louisenstr 39; ☎ 456 8525; www.espitas.de; ⏰ 11.00–01.00 Mon–Thu, 11.00–03.00 Fri, 10.00–03.00 Sat, 10.00–01.00 Sun
Not a very authentic Mexican cantina, but at least it's a funky modern building (on the corner of Alaunstr); there's a brunch buffet until 15.00. **$$**

🖵 **Habibi Café** Martin-Luther Str 37; ☎ 5635098; ⏰ 17.00–05.00 daily
At the junction with Louisenstr, this serves hummus, baba ganoush, sandwiches & a dish of the day, as well as coffee & cocktails, & *shisha* waterpipes. **$**

🖵 **Hot Spoon** Bischofsweg 6; ☎ 2134523; ⏰ 11.30–23.00 daily
At Königsbrucker Str, a great stand-up soup bar. **$**

✖ **Jaipur** Louisenstr 59; ☎ 456 8946; www.jaipur-dresden.de; ⏰ 11.00–14.30 & 17.00–midnight daily
A very good Indian restaurant (in a nice Baroque house), with a long menu including tandoori & vegetarian dishes. **$$**

✖ **La Casina Rosa** Alaunstr 93; ☎ 801 4848; www.lacasinarosa.de; ⏰ 17.30–23.30 Mon–Sat, also 11.45–14.30 Tue–Fri

A friendly family-run Italian place serving homemade pasta, saltimbocca romana, risotto, & on Wed/Thu fish. $$$. Also the Piccola Capri (⏲ 17.30–23.30 Mon–Sat; pizza $$).

✕ **La Rue** Görlitzer Str 11; ☏ 801 2977; ⏲ 18.00–02.00 daily
On the face of it a French café-bistro-crêperie, with a summer garden, but also a Jewish restaurant, specialising in gefillte fish. $$$

✕ **Le Petit Maroc** Bischofsweg 18; ☏ 3741336; ⏲ 11.30–16.00 & 18.00–23.00 Mon–Thu, 12.00–23.00 Fri/Sat
A nice little Moroccan restaurant. $$

✕ **Mãe Portugal** Sebnitzer Str 36; ☏ 0162 197 3989; ⏲ from 17.00 Mon–Fri, from 12.00 Sat/Sun & hols
Dresden's Portuguese restaurant. $$

✕ **Maharadscha** Kamenzer Str 62; ☏ 803 0407; ⏲ 17.00–23.30 Mon–Thu, 11.30–23.30 Fri–Sun
At Nordstr, serving Indian food from Maharashtra, the state of Mumbai. $$$

✕ **Orientalis** Alaunstr 72; ☏ 658 8788; ⏲ 12.00–20.00 Mon–Fri, 13.00–20.00 Sat
A pleasant place serving great-value Arab–Persian cooking, with a dish of the day (vegetarian on Thu) for €2.50–3, stuffed breads at the same price & tagine & vegetarian dishes for barely more. $

✕ **Pailin** Bautzner Str 34; ☏ 563 3388; ⏲ 11.30–14.30 & 17.30–23.00 Mon–Sat
Actually set back from the main road at the corner of Lessingstr & Holzhofgasse, this is a relatively pure Thai restaurant, but not at all expensive. $$$

💻 **Panino Die Baguetteria** Görlitzer Str 4; ☎ 563 8699; ⏰ 12.00–23.00 Mon–Thu, 12.00–01.00 Fri, 17.00–01.00 Sat, 17.00–22.00 Sun, closed hols
An attractive take-away/stand-up place selling huge ciabattas (€ 2–3), half-metre baguettes (€ 3–4), coffees, Glühwein & other drinks. **$**

✕ **Piccola Toscana** Louisenstr 34; ☎ 992 4929
A basic cheap Italian restaurant serving pizza, spaghetti, gnocchi & lasagne, with a beer garden too (serving Feldschlossen beer). **$$**

✕ **Plaka** Louisenstr 30; ☎ 801 9706
The Neustadt's best Greek eatery, on the corner of Alaunstr. **$$**

✕ **Planwirtschaft** Louisenstr 20; ☎ 801 3187; e planwirtschaft@t-online.de; www.planwirtschaft.de; ⏰ 09.00–01.00 Sun–Thu, 09.00–02.00 Fri/Sat
At the rear of a quiet courtyard, this is one of the oldest Neustadt pubs, with a funky café (with 20 types of tea too) & a beer cellar (with Guinness). The Planned Economy theme is represented by DDR-made vacuum cleaners & suchlike on the walls. Food includes a b/fast buffet (⏰ 09.00–15.00; € 8). **$$**

✕ **Raskolnikoff** Böhmische Str 34; ☎ 804 5706; e raskolnikoff-dresden@t-online.de; www.raskolnikoff.de; ⏰ 10.00–02.00 (food till midnight) daily
Formerly rather punky, this is now a very cool bar-restaurant serving Russian food such as *borsch* soup & *vareniki* (like ravioli), as well as a range of vodkas (& whiskies). There's also a pleasant garden (with fountain), open in summer to 22.00. **$**

📖 **Scheune Café** Alaunstr 36; ✆ 802 6619; e info@scheunecafe.de; www.scheunecafe.de; ⏰ 17.00–02.00 Mon–Fri, 10.00–02.00 (with brunch to 16.00) Sat/Sun & hols
The 'Barn' hosts punky gigs most nights, but there's also a large beer garden & a café (with a non-smoking area) serving cheap Indian food. $$

✕ **Serengeti** Alaunstr 60; ✆ 213 1393; e african-food@serengeti-dd.de; www.serengeti-dd.de; ⏰ from 17.00 Mon–Fri, from 15.00 Sat/Sun
You'll eat 'African food' (with South African wines) sitting in an African hut on zebra-striped seats. $$

📖 **Soul Food Sisters** Louisenstr 26; ⏰ 11.00–23.00 Mon–Sat
An excellent stand-up place (with a few seats) for panini & soup (€3–4.50 for a big bowl). $

📖 **Suppenbar** Rothenburger 37; ✆ 810 7130; www.suppenbar-dresden.de; ⏰ 11.30–22.00 Mon–Fri, 11.30–16.00 Sat
The original Neustadt soup bar, now also at Fetscher Platz near the University Hospital (⏰ 11.30–17.00 Mon–Fri) & in the Haus der Presse on Ostra Allee (⏰ 11.00–16.30 Mon–Fri); the soups are good & filling (also for take-away), & there are a few seats & newspapers. $

✕ **Trattoria Vecchia Napoli** Alaunstr 33; ✆ 802 9055; www.gastro-gagliardi.de; ⏰ 12.00–14.00 & 18.00–23.30 Mon–Sat
At the junction with Katharinen Str (with 3 other sites in the suburbs), a good Italian restaurant, with a wood-fired pizza oven. $$$$

THE SUBURBS

⌨ **Café Toscana** Schillerplatz 7, Blasewitz; ☎ 310 0744 ⏰ 11.00–19.00 Mon–Fri, 09.00–19.00 Sat, 12.00–19.00 Sun [map 1]
A very pleasant café/pastry shop with scrumptious cakes & a terrace overlooking the river & the famous Blaues Wunder (Blue Wonder Bridge). **$$$**

✗ **Historisches Fischhaus** Fischhausstr 14; ☎ 899100; e info@fischhaus.de; www.fischhaus.de; ⏰ 12.00–midnight Mon–Fri, 11.00–midnight Sat/Sun [map 1]
Founded in 1573 at the König-Albert-Park-Hotel, on the fringe of the Albertpark, northeast of the city (tram 11). Fish is now served in a Jugendstil hall or in the charmingly rural garden. **$$$**

✗ **Luisenhof** Bergbahnstr 8, Loschwitz; ☎ 214 9960; www.luisenhof.org; ⏰ 11.00–01.00 Mon–Sat, 10.00–midnight Sun
At the top of the funicular, this is a popular excursion for Saxon food with good wine & beer, especially in summer when the terrace gives great views. **$$$**

✗ **Marcolini** Bautzner Str 96; ☎ 862 7800; e info@restaurant-marcolini.de; www.restaurant-marcolini.de; ⏰ 15.00–23.00 Mon–Fri, 12.00–23.00 Sat & hols, 12.00–21.00 Sun [map 3]
Bizarrely located below a plastic surgery clinic, this is actually a lovely restaurant, looking out over the Elbe Meadows (& easily reached along the cycle route) & serving seasonal & vegetarian specialities. **$$$**

✗ **Parkcafé Pillnitz** Landhaus Carus, Orangeriestr 26; ☎ 261 8233; e restaurant.parkcafe@t-online.de; www.parkcafe-pillnitz.de

In addition to the fine restaurants at the Schlosshotel Pillnitz, there's the Parkcafé, on the main road through the village, serving Saxon cuisine & seasonal specialities in the summer home of the royal doctor. $$

✕ **Prinzenkeiler im Schloss Albrechtsberg** Bautzner Str 130; ☎ 216 7545; e info@prinzenkeller.de; ⏰09.00–midnight Mon–Fri, 11.00–midnight Sat/Sun [map I]
Actually in the cellar of the castle gatehouse, this is a bistro during the day & a French restaurant in the evening; it's run by catering students & is great value. $$

✕ **Schillergarten** Schillerplatz 9, Blasewitz; ☎ 811 9922; e info@schillergarten.de; www.schillergarten.de; ⏰11.00–01.00 daily [map I]
Famous long before the Blue Wonder Bridge was built, this was where the great Romantic Friedrich Schiller fell in love in the 1780s with the waitress, Justine Segedin, immortalised as Gustel von Blasewitz in his *Wallenstein*. Now it's a beautiful Jugendstil restaurant with dark wood & leather & modern Saxon cuisine, as well as a café-patisserie & a garden with seating for a thousand. $$

✕ **Schlossrestaurant im Hotel Schloss Eckberg** Bautzner Str 134; ☎ 80990; e info@schloss-eckberg.de; www.schloss-eckberg.de; ⏰11.30–14.00 & 18.00–23.00 daily [map I]
If visiting the Elbe castles you can have a good meal of light Mediterranean-style food here in the wood-panelled hall or the winter garden, or in summer on the terrace with fantastic views of the Elbe bend & Dresden. $$$$

✕ **Schmidt's Restaurant** Moritzburger Weg 67; ☎ 804 4883; e info@koenig-albert.de; www.koenig-albert.de; ⏰11.00–23.00 Mon–Fri, 17.00–23.00 Sat

On the southern edge of the garden suburb of Hellerau (tram 8 to Am Hellerand), this offers fine modern French-based fusion cuisine. $$$$

🍺 BARS AND BEER GARDENS

NEUSTADT The Aussere Neustadt is *the* place to go for a drink, unless you're happy to relax in your hotel's bar. Most bars there are actually *Kneipen* or pubs, concentrating on drink but selling solid food too – the website www.kneipensurfer.de has a good interactive map of the current choices (there are plenty, and they have a fairly high turnover). Equally, many of the establishments listed in the previous section would be perfectly good places to have a drink without eating.

🍺 **Augustus-Garten** At the northeastern end of the Augustusbrücke [map 4]
An unassuming & little-known beer garden with views of the meadows & Altstadt.

🍺 **Bar Pawlow** Görlitzer Str 34 [map 5]
Below Lollis hostel at the corner of Sebnitzer Str, this is described as a punky pub, although in fact there's no music but pleasantly funky décor.

🍸 **Canapé** Alaunstr 61; ✆ 810 7301; e ow@canape-bar.de; www.canape-bar.de; ⏰from 19.00 to at least 01.00 Mon–Sat, from 20.00 Sun & holidays [map 5]
A fairly chic bar with a courtyard terrace, serving coffee, cocktails (all at €5.50) & fingerfood.

♀ **Efes Shisha Café** Louisenstr 33; ✆ 888599 [map 5]
A place to smoke waterpipes.

♀ **El Cubanito** Sebnitzer Str 8B; ✆ 804 7870; ⏱ 19.00–01.00 daily, to 02.00 Fri/Sat [map 5]
Across Görlitzer Str from the Pawlow, this serves lots of rum cocktails (inc non-alcoholic ones) & pilsner & dark beer; although the music is relatively quiet, it does attract plenty of Afro-Caribbeans.

♀ **Hebedas** Rothenburger Str 30; ✆ 895 1010; e post@hebedas.de [map 5]
A small retro bar with billiard table, playing lounge/dance music.

🍺 **Hieronymus** Alaunstr 61; ✆ 801 1739; www.cafe-hieronymus.com; ⏱ 19.00–02.00 daily [map 5]
A good honest pub, with Becks beer, wines & whiskies, plus snacks. There's often live music.

🍺 **Katy's Garage** Alaunstr 48; www.katysgarage.de [map 5]
On the corner of Louisenstr, marking Dresden's party central, there are gigs every night (student night Mon, reggae Thu), as well as table football & a beer garden.

🍺 **Kontinental** Gorlitzer Str 1; ✆ 801 3531; ⏱ always [map 5]
On the corner of Louisenstr, this 24hr bar is where you'll end up when everywhere else is closed, or where you'll get b/fast after an early arrival in the Neustadt (lunch & dinner also available).

♀ **Lebowski Bar** Görlitzer Str 5; www.dudes-bar.de; ⏱ 19.00–05.00 daily [map 5]
The homage to bowling & the Coen Brothers film is not overdone; this is a good drinking bar, with cocktails (from €4.50), wine, beer & cigars.

Madness Louisenstr 20; ☎ 899 6135; e info@madness-dresden.de; www.madness-dresden.de; ⏲19.00–03.00 daily, to 05.00 Fri/Sat [map 5]
Live bands (unless it's bingo night!).

Pinta Louisenstr 49; ☎ 810 6761; ⏲18.00–03.00 Mon–Sat [map 5]
Dresden's oldest cocktail bar, with a range of over 150 drinks (all at €4.50 19.00–21.00 Sun–Thu).

The Red Rooster Rähnitzgasse 10; ☎ 272 1850; ⏲from 17.00 to at least 03.00 daily, also 11.30–14.30 Mon–Fri [map 4]
A traditional pub serving Veltins Pilsner & various whiskies; there's also Wi-Fi.

Shisha Lounge Louisenstr 58; www.shisha-dresden.de; ⏲from 19.00 daily [map 5]
As the name implies, a place to lounge with a waterpipe (€4).

Tir Na N'og Bischofsweg 34; ☎ 810 3639; www.tirnanog-pub.de [map 5]
A better Irish pub than the Shamrock in the Altstadt, with Guinness & Kilkenny beers, plus frequent folk & blues acts.

Trotzdem Alaunstr 81 [map 5]
'Nevertheless' is a cheap alternative pub, showing free films on Sun at 22.00.

U-Boot Bautzner Str 75; ☎ 802 3254; ⏲23.00–05.00 daily [map 5]
A late-night dancebar (student night Wed).

♀ **Zora** Priessnitzstr 12; ✆ 204720; ⏰ from 15.00 Tue–Sun [map 5]
A stylish modern café-cocktail bar next to the Carte Blanche drag revue (see page 137).

ELSEWHERE

🍺 **Brauhaus Watzke** Kötzschenbroder Str 1; ✆ 852920; e dresden@watzke.de; www.watzke.de;
⏰ 11.00–midnight daily [map 1]
At Leipziger Str 1km from Pieschen S-Bahn station, this is the microbrewery of the Neustadt's Watzke Café (see page 114); in addition to sampling the product in the riverside beer garden you can also take tours (€5). There's also an 1880s' ballroom which hosts regular dances.

🍺 **Brauhaus am Waldschlösschen** Am Brauhaus 8B; ✆ 652 3900; e info@waldschloesschen.de;
www.waldschloesschen.de; ⏰ 11.00–01.00 daily, with live music Mon–Sat evenings [map 1]
Housed in an imposing Tuscan-style building high above the Elbe, the Brauhaus am Waldschlösschen was Germany's first joint-stock brewery, established in 1836. It makes a great excursion from the city, walking or cycling along the river, & can easily be combined with visits to the the Elbe castles. The 5m-high bronze beer fountain delivers unfiltered Zwickelbier, pale filtered Hell, yeasty Hefe & dark Dunkel beers; there's filling Saxon food too.

🍺 **Elbterrasse Wachwitz** Altwachwitz 14; ✆ 269610; e elbterrasse-wachwitz@t-online.de;
www.elbterrasse-wachwitz.de; ⏰ 11.00–midnight daily
On the way to Pillnitz (bus 83), a classic riverside beer garden which also does food (€8–14).

🍺 **Fährgarten Johannstadt** Käthe-Kollwitz-Ufer 23B; ✆ 459 6262; e info@plattenserviceundmehr.de;
www.faehrgarten.de; ⏰ Apr–Oct 10.00–01.00 daily [map 1]

One of Dresden's favourite beer gardens, where you can watch the ferry go to & fro as you drink your Radeberger.

🍺 **Gare de la Lune** Pillnitzer Landstr 148, Wachwitz; ☎ 267 8554; e garedelalune@gmx.de; www.gare-de-la-lune.de
A lovely riverside beer garden, with dances (indoors) at w/ends plus tango on Wed.

🍺 **Körnergarten** Friedrich-Wieck-Str 26, Loschwitz; ☎ 268 3620; www.koernergarten.de; ⏰ 11.00–midnight daily
A historic tavern & beer garden.

7 Entertainment and Nightlife

Dresden is of course known for its high culture, above all music and opera, but the Aussere Neustadt is home to a lively alternative scene, with cutting-edge music, dance and theatre all important.

FESTIVALS

Dresden's best festival is, in a way, the **Striezelmarkt** or Christmas Market, which takes over the Altmarkt from the end of November to Christmas Eve (see box, page 146).

Every February the anniversary of the bombing of Dresden is commemorated, with the city's bells tolling in the evening of the 13th for the 20 minutes that the RAF's bombs fell on the city. In the morning there's the **Friedenslauf** (Peace Run), a jog (maximum speed 10km/h) from Münchner Platz to the Heidefriedhof (Heath Cemetery), for a wreath-laying ceremony, and back.

The **Elbhangfest** (Elbe Slope Festival; *www.elbhangfest.de*), on the last weekend of June, takes over the 7km-long stretch of riverbank from Loschwitz to Pillnitz with concerts, drama, art exhibitions, craft markets, fairs and children's events. This is followed in July by the **Vogelwiese** or Dresden Stadtfest (City

Festival), on the Elbe Meadows west of the railway bridge, a funfair which is over 400 years old.

The Dresdner **Musikfestspiele** (Dresden Music Festival; *www.musikfestspiele.com*), held every year in late May and early June, is one of Germany's most important music festivals, with concerts featuring leading performers from across the world in many of Dresden's most beautiful buildings and gardens. In early October there's the Dresden **Festival of Contemporary Music** (*www.zeitmusik.de*), and in mid May the **Dixieland Festival** (*www.dixieland.de*), the world's second largest, with half a million people listening to bands on Prager Strasse and on river steamers as well as in concert halls. Also in May the Tante Ju club holds its **Blues Festival**.

More specialised offerings include **Filmfest Dresden** in mid April (there are also open-air screenings by the river on the Königsufer from July to September), the Dresden **Gay Pride** parade in June, **Tanzwoche** (Dresden International Dance Week; *www.tanzkalender-dresden.de*) in April and **TANZherbst** (Dance Autumn; *www.tanzherbst.de*) at the Festspielhaus Hellerau in November.

The **'White Fleet'** or Sächsische Dampfschiffahrt (Saxon Steamship Company) turn out their nine historic paddle-steamers for a parade on May Day, and also on 19 August.

♪ MUSIC

CLASSICAL Dresden is fortunate to have two great orchestras, a fine opera house and a wealth of church music. The **Sächsische Staatskapelle Dresden** (Dresden State Orchestra of Saxony or SSKD), founded in 1548, has almost always been in the top rank of the world's orchestras; it's based at the Semperoper. There's also the **Dresdner Philharmonie** (Dresden Philharmonic Orchestra), founded in 1870, which performs regularly in the Kulturpalast.

The opera's ticket office is in the Schinkelwache [map 2], the former guardhouse on the far side of Theaterplatz from the opera house itself (✆ 491 1705; e bestellung@ semperoper.de; www.semperoper.de/en/oper/spielplan.html; ⊕ 10.00–18.00 Mon–Fri, 10.00–13.00 Sat/Sun & hols). Tickets for the Dresdner Philharmonie (www.dresdnerphilharmonie.de) can be booked at Ticketcentrale (in the Kulturpalast at Schlossstrasse 2; ✆ 486 6866; e ticket@dresdnerphilharmonie.de; ⊕ 10.00–19.00 Mon–Fri, 10.00–14.00 Sat [map 2]) , through the tourist offices in the Schinkelwache on Theaterplatz [map 2] and at Prager Strasse 10 [map 2] (both ✆ 4919 2233; e info@dresden-tourist.de; www.dresden-tourist.de, go to Onlinebuchung), at the Konzertkasse in der Schillergalerie (Loschwitzer Str 52A; ✆ 315870), SAX Ticket (Königsbrücker Str 55 – in the Schauburg cinema; ✆ 803 8744) and at travel agents such as Thomas Cook Reisebüros.

Tickets for the opera can be in short supply (most are bought in advance and there's only a small Abendkasse in the foyer (open an hour before performances), which may have only standing tickets available; but if the tickets on offer are, as so often, too expensive, you might settle for a Hörplatz or listening place, which in fact allows you to see half the stage. Standing tickets give you a rail to lean on, and often a seat at the back with no view; some of the seats squeak and there's a lot of coughing because lots of the audience are smokers, but the atmosphere easily compensates. Productions are in a good, clean, modern style but with the huge choruses that only seem to be possible nowadays in the ex-communist countries. Concerts by the orchestra may see conductors of the stature of Sir Colin Davis, Charles Dutoit, Danielle Gatti, Daniel Harding, Vladimir Jurowski and Myung-Whun Chung, and singers such as Angelika Kirchschlager, Kurt Moll and Ben Heppner. The Semperoper is especially associated with Richard Strauss, having staged the premieres of no fewer than nine of his operas; most are still in the repertory, and they occasionally stage ten Strauss operas in ten days, an unprecedented feast for lovers of his lush late-Romantic sound and histrionic plots.

The Staatskapelle also use the **Kleine Szene** (*Bautzner Str 107* [map 1]) as a chamber theatre and studio. The Philharmonie also puts on concerts at Schloss Albrechtsberg (see page 181), where the Kronensaal is considered the city's finest chamber-music venue; there are also Sunday concerts here, often by students of the Heinrich-Schütz Konservatorium (the music conservatoire). There are also summer concerts here, on the terraces or a floating stage at the Roman Bath. The Konservatorium also puts on concerts at its home, Glacisstrasse 30 (↘ *828260;* e *hskd@musik-macht-freunde.de; www.musik-macht-freunde.de* [map 4]). Similarly, students of the Hochschule für Musik Carl Maria von Weber or Dresden University of Music perform (often at lunchtime) in the former Gymnasium Wettinianum, Wettiner Platz 13, where a very modern new hall is under construction. There are also concerts in the Ballsaal of the Four Points Hotel Königshof (on Wasaplatz in Strehlen [map 1]), in many of Dresden's churches and elsewhere.

If the opera is too highbrow for you, you could try the **Staatsoperette Dresden**, in the eastern suburbs at Pirnaer Landstrasse 131 (↘ *207 9929;*

e *besucherdienst@staatsoperette-dresden.de; www.staatsoperette-dresden.de*), where tickets cost only €7.50–23 – but in fact you're likely to understand even less unless your colloquial German is very good. Take tram 1 or 6 or bus 73 or 89 to Altleuben.

CHOIRS AND CHURCH MUSIC The city's best choir (and its best known, having been active for over 500 years) is the **Dresdner Kreuzchor**, based in the Kreuzkirche (↘ *496 5807;* e *konzert.kreuz@arcor.de; www.kreuzchor.de*), which sings at Saturday vespers (at 18.00 in summer, 17.00 in winter); the Kapellknaben or Cathedral Boys Choir sings in the Hofkirche on Sundays and holidays at 10.30, and both give concerts elsewhere. On church High Holidays the Kapellknaben perform with the full cathedral choir and members of the Staatskapelle orchestra for the 10.30 service.

The **Orgelzyklus** (Organ Cycle) is a programme of organ recitals in the Kreuzkirche, Frauenkirche and the Roman Catholic cathedral; they take place on Wednesdays at 20.00 and tickets (€5) go on sale at 19.15 – there are no advance bookings, but for information contact the cathedral's Dompfarramt at Schlossstrasse 24 (↘ *484 4712;* e *info@kathedrale-dresden.de; www.bistum-dresden-meissen.de*). The Silbermann organ in the cathedral is superb and it can also be heard on Wednesdays and Saturdays (11.30–12.00, except on holidays) and at vespers on Saturdays (16.00).

J S Bach is a staple of both choral and organ performances, but many other composers are represented. Tickets for events at the Kreuzkirche can be bought at the Konzertkasse in the Haus an der Kreuzkirche (*An der Kreuzkirche 6;* ☎ *496 5807;* e *konzert.kreuz@arcor.de;* ⏰*09.00–13.30 & 14.00–17.00 Mon–Wed, to 18.00 Tue, to 16.00 Fri*) and an hour before concerts.

JAZZ In addition to the Dixieland Festival (see above) there are two good jazz clubs. The Jazz Club Tonne holds a couple of gigs a week in the Kulturrathaus, Königstrasse 15 (☎ *802 6017;* e *post@jazzclubtonne.de; www.jazzclubtonne.de* [map 4]), starting at 21.00. The Blue Note, at Görlitzer Strasse 2B (☎ *801 4275; www.jazzdepartment.com* [map 5]) has live music most nights (21.00–23.00); the bar is open until at least 05.00, and some gigs are actually smoke-free.

DANCE

Throughout the 18th century, Dresden's Augustan period, dance played a major role in court festivals, and August the Strong himself is said to have danced in an allegory apotheosis. In the late 19th century ballet was staged at the opera, and again after 1985.

The Swiss dance teacher Emile Jacques-Dalcroze, who had been developing his ideas on eurhythmics (or rhythmic gymnastics) from 1900, taught in the garden suburb of Hellerau in 1910–14 and put on an annual festival which in 1913 drew George Bernard Shaw, Upton Sinclair, Max Reinhardt and Reiner Maria Rilke. Mary Wigman, who had studied at Hellerau and then with Rudolf von Laban near Ascona, helped Dalcroze develop Ausdruckstanz (Expressionist Dance), and in 1920 founded her own school of free dance on Bautzner Strasse, closed down in 1942 (and now the Kleine Szene). Her dancers wore masks and accompanied themselves with bells, gongs and drums. Her pupil Greta Palucca set up her own equally influential Palucca School in 1925, and continued teaching to the early 1990s; the school (*www.palucca-schule-dresden.de*) is still active and influential.

The American dancer and choreographer William Forsythe (born 1949) made his name at the Frankfurt Ballet, which closed in 2004; with the support of the cities of Frankfurt am Main and Dresden and the Länder of Saxony and Hesse he founded the Forsythe Company (*www.theforsythecompany.de*), based in Frankfurt and at the Festspielhaus in Hellerau, where they perform regularly to a devoted audience. Meanwhile the resident choreographer of the Semperoper Ballet is now the British David Dawson, who plans to co-operate with Forsythe.

Tickets for ballet at the Semperoper can be booked in the same way as opera tickets (see above); tickets for the Forsythe Company (€ 15–20) can be booked through Ticketcentrale at the Kulturpalast (see above), or from an hour before the performance at Hellerau.

See above for details of Dresden's two dance festivals.

THEATRE

Dresden's leading theatre is the **Schauspielhaus** (*Ostra Allee 48; www.staatsschauspiel-dresden.de* [map 2]), built in 1912–13 and rebuilt in 1948 and 1995–96, which has the world's oldest fully functional hydraulic stage equipment. It now incorporates the **Theater Oben** (Upper Theatre), a studio space; the **Kleines**

Haus (which also incorporates a studio space) is its Neustadt outpost, at Glacis Strasse 28 (a 19th-century villa extended in 1860). Box offices are in the main theatre (⊕10.00–18.30 Mon–Fri, 10.00–14.00 Sat) and the Kleines Haus (⊕14.00–18.30 Mon–Fri) and for an hour before performances; you can also book by phone or email (✆ 491 3555, free 0800 491 3500; e tickets@staatsschauspiel-dresden).

The **Societaets Theater** (✆ 803 6810; www.societaetstheater.de [map 4]), in the courtyard of Hauptstrasse 19 in the Neustadt, was Germany's first citizens' theatre (founded in 1776) and reopened in 1999. It's a chamber theatre, staging contemporary but not too experimental work. On Thursday tickets cost €6; otherwise they're €10–15 (reductions €6–10). There's also the **Komödie Dresden** (✆ 866410; e kasse@komoedie-dresden.de; www.komoedie-dresden.de [map 2]) in the World Trade Centre (by the Freiberger Strasse S-Bahn station); the box office is open 10.00–18.00 Monday to Saturday and an hour before performances.

One of the most interesting theatre companies is in fact based in the western suburb of Radebeul and tours all over the state of Saxony; it's the **Landesbühnen Sachsen** or Saxon State Stage (Stammhaus, Meissner Str 152, 01445 Radebeul; ✆ 895 4239, tickets 895 4214; e info@dresden-theater.de; www.dresden-theater.de), which is Germany's second-largest subsidised repertory theatre, performing everything from straight drama to operetta, musicals and even concerts. Its state subsidy was cut in 2006 but the company agreed to forgo their usual Christmas bonuses, in effect taking an 8% pay cut to keep the show on the road; only top ticket prices are being raised, and not by much. In summer half the company is based at the open-air Felsenbühne Rathen (*Amselgrund 17, Kurort Rathen;* ☏ *035024 7770*) in Saxon Switzerland, 2km from the Rathen S-Bahn station (see page 268).

At Materni Strasse 17, between the Altstadt and the Freiberger Strasse S-Bahn station, is the **Wechselbad der Gefühle** (e *info@orphee-event.de; www.theater-wechselbad.de* [map 2]), which hosts touring performers of various kinds and the **Mimenbühne Dresden** (Mime Stage) (☏ *796 1400;* e *mimenstudiodd@aol.com; www.mimenstudio.de*). Tickets can be booked at the box office (⊕ *10.00–19.00 Mon–Fri; 14.00–19.00 Sat*), by phone (☏ *796 1155*) or from an hour before performances.

In the Aussere Neustadt the **Projekt Theater** at Louisenstrasse 47 (☏ *803 3548; www.projekttheater.de* [map 5]) stages fringe theatre, modern dance and some jazz.

The former Rundkino (Circular Cinema) (*www.rundkino-dresden.de*) at Prager Strasse 6 in the Altstadt is now home to the **Theater Junger Generation** (☏ *496 5370;* e *service@tjg-dresden.de; www.tjg-dresden.de* [map 2]), a lively youth theatre, and the **Puppen Theater** (Dresden State Puppet Theatre) (e *puppentheater@tjg-dresden.de* [map 2]) – and to a Pizza Hut, which is the easiest way of finding the place. Tickets are sold here (⊕ *14.00–18.00 Tue–Fri and an hour before performances;* €*6*).

Germany has a fine tradition of cabaret and satirical theatre, which can be experienced at the floating **Theaterkahn** (see page 107), Terrassenufer (*by the Augustusbrücke;* ☏ *496 9450;* e *theaterkahn@t-online.de; www.theaterkahn-dresden.de*); **Kabarett Die Herkuleskeule**, Sternplatz 1 (☏ *492 5555;* e *ticket@herkuleskeule.de; www.herkuleskeule.de*); and **Kabarett Breschke & Schuch**, Wettiner Platz 10 (*entry on Jahnstr, near Mitte station;* ☏ *490 4009;* e *ticket@kabarett-breschke-schuch.de; www.kabarett-breschke-schuch.de*). You do need a good understanding of German.

Carte Blanche, at Priessnitz Strasse 10 (☎ 204720; www.carte-blanche-dresden.de), hosts a drag revue that's a lot of fun and doesn't require fluent German (although it helps); the two-hour shows (€25) start at 20.00 Wednesday to Friday, 19.00 and 22.30 Saturday, 16.00 and 20.00 Sunday, and there's also a restaurant.

Other venues, putting on occasional events (including rock concerts), include the Kulturpalast (see page 159); Freilichtbühne Grosser Garten (the open-air stage in the Grosser Garten); the Alter Schlachthof (Old Slaughterhouse) (*Gothaer Str 11;* ☎ 563 6567; e info@first-class-concept.de; www.alter-schlachthof.de); ARTEUM, at the Waldschlösschen (*Am Brauhaus 3;* ☎ 563 6555; e info@arteum-dresden.de; www.arteum-dresden.de); and the Messe (Trade Fairground) (*Messering 6;* ☎ 44580; e info@messe-dresden.de; www.messe-dresden.de). Tickets for events here can often be bought at the Konzertkasse im Florentium at Ferdinandstrase 12 (☎ 866600; www.konzertkasse-dresden.de). At the Societaets Theater you can also buy tickets for a range of events (☎ 803 6810; www.ticket2day.de).

CINEMA

Modern multiplex cinemas include the **UFA Cinema Center** [map 5] between the Walpurgisstrasse tram stop and Prager Strasse (opened in 1998 and known as the Kristallpalast due to its very striking deconstructivist entry) and **Cinemaxx**, Schillerplatz (☎ 315 6868; www.cinemaxx.de [map 2]). The leading art cinema is the **Schauburg**, Königsbrücker 55 (*at Bischofsweg;* ☎ 803 2185; www.schauburg-dresden.de [map 5]), which charges just €4 (or €6 after 18.00 Thu–Sun), and also

Entertainment and Nightlife CINEMA

7

has a fine bar). More occasional films are shown at **Metropolis** (*Am Brauhaus 8, Waldschlösschen;* ☎ *816 6721/2; www.metropolis-dresden.de*), **KIF** (Kino in der Fabrik) (*Friedensstr 23;* ☎ *804 2924; www.casablanca-dresden.com*), the **Technische Sammlungen** (*Junghans Str 1–3;* ☎ *488 7272; www.tsd.de*) and at the university **Kino im Kasten** (*Weberbau, August-Bebel-Strasse 20;* ☎ *463 36463;* e *info@kino-im-kasten.de; www.kino-im-kasten.de;* ⊕ *Mon 18.00*).

Filmenächte am Elbufer is a summer series of open-air films (and concerts) on the Elbe embankment right opposite the Altstadt, from 28 June to 26 August 2007 (*www.filmnaechte-am-elbufer.de*).

☆ NIGHTCLUBS

The pubs of the Aussere Neustadt are probably enough for most people, with the action going on until 05.00 many nights; however, the local youth has a lively clubbing scene, with live music and dancing.

INDUSTRIEGELÄNDE The hot area at the moment is Industriegelände, north of the city (reached by trams 7 and 8 and trains including S2 to the airport [map 6]), where industrial buildings are being taken over.

☆ **Action Halle** Werner-Hartmann-Strasse 3; www.action-dresden.de. Punky & possibly neo-Nazi.
☆ **Das Eventwerk** Hermann-Mende-Strasse 1 (at the east end of the footbridge from the station); ☎ 563 6567; e info@eventwerk-dresden.de; http://eventwerk-dresden.de. This venue houses the Washroom

(*www.washroom.de*; ⏱ *from 22.00 Fri–Sat*), which boasts liquid sounds, an indoor beach & an 8m x 16m swimming pool.

☆ **Strasse E** Werner-Hartmann-Strasse 4; www.strasse-e.de. Hosts poker (!) followed by indie/alternative music on Wed, Goths on Thu, techno music on Fri, & gigs & special club nights on Sat.

☆ **Strassen Café** Werner-Hartmann-Strasse 2; www.strassencafe.de; ⏱ from 17.00 daily. A place to warm up with billiards & darts.

☆ **Tante Ju** An der Schleife 1; ☎ 0172 363 1539; www.tanteju.com. Stages blues bands & other rather more grown-up types of music.

☆ **Terminal 1** Flughafenstr 100; ☎ 481 2340; www.terminal1.tv. There's a great venue in the airport's former Terminal 1, to the west of the present terminal, which plays house, electro & neo-pop, & hosts international DJs.

☆ **X-Side Club** Werner-Hartmann-Strasse 1; www.x-side-club.de. Focuses on electronica.

AUSSERE NEUSTADT In the Aussere Neustadt [map 5] the centre of the action is at Katharinen Strasse 11–13, shared by Groove Station (☎ *801 9594; www.groovestation.de*), Downtown (*www.downtown-dresden.de*) and LOFThouse (☎ *810 3923; www.lofthouse-dresden.de club*), all active on Friday and Saturday nights. You could also try the following:

☆ **AZ Conny** Rudolf-Leonhard Str 39; ☎ 804 5858; www.azconni.de. An alternative youth centre, with bar, ping-pong, table football, free internet & gigs.

☆ **Flower Power** Eschenstr 10; ☎ 804 9799; www.flower-power.de; ⏱ from 20.00 daily [map 5]. Free entry, nightly from 20.00. Student night Mon, karaoke Thu.

☆ **Katy's Garage** Alaunstr 48 (at Louisenstrasse); ☎ 656 7701; www.katysgarage.de [map 5]. Hosts gigs — student night Mon, reggae Thu.

☆ **Metronom** Louisenstr 55; ☎ 428741; www.metronomclub.de [map 5]. Salsa Tue, student night Wed, funk, soul & hip-hop Fri, themed nights Sat.

☆ **Scheune** Alaunstr 36; ☎ 8045858; www.scheune.org [map 5]. Music & events 4 or 5 nights a week, & a good café (see page 120).

OUTSIDE THE NEUSTADT

☆ **Arteum Club and Lounge** Am Brauhaus 3, Waldschlösschen; www.arteum-dresden.de. Hosts the regular Pacha Party (*www.pachadresden.de*) & less regular nights such as Puro & Winter Chillout.

☆ **Dance Factory** Bautzner Str 118; ☎ 802 2451; www.factory-diskothek.de. Take tram 11 or bus 91 to Angelikastr. Plays all kinds of music on 4 floors.

☆ **Der Felsenkeller** Am Eiswurmlager 1C; ☎ 417 3857; e info@felsenkeller.tv; www.felsenkeller.tv. Plays all types of music on Fri & '80s/90s & cult tunes on Sat.

☆ **Glory Club** Bautzner Str 153; www.glory-club.de. Hosts mainly live acts, usually electronica.

☆ **Puschkin Club** At the junction of Leipziger Str & Erfurter Strasse (tram 4 or 9 to A-Puschkin-Platz); ☎ 205 4587; www.puschkin-club.info; ⏰from 21.00 Thu–Sat. A recent addition to the scene.

☆ **Saloppe** Brockhausstr 1; www.salopp.de. Puts on open-air dancing on summer nights.

☆ **Showboxx** Leipziger Str 31 (at the Alte Schlachthof stop of trams 4 & 9); www.showboxx.de. Once a largely gay disco this club is now open to all. Also here is **City Beach** (*www.citybeachdresden.de*), with beach volleyball & table-tennis facilities.

SOUTH OF THE RIVER

☆ **Club Aquarium** St Petersburger Str 21; www.club-aquarium.de; ⏰21.00–01.00 Mon–Fri [map 2]. More of a bar with live acts.

☆ **Motown Club** Robotron Bürozentrum, St Petersburger Str 9; ☎ 487 4150; e info@motown-club.de; www.motown-club.de; ⏰21.00–05.00 Wed–Sat [map 2]. Plays black music, with African Beat Night on Fri & a Black is Beautiful party on Sat.

CENTRAL ALTSTADT

☆ **Haus Altmarkt** Wilsdruffer Strasse 19; www.haus-altmarkt.de [map 2]. A rather tackier disco for an older age group.
☆ **M.5 Tanzbar & Diskothek** Münzgasse 5; ☎ 496 5491; www.m5-nightlife.de [map 2]. Similar to the above.

GAY NIGHTLIFE

There are plenty of visible gays in Dresden, especially in the Neustadt; in fact they are so well established that many of them see little need for specifically gay bars or clubs, going wherever the best gigs or the cheap drinks are. Those who want livelier (and more anonymous) action are likely to head for the fleshpots of Berlin, just a couple of hours away.

☆ **BOYS** Alaunstr 80; ☎ 563 3630; www.boys-dresden.de [map 5]. Perhaps the best of the bunch. Lively Tue–Sat (⏰20.00–05.00).
☆ **Bunker-LCD** Priessnitzstr 51; ☎ 441 2345; www.lederclub-dresden.net; ⏰from 22.00 on Fri/Sat nights only; open to all Fri, dress code Sat [map 5]. A leather club with a darkroom.

☆ **Café Sappho** Hechtstr 23; ✆ 404 5136; www.sappho-dresden.com; ⏰from 18.00 daily, 09.30 Sun brunch [map 5]. Specifically for women.

☆ **Cat Club** Werner-Hartmann-Str 3, Industriegelände. Hosts mixed crowds.

☆ **Der Blaue Salon** In the lobby of the Parkhotel, Bautzner Landstrasse 7; ✆ 804 4238; e info@ blauersalon.com; www.blauersalon.com, www.8seasons-dresden.de [map 5]. Plays electronica music for dancing.

☆ **DownTown** Katharinen 11 [map 1]. Also hosts mixed crowds.

☆ **Duplexx** Försterei Str 10; ✆ 658 8999; www.duplexx-club.com; ⏰15.00–03.00 daily; entry €8 [map 5]. A sex shop with video cabins.

☆ **Klara Fall Frauenkneipe** Angelika Str 1; ✆ 804 1470; ⏰19.00–01.00 Thu–Sat [map 5]. Specifically for women.

☆ **Man's Paradise** Friedensstrasse 45; ✆ 802 2566; www.mans-paradise.de; ⏰12.00–01.00 daily [map 5]. A gay sauna club.

☆ **Queens** Görlitzer Str 3; ✆ 810 8108; www.queens-dresden.de; ⏰20.00 daily [map 5]. Intimate; holds popular themed nights.

The local gay rights organisation is Gerede, based at the Stadtteilhaus (community centre), Priessnitzstrasse 18 (✆ 802 2250/1; e kontakt@gerede-dresden.de; www.gerede-dresden.de; office & information ⏰15.00–17.00 Mon–Fri). There's a library here, for free video/DVD loans, the Kontakt Café (⏰15.00–21.00), and even a running group (✆ 802 2251; ⏰18.30 Tue). *Gegenpol* is a free monthly magazine (✆ 486 7777; www.gegenpol.net), available here and at Neustadt bars and shops; there are also 'pink pages' online (*http://gaydresden.de*). For HIV issues, AIDS-Hilfe Dresden is at Bischofsweg 46 (*office* ✆ 441 6142; e info@aidshilfe-dresden.de; *www.aidshilfe-dresden.de*).

8 Shopping

OPENING HOURS AND VAT

Shopping hours in Germany, although slightly less tightly regulated than they were, are still pretty unvarying, with most shops open Mondays to Fridays from 09.30 or 10.00 to 19.00 or 20.00, and on Saturday to 16.00 (in winter to 18.00), and shopping centres like Karstadt or the Altmarkt Galerie to 20.00. On Sundays the only shops that can legally open are at railway stations and the airport, as well as restaurants.

Value added tax (MWST) was increased from 16% to 19% at the end of 2006, leading to a fall of almost 10% in retail sales. There is also a lower rate of 7% on food and agricultural products. Those resident outside the European Union are entitled to a refund of VAT, by asking the retailer for a special invoice (Ausfuhr- und Abnehmerbescheinigung) which must be checked, with the purchases, by customs officers when leaving the country (no more than three months after the date of purchase). You may receive the refund at a major airport, or else will have to post the form and wait perhaps some months.

SHOPPING AREAS

Dresden's main shopping areas are in the rebuilt areas of the Altstadt, along Prager Strasse (rebuilt after the war and now just like anywhere in western Germany, or indeed Plymouth or Coventry) or in the Altmarkt Galerie, built in 2001–03 just south of the Altmarkt. Germany's leading department store is **Karstadt** (*www.karstadt.de*), founded in 1881; its central Dresden branch at Prager Strasse 17 (⊕09.30–20.00 *Mon–Sat* [map 2]) contains a deli, wine shop, travel agency, sections selling clothes, books, electronics, kitchen, garden and photo equipment, and a restaurant. It actually moved across the road in 1995 from the striking aluminium-clad building, built in the 1970s and now sadly disused.

HANDICRAFTS AND LOCAL SPECIALITIES

Apart from the Christmas market specialities (see box, page 146), the obvious thing to buy in Dresden, if you can stomach it, is Meissen porcelain. The **Meissener Porzellan Manufaktur** has authorised shops in the Hilton (✆ 864 2964; e *dresdenh@meissen.de*; ⊕09.30–19.00 *Mon–Fri, 09.30–18.00 Sat/Sun & hols* [map 2]), in Karstadt (*Prager Strasse 12;* ✆ 490 6833; e *dresdenk@meissen.de*; ⊕09.30–20.00 *Mon–Sat* [map 2]) and at Silke Havlik jewellers (*Wilhelmine-Reichert-Ring 1;* ✆ 1 881 5240 [map 2]). There are other porcelain shops in the Hilton and elsewhere, but only wares with the blue crossed swords on the bottom are genuine Meissen. The less glamorous **Dresdner Porzellan** (see page 174) has its shop in the Neustadt's

Kunsthandwerker-Passage (Craftsmens' Passage) at Hauptstrasse 17 (℡ 563 5150 [map 4]). Also in the Altstadt, look in the **Haus am Zwinger** (*Kleine Brüdergasse 1* [map 2]), for shops selling leatherware and other expensive clothing. **Kunsthandwerk an der Kreuzkirche** (*An der Kreuzkirche 6;* ℡ 496 4840 [map 2]) has a pretty kitschy range of crafty gifts.

Across the river, Königstrasse is home to pricey commercial art galleries such as **Galerie Königstrasse** at no 16 [map 4], as well as expensive clothes boutiques; smaller shops can be found in the **Antiquätenspassage** [map 4] at Königstrasse 5 (mostly antiques) and at Kunsthof-Passage 165, between Görlitzer Strasse 21–25 and Alaunstrasse 70 (smaller and more artsy studios). The **Aussere Neustadt** (Alaunstrasse and nearby) [map 5] has a great variety of underground clothing and music stores, head shops, shops selling homemade paper and candles, and almost anything else you can think of.

BOOKS AND MUSIC

Internationale Buch (*Altmarkt 24;* ℡ 656420; ◷ *09.30–20.00 Mon–Fri, 09.30–18.00 Sat* [map 2]) has a wide range of German books plus English guides to the Frauenkirche, Semperoper, Old Masters Picture Gallery and Green Vault.

Buch & Kunst (*www.buch-kunst.de*) has lots of branches throughout Saxony including six in Dresden, at Hauptstrasse 26 [map 4], Hüblertstrasse 3, Peschelstrasse 31 (Elbe-Park) [map 1], Borsbergstrasse 27B, Dohnaer Strasse 246 (KaufPark Nicken) and Königsbrücker Landstrasse 58 [map 1]. At the

STRIEZELMARKT

Dresden's Advent market is the oldest example of this great German institution, founded in 1434. Originally held on the Altmarkt for one day, it now occupies much of the Old Town and lasts from late November until Christmas Eve (⏲ 10.00–20.00 daily, to 21.00 Fri/Sat).

Its name derives from Strüzel, the cake now known as *Stollen* (see page 102), and its highpoint is the Stollenfest, held on the Saturday before the second Sunday of Advent (www.stollenfest.com has information in English), when a giant *Stollen*, at least three tonnes in weight (a record 4.2 tonnes in 2001), is taken by carriage from the Zwinger to the Altmarkt, accompanied by the city's bakers and pastry-makers, and by chimney sweeps, soldiers in 18th-century uniforms and brass bands. It is then cut by the Master Baker and the Stollenmädchen or *Stollen* maiden, a beauty queen who works in one of the city's bakeries, and divided up and sold for charity. The giant *Stollen* is of course cut with the giant Stollenknife, 1.2m long, a porcelain-handled replica of one made for August the Strong in 1730.

It may seem paradoxical to say that a market isn't commercial, but most people are here to eat, drink and have a good time with friends. Stalls sell Christmas-tree ornaments and other handicrafts, but nothing's very expensive and trashy plastic products are simply not allowed.

The tradition of hand-carving wooden ornaments in the Erzgebirge (Ore Mountains) dates from the Peasants' War of 1524–25, when many miners lost their jobs. Among the most typical pieces are nutcrackers (painted with a red jacket like a soldier), the Räuchermann (Smoking Man, with smoke from a hidden incense candle emerging through his pipe) and the Schwibbogen, an arch-like candle-holder seen in the window of just about every Dresden home during Advent.

Rather larger are the candle pyramids, two- or three-tier tapering towers, with the heat from the candles driving a rotor to turn each tier with its carved figures. Normally these are about half a metre high, but you'll see some bigger ones, notably the world's tallest, at the centre of the Altrnarkt, which is 14m high.

Other products include indigo-dyed textiles and ceramics from Lusatia, lace from Plauen, advent stars from Herrnhut and glass tree ornaments from Lauscha.

Food is also important, of course – Pflaumentoffel (Plum Devil) is a chimney-sweep figure made of dried prunes, and Pulsnitzer Pfefferkuchen (Peppercakes) is gingerbread, which has been made in Pulsnitz, about 50km from Dresden, since 1558. It in fact contains no pepper or ginger, but rather nutmeg, cinnamon, cloves and allspice, and is filled with jam and covered with chocolate. Stalls also sell roasted nuts, Quarkbällchen (curd cheese balls), waffles, crêpes, sausages of course, and Pilzpfanne (sautéed mushrooms), ideally served in a hollowed-out loaf, but usually just on a cardboard plate.

There's also Glühwein ('Glow-wine'), hot red wine mulled with cinnamon and cloves, Jägertee (tea with rum) and Grog (hot water and rum with lemon or lime juice, cinnamon and sugar). Beer is not a big feature of Striezelmarkt.

university, the **Buchhandlung TU** (*Rugestr 6;* ℡ *471 5078*) has a large range of mainly academic texts, mainly in German.

Other bookshops (which put on book readings and other events) include **Buchhandlung im Kunsthof** (*Görlitzer Str 23* [map 5]), **Buchhandlung Lesezeichen** (*Priessnitz Str 56* [map 5]), **Buchhandlung Pusteblume** (*Martin-Luther-Platz 23* [map 5]), **Kommissariat** (*Louisenstr 38* [map 5]), **LeseLust** (*Louisenstr 24; www.leselust-dresden.de* [map 5]), specialising in photography and eroticism, **Rebecca-Brunnen** (*Hinter der Dreikönigskirche* [map 5]) and **KulturHaus Loschwitz** (*Freidrich-Wieck-Str 6A*).

Dresdner Antiquariat is a large secondhand bookshop at Wilsdrufer Strasse 14, on the west side of Kleine Kirchgasse (℡ *490 4583;* e *buch@dresdener-antiquariat.de;* ⊕ *10.00–19.00 Mon–Fri, 10.00–16.00 Sat* [map 2]); across the river in the Neustadt, **Historica Antiquariat** (*Heinrichstrasse 22* [map 4]) is a smaller secondhand bookshop.

There are some excellent old-style record stores, with LPs and turntables to listen to them on, in the Aussere Neustadt [map 5], including **Fenders** (*Rothenburger Str 26;* ℡ *495 3124*); **Laconic Records** (*Rothenburger Str 13;* ℡ *206 9088*), which also sells studio equipment); **Backstock Records** (*Böhmische Str 14;* ℡ *652 3909*); Dropout Records (*Alaunstr 41;* ℡ *804 2862*); and **Popcorn Records** (*Alaunstr 20;* ℡ *801 2829*).

For classical music (including scores, books and DVDs, and jazz and world music) head for **Opus 61** (*Wallstr 17;* ℡ *486 1748;* e *dresden@opus61.de; www.opus61.de;* ⊕ *10.00–20.00 Mon–Fri, 10.00–18.00 Sat* [map 2]) opposite the Altmarkt Galerie.

FOOD SHOPS AND MARKETS

There's no shortage of small supermarkets in fairly central locations, usually run by **Konsum** or **Plus**, and of a pretty good standard; bigger Lidl and Aldi supermarkets are usually further from the centre, and less good. On the west side of the Altstadt [map 2] there's a Konsum at Annenstrasse 12 and another in the atrium of the World Trade Centre (both ⊕08.00–20.00 Mon–Fri, 08.00–14.00 Sat) as well as an Aldi and other shops.

On the main drag of the Aussere Neustadt [map 5] there's a Konsum at Alaunstrasse 21 (⊕08.00–20.00 Mon–Sat), almost opposite a **Spar** at no 6 (⊕07.00–21.00 Mon–Sat). The Plus supermarket at Rudolf-Leonhardt-Strasse 12 is handy for Die Boofe hostel.

Perhaps the nicest place to shop for food in the Neustadt [map 4] is the **Neustädter Markthalle** (Metzer Str 1; ✆ 810 5445; www.markthalle-dresden.de; ⊕08.00–20.00 Mon–Fri, 08.00–18.00 Sat/Sun), which houses delis, wine shops, Asian and other fast-food stalls (definitely not of the mass-market chain persuasion), as well as ATMs, toilets, and a branch of Konsum in the east end (⊕same hours Mon–Sat).

For organic and health foods there's **Bio-Sphäre Naturkost** (Königsbrücker Strasse 76; ✆ 804 4466 [map 4]) and the **Fairtrade Kontor** (Schillingstrasse 7, off Tharandter Strasse, Plauen; ✆ 464 4977; ⊕12.00–20.00 Mon–Fri, 14.00–20.00 Sat/Sun [map 1]), a non-smoking café selling organic and fairtrade products including tea and coffee.

For Italian foods and wines, go to the alimentaria-osteria **La Villetta** (Augsburger Strasse 43, Striesen; ✆ 315990 [map 1]), which stocks 150 Italian wines, among other things; **Weine aus Georgien** (*Bautzner Strasse 67;* ⏰*12.00–18.00 Tue–Thu, 12.00–20.00 Fri, 10.00–18.00 Sat* [map 5]) has wines from Georgia and the Caucasus.

Other than the **flea market**, under the south end of the Albertbrücke on Saturdays [map 2], and the famous **Advent markets** (see box, pages 146–7) there aren't any markets of significance in Dresden.

OUTDOOR AND HIKING GEAR

Karstadt-Sport and **Jack Wolfskin** are at Prager Strasse 2 [map 2], at the street's south end appropriately close to a transparent gym. In the Neustadt, **Die Hütte** hiking gear shop is at Bautzner Strasse 39 [map 5], along with the outdoor tour company **Schulz Aktiv Reisen** (*www.schulz-aktiv-reisen.de*), just west of Pfunds Molkerei (*both* ⏰*10.00–19.30 Mon–Fri, 09.00–14.00 Sat*).

9 Walking Tours

Dresden is an ideal size for walking, and you can easily see the Altstadt (Old Town) in a couple of hours, although this tends to be extended hugely by visiting the many museums. Afterwards you can cross the river to see the Neustadt, or head into the suburbs in various directions.

WALK I: THE ALTSTADT [maps 2 & 3]

Dresden's Old Town is the Baroque jewel that you came here to see, even though much of it has been rebuilt in the last couple of decades. The place to start is **Theaterplatz**, the tarmac expanse between the opera house, Zwinger, Hofkirche (Roman Catholic cathedral) and Residenzschloss (Royal Castle). It's at the south end of the Augustusbrücke (Augustus Bridge), traversed by trams 4, 8 and 9 (line 8 coming from the Hauptbahnhof or main railway station).

The bridge was built in 1727–31 by Matthäus Daniel Pöppelmann (1682–1737), the great architect of Baroque Dresden, and named after August the Strong; it was rebuilt in 1907–10 to Pöppelmann's design. Between it and Theaterplatz is the **Italienisches Dörfchen** or Italian Village, named after the artisans who lived on this site while building the cathedral; it was built in 1911–13 by Hans Erlwein, and refurbished with a historically accurate interior in 1993. In the centre of the square is an equestrian statue of King Johann by Johannes Schilling (1889).

The **Semperoper**, as the opera house is always known, after its architect Gottfried Semper, is revered as the birthplace of German opera. Carl Maria von Weber was director of the Court Opera and wrote *Der Freischütz* here, although Dresdeners conveniently forget that the opera was premiered in Berlin in 1821, the year before it was staged here; this also ignores Mozart's *Magic Flute* and other German-language operas. In any case, it was *Der Freischütz* that closed the 1944 season and that reopened the Semperoper after its rebuilding in 1985, and it's still in the repertory. The opera house was built in 1838–41, burnt down in 1869, and was rebuilt in 1871–78 by Semper's son Manfred to the same neo-Renaissance style; it was again destroyed in 1945 and again rebuilt in 1977–85. In the centre of the imposing two-storey arcade is a grand portal topped by a quadriga, a bronze chariot drawn by four panthers, by Johannes Schilling.

If you can't catch a performance (see page 130) you can enjoy a tour, running frequently but somewhat irregularly and lasting 45–60 minutes (✆ 491 1496; *www.semperoper-fuehrungen.de;* ⏲ 14.00–15.30 Mon–Thu, 09.00–11.00 Sat, & on some Suns; €6, reduced €3, family €12, photos €2). Don't miss the wonderful digital clock above the proscenium arch which uses Roman numerals for the hours and moves in five-minute increments.

To the southwest of Theaterplatz is the **Zwinger** (often translated as Kennel, although Outer Ward is more accurate, meaning the space between the inner and outer rings of the city walls), as fine an array of Baroque architecture as you'll find anywhere (✆ 491 4601; e zwinger@schloesserland-sachsen.de; ◷06.00–22.00 daily; free). In 1709 Pöppelmann was commissioned by August the Strong to build an orangery, but the project snowballed so that by 1719 (when the marriage of Friedrich August to the Habsburg Emperor's daughter Maria Josepha was celebrated here) he and the sculptor Balthasar Permoser (1651–1732) had laid out an enclosed space for festivities and surrounded it on three sides with

Zwinger

galleries and pavilions, tucked inside the city's fortifications. The buildings were not finished until 1728, when the royal collections began to be displayed here, and the Zwinger is still home to several fine branches of the State Museums (*closed Mon*), although they are still being moved around. It was damaged in the Prussian siege of 1760 and rebuilt two decades later; after long debates about how to close off the Zwinger and complete the Theaterplatz, Semper's rather heavy neo-Renaissance art gallery was built in 1847–55 along the northeastern side. The Zwinger was destroyed in 1945 but rebuilt relatively soon after the war.

Entering from Theaterplatz you'll pass under the Semperbau, with the entrance to the **Old Masters Gallery** (see page 197) on your right and the **Rustkammer** (Armoury Museum) (see page 223) on your left. In the centre of the courtyard is a pool with fountains; going around to the right/west you'll pass the present location of the Sculpture Gallery in the northeastern gallery, then the Wallpavilion (Ramparts Pavilion), heavily laden with sculpted gods and heroes and on top the demigod Hercules bearing the globe. Hidden away to the right (behind the northeastern gallery) is the Nymphenbad (Nymphs' Bath), modelled on Roman originals and surrounded by female figures in sandstone; severely damaged by the 2002 floods, it has now been restored. The southwestern pavilion houses the Mathematical and Physical Salon, on the site of the Grottensaal (destroyed in 1813), home to trick fountains and Permoser's statues of Apollo and Minerva, now in the Sculpture Gallery. The southwestern side of the Zwinger, alongside the moat, is formed by the Langgalerie (Long Gallery) with the Kronentor (Crown Gate) in the middle, its onion dome topped by a Polish crown supported by four eagles. In the gallery to the right of the gate is the Museum of Minerals and Geology, while the entire southeastern side of the Zwinger is occupied by the Porcelain Collection. This is entered from inside the Glockenspielpavilion or Carillon Pavilion, so called because of the chime of bells of Meissen porcelain added in 1924–36.

To the northwest the terrace overlooks the Zwingerteich (Zwinger Pond) and gardens laid out in the 1820s, along with the pools and fountains in the Zwinger courtyard.

Leaving the Zwinger to the southeast, under the Glockenspielpavilion, you'll find yourself opposite the **Taschenberg Palais**, now a luxury hotel (see page 86). In 1705 August the Strong bought two houses and had them rebuilt as one by Pöppelmann for his mistress Anna Constantia von Brockdorff, soon to be better known as Gräfin (Countess) von Cosel. Extended for the Crown Prince in 1756–63, when the east and west wings were added, it was destroyed in 1945 and rebuilt in 1993–95 as a Kempinski hotel.

Heading to the left/north from the Zwinger, you'll pass the **Schinkelwache** or Altstädter Wache (Old Town Watchhouse), built in 1830–33 by Karl Friedrich Schinkel, the great architect of neo-Classical Berlin; destroyed in 1945, it was rebuilt in 1955–56 and again in 1995–96 when it became a tourist information centre and booking office. Across the road is the **Residenzschloss** (Royal Castle), housing other State Museums (*closed Tue*). Although inner parts date back to the 12th century, it was largely rebuilt in 1717–19 and in 1889–1901, when a unified neo-Renaissance façade was added. Destroyed in 1945, rebuilding began in 1989 and is more or less complete. When the inner court opens you'll be able to admire its Italian-inspired *sgraffito* decorations and spiral staircase tower. The main entry is at the southwestern corner, leading to the Green Vault museums and the Kupferstichkabinet (see page 205); there's also the visitor centre of the State Art Collections (⊕ *11.00–18.00 Mon–Fri, 10.00–18.00 Sat/Sun & hols*) on the southeastern corner, at Schlossstrasse, which leads north under the Georgenbau. This connects the main block of the castle to the Stallhof (Stable Yard), once used for jousting tournaments (⊕ *07.00–20.00 daily, free except for special events*).

To the north of the Georgenbau is the **Hofkirche** or Roman Catholic cathedral (literally, 'court church'; see page 206), more directly reached from Theaterplatz and the north side of the Residenzschloss, passing the castle's 100m-high Hausmannsturm, built in 1674–76 and rebuilt in 1991 with its distinctive copper Baroque cupola.

Across the pedestrianised Schlossplatz (Castle Square) to the east of the cathedral is the **Ständehaus**, built in 1901–07 by Paul Wallot, architect of the Reichstag in Berlin, as the Landtag or state parliament; it's now the state Appeal Court. To its right you'll see the **Fürstenzug** or Procession of Princes, a 102m-long depiction of all 35 rulers of the Wettiner dynasty, from 1124 to 1904. This was painted in *sgraffito* in 1876–78 and replaced with 25,000 porcelain tiles in 1907; it's the world's largest porcelain mosaic. Beyond this Töpfergasse, leading to the Frauenkirche, is lined with modern buildings, so it's a better idea to go to the north of the Ständehaus and climb the steps (flanked by four statues by Schilling, erected in 1868) to the **Brühlsche Terrasse** (Brühl Terrace), laid out in 1739–48 by the Prime Minister, Count Brühl, on the city ramparts and opened to the public in 1814. Statues and fountains appeared, as well as fashionable coffee houses, leading to its being known as the Balcony of Europe, with its views over the Elbe extending from the Neustadt east to the hills behind Loschwitz.

The next building east of the Ständehaus is the **Secundogenitur Palace**, dating from 1896–97, an anachronistic neo-Baroque pile with a green copper roof; built to hold Brühl's library and graphic collection, and now housing restaurants, its name is due to the fact that it belonged to the king's second son. The sculpture in front of it is Schilling's monument to his teacher Ernst Rietschel.

Passing the so-called Painters' Corner above Münzgasse, you'll come to the **Kunstakademie** (Art Academy) and Kunstverein (Art Association), heavier, less attractive neo-Renaissance buildings also built in the 1890s by Constantin Lipsius, dominated by a glass dome known for obvious reasons as the 'lemon squeezer'.

Beyond this the Brühl Terrace ends in the Brühlscher Garten, a small park in the corner of the city walls; there are various monuments here, including a Modernist one to the painter Caspar David Friedrich, consisting of stainless-steel representations of an easel, chair and window. Around the corner (at the Semper Monument, also by Schilling) steps lead down to the right, to the entrance to the Festung or citadel (see page 214), under the garden. On the far side of the steps is the **Albertinum**, another heavy pile built in 1884–87 for the royal collections. It's closed for refurbishment until 2008 but will then house the New Masters and State Sculpture collections.

It's well worth an excursion to the strikingly modern **New Synagogue** below the ramparts at Hasenberg 1; looping around the simple Baroque Pfarrhaus (Lutheran Parish House), opposite the Albertinum, you'll pass a monument on the site of the previous synagogue, built by Gottfried Semper in 1840 and burnt down by the Nazis on Kristallnacht, 9 November 1938. The New Synagogue, designed by the Saarbrücken architects Wandel Höfer Lorch & Hirsch, was consecrated in 2001 and won the Arup World Architecture Award for European Building of the Year. Here in September 2006 the first rabbis were ordained in Germany since World War II. To the right is the parish house, with the Café Schoschana (↘ 482 0398; www.cafe-schoschana.com; ⊕ 12.00–18.00 Sat–Thu), although this always seems moribund, and a desk where you can book a tour (↘ 802 0489; around 14.00 Sat–Wed, with up to 4 on Sun afternoons; €4), which is the only way to see the synagogue (other than by attending a service).

To the left/north is the synagogue itself, a minimalist cube with a golden Star of David, the only remaining piece of Semper's synagogue, hanging over the door. Inside, hatless men can borrow a skullcap; it's much like the exterior, with plain walls and a concrete cassette ceiling. The actual prayer room is formed by a metal net curtain around something reminiscent of a portable school gym or theatre, with a gallery at the west end and a small organ. There's not a lot to see, but you'll be given a long talk about Jewish traditions and rituals. This is a Liberal congregation of about 700 members, sharing a rabbi with Leipzig (where there are around 1,200 Jews) and Chemnitz.

Going around the rear of the Albertinum on Rampische Strasse, it's a short step westwards to the **Frauenkirche** (Church of Our Lady; see page 193), the symbol of Dresden's slow recovery from the devastation of World War II and a prominent landmark all over the city. It's also the most important stone-cupola church north of the Alps, and the largest Protestant church in Germany. The Neumarkt, south of the church, is now the focus of rebuilding work, as something akin to Bellotto's townscapes of 1749–51 is recreated, although with modern concrete frames hidden inside the repro-Baroque buildings, and car parking under the cobbled square. The **Coselpalais**, by the Frauenkirche north of Salzgasse, was built in 1762–64 for August the Strong's son by Countess Cosel and reopened in 2000 with a café, restaurants and offices. The so-called QF (Quartier an der Frauenkirche) development, immediately west of the Frauenkirche, opened in 2006, with Q2, to the east between Rampische Strasse and Salzgasse, following in early 2007, and then Q3, south of Rampische Strasse, and Q5 to Q8, on the west side of the Neumarkt, where the Old Gewandhaus (Cloth Hall, demolished in 1791) will be replicated by the end of 2008, with luck, returning the Judenhof to the form it had in Bellotto's paintings. The Neumarkt will be slightly smaller than before World War II, but sightlines will still lead to the Frauenkirche dome. The **Johanneum**, to the north of the Judenhof, was built as stables in 1586–91 and converted to a picture gallery by August the Strong in 1729–30; it's now the Transport Museum (see page 226). The Q3 site, south of Rampische Gasse, was occupied by the hideous 1970s' Police Praesidium; on Q4, to its southwest, is a replica of the Hotel de Saxe where Clara Schumann premiered her husband's piano concerto in 1845.

To the south of the Neumarkt, however, there are no plans to remove the communist **Kulturpalast** (Palace of Culture), a glass-and-concrete aluminium-framed box built in 1962–69. There are fine Socialist Realist mosaics on its west side and upstairs, and bronze doors by Gerd Jaeger relating scenes from the city's history. It houses a concert hall and one of the city's main ticket agencies. On the roof, incidentally, is a webcam panning across the Neumarkt; go to: http://panorama.dresden.de to see the changes over the last couple of years. There's also the Neumarkt Pavillon (⊕ 11.00–18.00 daily) in a temporary building just north, with a display on the rebuilding project.

On the south side of the Kulturpalast, Wilsdruffer Strasse is a major axis (widened in 1912, then again in 1953 to allow parades), leading from the public transport interchange of Postplatz to the west to the Landhaus, now housing the Stadtmuseum (City Museum; see page 209), to the east. It's lined with communist-era shops and apartment blocks, and opens to the south into the **Altmarkt**, also expanded in 1953 when its east and west sides were rebuilt in a local neo-Baroque-socialist style. On Shrove Tuesday of 1349 the Margrave of Meissen ordered the burning of all Dresden's Jews in the Altmarkt, probably on a charge of spreading the plague; on Shrove

Tuesday of 1945 another auto-da-fé began with a flare dropped by RAF Pathfinders on the Altmarkt, followed ten minutes later by the first wave of 529 Lancasters dropping high explosive and incendiaries and creating a firestorm within 45 minutes.

For much of the year the Altmarkt is used for car parking but from late November until Christmas it is occupied by the Striezelmarkt, Germany's oldest Christmas market (see box, pages 146–7). Its southern end was finally filled in 2000 by an office block; to its east, at the corner of the Altmarkt, is the Kreuzkirche (Church of the Cross; see page 228), the city's main Lutheran church.

Behind the church the **Rathaus** (City Hall) occupies a whole city block with six inner courtyards; built in 1905–10 by Karl Roth and destroyed in 1945, it was rebuilt in 1962–65. On Kreuz Strasse you'll pass the entry to the Rathausturm, a tower with a viewing platform 68m above street level (⊕ *Apr–Oct 10.00–18.00 daily; adult €2.50, children & Dresden-Card holders €1.50, family €6*) and a small exhibition. The tower is 100.2m in all, including the golden *Rathausmann* statue (by Richard Guhrs, modelled on the wrestler and artiste Ewald Redam) that is one of the symbols of the city. The main entrance is on the south side, but the historic portal is to the east, looking out over the ring road, where gilded wrought ironwork leads to a low entry hall (with free toilets) and impressive stairs with an unimpressive ceiling mural.

Immediately north is the **Neues Gewandhaus** (New Cloth Hall), now the Radisson SAS Hotel. Built in 1768–70 by Johann Friedrich Knöbel, it was rebuilt in 1965–66 and is an acceptable reproduction of a Baroque townhouse on the outside but less so inside, with a covered atrium in an obviously fake Baroque courtyard.

Continuing south from the Kreuzkirche or Altmarkt, it's 500m along Prager Strasse to the **Hauptbahnhof** (central station); this area was more comprehensively flattened than the rest of the city in February 1945 and when it was rebuilt in 1963–70 was laid out as a modern pedestrian boulevard for socialist man. Damaged by flooding in 2002, it was refloored in 2004 and is now a busy and attractive shopping boulevard. This tour ends at the Hauptbahnhof, from where you can continue south (see page 170) or take a tram or train to anywhere in the city. When the Hauptbahnhof opened in 1898 it was one of the biggest and grandest stations in Germany; destroyed in 1945 it was soon rebuilt and is again being rebuilt in 2001–08. The main feature is a fairly unobtrusive high-tech roof by Lord Norman Foster (who is what the Germans call a Starchitect) consisting of 33,000m² of Teflon membrane that either lets light through or reflects it, depending on its intensity. Above the entrance hall, where more retail outlets are being installed, the glazed cupola has been restored and provides natural ventilation to the whole station; the pair of clock towers has also been replaced.

Facing the station to the north on Wiener Platz is the Kugelhaus or Globe Cube House, built in 2004–05; lifts rise above the entry into what looks like a glass bowling ball that houses shops.

WALK 2: THE NEUSTADT [maps 4 & 5]

The Neustadt (New Town) is, as explained in *Chapter 1*, older than the Altstadt; Altendresden, as it was known, was absorbed by Dresden in 1549. It was burnt down in 1429 by the Hussites and then in 1685; a new plan was drawn up in 1730, incorporating the new bridge over the Elbe (opened in 1731) and a main road north, a new cemetery, town hall and a church (consecrated in 1739). Much was destroyed in February 1945, some being replaced by communist blocks but other areas being rebuilt more recently in Baroque style.

Walking north from the north end of the Augustusbrücke you'll at once see on your left the **Blockhaus** or Neustädter Hauptwache, built to control traffic over the bridge. It was begun in 1732 by Zacharias Longuelune, and finally completed in 1753 by Johann Cristoph Knöffel. It's a fine Baroque townhouse (rebuilt in 1977–81) now housing the Saxon Academies of Art and Science and the Saxon Foundation for Nature and the Environment, which sometimes puts on exhibitions here.

Immediately to the north is the Neustädter Markt, not now used as a market square; at its centre is the statue known as the **Goldener Reiter** (Golden Rider), an equestrian statue of August the Strong by Jean-Joseph Vinache, finished in 1736, three years after August's death.

Golden Rider

Hauptstrasse leads north from here, a pedestrian street lined with communist-era shops and apartment blocks, with some rebuilt Baroque buildings on its west side further up, including the Kunsthandwerker Passagen (Craftsmen's Passages) and the Tschechisches Zentrum (Czech Centre), which promotes Czech culture with exhibitions and events. You can go straight up

Haupststrasse to Albertplatz, but it may be worth detouring west. On the far side of the Westin Bellevue Hotel, immediately west of the Blockhaus, a path leads down to the riverside meadows, with plaques marking the site where poet and dramatist Friedrich Schiller lived in 1786–87 with his friend Christian Körner and the birthplace in 1791 of Christian's son, the poet Theodor Körner, who died in 1813 fighting for German freedom from Napoleon. Just beyond is the **Japanisches Palais**, built in 1715; it was bought by August the Strong in 1717 from his Prime Minister Jacob Heinrich, Count Fleming, and by 1721 he had housed 13,000 pieces of Chinese and Meissen porcelain there. It was transformed in 1727–37 by Pöppelmann, Longuelune. Knöffel and de Bodt, expanding it from one wing to four; it became known as the Japanese Palace because of the grotesque caryatids in the court. It now houses the Museums of Ethnography, Prehistory and Natural History (see page 222).

Across Palais Platz is the start of Königstrasse, leading to the so-called **Kunstquartier** (Art Quarter) or Baroquequartier, laid out by Pöppelmann in 1731. With its regular wide streets, this is a quintessentially Baroque townscape, unlike the more haphazard and congested Altstadt; it's becoming increasingly popular with upmarket antique shops and eateries and has little in common with the better-known bohemian part of the Neustadt further north. To the right is Rähnitzgasse, with chic art galleries and shops, and Heinrichstrasse, a boutiquey street (rebuilt only in 1997), leading through a passage to Haupststrasse next to the **Dresdner Fussball Museum** (Dresden Soccer Museum; *Hauptstr 7;* \ *0174 671 6336 for tours;* ⊕ *11.00–19.00 Mon, Wed–Sat, 12.00–18.00 Sun;* €*2.50, children* €*1*), essentially a shop selling strips and books, leading to a fairly bare room of mementoes of local interest, as well as 1930s' Coca-Cola posters, programmes and so on.

At Hauptstrasse 13, the **Kügelgenhaus** (see page 216), dating from the 1690s, is home to the Museum of Romanticism in Dresden, concerned with the major role played by the city in the development of the 19th century's principal artistic movement (see page 25). At the rear of no 19 is the Societaets Theater (see page 164), founded in 1776 as the first citizens' theatre in Germany; it's housed in a Baroque pavilion by Permoser's pupil Benjamin Thomae, who lived at no 17.

Just north of the theatre is the **Dreikönigskirche** (Three Kings church; see page 227), the Neustadt's main church, facing the Neustädter Markthalle (1901) across Hauptstrasse. North of the church Hauptstrasse continues to **Albertplatz**, marking what used to be the boundary of the Neustadt; it's now principally a tram interchange, but was far more exotic a hundred years ago, as shown in Kirchner's painting of banana trees growing at the Artesian Well. The well at least is still here, beneath a round neo-Classical temple erected by Erlwein in 1905–06 and rebuilt in 1992 in front of the Nudelturm (Noodle Tower). Facing it, on the west side of Königsbrücker Strasse, is a more substantial piece of modern architecture, the **Hochhaus am Albertplatz** (Towerblock on the Albertplatz), which was the city's first skyscraper, built in 1929 for the Saxon National Bank. It survived World War II and was the headquarters of Dresden transport services until 1997, since when it has stood empty. Just west of it is the well-house of the Artesian Well, bored in 1832–36, opposite the Erich Kästner Museum, commemorating the author of *Emil and the Detectives* (see page 213). On the other side of Albertplatz, at

Georgenstrasse 6, the Dresdner Volksbank Raffeisenbank occupies the **Villa Eschebach**, built in 1901 by Herman Thüme for a manufacturer of kitchen equipment; burnt down in 1945, it was rebuilt in 1957, and the bank's tills are housed in what seems to have been an Eiffelesque orangery. There's also often a show here by a local artist (⏰08.30–16.00 Mon/Wed, 08.30–18.00 Tue/Thu, 08.30–13.00 Fri).

To the north of the Albertplatz is the **Aussere Neustadt** (Outer New Town) [map 5], also known as the Szenesviertel or Cool Quarter (*www.dresden-dresden.de/szene*); it's the bohemian area, home to the happeningest bars and the hippest people. Its main axis is Alaun Strasse, lined with bars, record shops and a few art galleries; be sure to duck through into the **Kunsthof Passage** (Art Court Passage; *www.kunsthof-dresden.de*) at Alaun 70, emerging to the east at Görlitzer Strasse 21–25. This is a group of connected courtyards, each themed (the courts of Mythical Creatures, of the Elements, of Light, of Metamorphoses, and of Animals) and imaginatively decorated to match, each in a different style (don't miss the drainpipes in the *Hof der Elemente*). There are secondhand clothes and bookshops here plus feng shui, a vinothek and the excellent Perro Borracho Spanish café-restaurant. On Görlitzer Strasse (one-way southbound except for two-way bikes and trams) no 21 has a nice elephant and camel frieze above the ground floor and no 25 is a Secession apartment block.

Go back south to Louisenstrasse (the main east–west street of the Aussere Neustadt, with more cafés, soup bars and funky shops and a fire station, opened in 1916, at no 14) and head east to Priessnitz Strasse; just to the right/south (opposite

Pulsnitzer Strasse 5) is the **Alte Jüdischer Friedhof** (Old Jewish Cemetery), which was in use from 1751 to 1869. The oldest surviving Jewish cemetery in Saxony, it contains over a thousand small tombs, a few with stones on top; ask at HATiKVA, Pulsnitzer Strasse 10 (☏ 802 0489; e info@hatikva.de), who also organise the synagogue visits (see page 157) and other cultural events.

There's not much to see on Martin-Luther-Platz, just west, other than the Martin-Luther church in the centre, built in 1883–87 in a largely neo-Romanesque style (home to the Dresdner Bachchor or Dresden Bach Choir; www.mmlk.de). You might as well go back to Priessnitz Strasse and turn right and then cut through a car park on the right to reach **Pfunds Molkerei** (Pfund's Dairy) at Bautzner Strasse 79 (☏ 810 5948; www.pfunds.de; ⊕ 10.00–18.00 Mon–Sat, 10.00–15.00 Sun & holidays), probably the most beautiful cheese shop you'll ever see. Paul Pfund opened a dairy in 1880; having invented condensed milk in 1886, he opened his new shop in 1892, covered all over with ornate neo-Renaissance tile paintings from the Dresden company Villeroy und Boch (he went on to invent long-life pasteurisation in 1900). However it's very small and very popular with tour groups – if there's more than one bus outside, don't bother. You can still go upstairs to the restaurant (⊕ 10.00–20.00 daily), for all things cheese-laden, such as raclette and fondue, but it's plain and modern in style.

From here you can head west to Albertplatz, walk or take tram 11 east to the Elbe castles (see page 181), or cut down to the riverside. Beyond the Albertbrücke you'll pass the Saxon State Chancellery and Staatsregierung or Finance Ministry, two very imposing piles built around 1900 on either side of the Carolabrücke.

Starting from Theaterplatz again, follow the embankment west to the **Sächsischer Landtag** (Parliament of Saxony), built in 1991–94 by Dresden architect Peter Kulka, mainly of glass and very striking at night. The architecture epitomises democratic transparency and openness, and free tours are available (*Bernhard-von-Lindenau-Platz 1;* ℡ *493 5136;* e *infodienst@slt.sachsen.de; www.landtag.sachsen.de;* ◷ *10.00–18.00 Mon–Fri, 10.00–16.00 Sat/Sun*). It adjoins the former Landesfinanzamt (State Finance Ministry), built in 1931 in Bauhaus style. On the embankment nearby are statues of Dostoyevsky (who lived here in 1867–71) and *Nike '89 Für Freiheit und Demokrätie das Land Sachsen* (just recognisable as *Winged Victory*).

Immediately to the west is the **Hotel Maritim Congress**, a conversion of one of Germany's first reinforced-concrete buildings, built by Hans Erlwein in 1914 as a tobacco warehouse. It's linked by a tunnel to the International Congress Centre to its west, another striking modern building (opened in 2004), with its sweeping glass curves overlooking the Elbe.

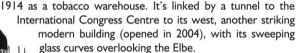

Yenidze

Literally on the wrong side of the tracks the mosque-like **Yenidze building** was built in 1908 and in fact modelled on a tomb in Cairo, with some Jugendstil elements; it was Germany's first reinforced-concrete-framed building. Named after the Yenissea tobacco-growing region of Turkey, it was built as a cigar factory (at a time when Dresden was the centre of the German tobacco industry, with around 60 companies based here). Largely destroyed in 1945, it was rebuilt only in 1996 and now houses offices and a restaurant in the cupola (see page 111).

Beyond this Magdeburger Strasse leads west past a stadium and ice rink and an artificial hill created in the 1890s with the soil excavated to form the Alberthafen docks, immediately beyond. To the right on Schlachthof Strasse is the Fischhaus Alberthafen restaurant (see page 106), an attractive terminal-style building (1895) with just beyond it an open-air museum, consisting of the Elbe barge *Waltraut* (1913), a dockside crane (1964) and a pair of railway vans (1910), which is worth a quick look. Visible to the west is the 64m-high Bienertsche Hafenmühle, another early reinforced-concrete industrial building, dating from 1912–14. To the north on the Ostrainsel (Ostra Island), beyond the flood-meadows of the Grosser Ostra-Gehege (now a nature reserve with pleasant cycle tracks), the **Messe** or Trade Fair Grounds (2001) incorporates the Schlachthof or slaughterhouse, a complex built by Erlwein in 1906–10 and expanded in 1929–30. From here bus 75 will take you back to town.

Turning south, you'll very soon reach the western end of Friedrichstrasse, the main street of the city's oldest suburb, established in 1670; it was home to the Brücke group of artists, who opened a gallery here in 1905. Returning towards the Altstadt, you'll soon pass the small Baroque Matthäuskirche (Lutheran Church of St Matthew; ⊕*16.00–18.00 Thu*), where the architect Pöppelmann was buried in the crypt in 1736; its cemetery (⊕*winter to 18.00/summer 19.00 daily*) is like a pleasant little park. Immediately beyond is the Friedrichstadt Hospital, built as the **Marcolini Palace** in 1727–28 by Johann Christoph Nauman and extended by Johann Cristoph Knöffel in 1774–78 for Count Marcolini. Napoleon lived here from June to August of 1813, agreeing a peace treaty with Count Metternich of Austria (in the Napoleonzimmer, which should open as a museum in 2007 or 2008), as did Richard Wagner in 1847–49, composing *Lohengrin* and other works.

The palace's 200m-long Baroque façade is imposing but not ornate; don't miss the lions holding the chains in front. Behind it are more recent hospital buildings, but you can still go through to the former French garden and the Neptunbrunnen (Fountain of Neptune) near its southwestern corner; made by Lorenzo Mattielli in 1741–44, it's rather worn but still impressive. Opposite the hospital (*Friedrichstr 54*) is the Old or Inner Roman Catholic Cemetery, last resting place of J B Casanova (brother of the libertine), the Baroque sculptor Balthasar Permoser, the painter Gerhard von Kügelgen, Friedrich von Schlegel (founder of the German Romantic movement), various Polish exiles, and of composer Carl Maria von Weber, who died on a visit to London in 1826. Wagner had his bones brought back and reinterred here in 1844, composing a beautiful choral ode to be sung over the tomb.

To the east of the hospital is Seminarstrasse, with the Schulmuseum (School Museum) in the courtyard of no 11 and a fine Jugendstil block at no 8; at its east end is the Mitte station, next to a market hall built at the end of the 19th century and now a discount furniture store. Beyond it, re-entering the Altstadt, the **Kraftwerk** (*Wettiner Platz 7*) is a museum of the energy and water distribution industries (see page 215); just to the north at Schützengasse 16 are the Umweltzentrum

(Environment Centre) and the Brenn Nessel vegetarian restaurant. Just beyond, An der Herzogin Garten (the Duchess's Garden) is the site of a garden laid out at the end of the 16th century in the Italian style, with a small summerhouse, then an orangery with a grotto, fountain and obelisks. It's now utterly abandoned.

To the south Althus Strasse leads to the **Annenkirche** (Church of St Anne); founded in 1578 and rebuilt in 1768 after the Seven Years War, it's a big Baroque hall church that managed to survive World War II (indeed, a thousand people survived the 1945 bombing in the church), although the tower was not rebuilt until 1997. It has a dramatic interior with big windows and galleries that's ideal for concerts (✆ 0351 318640).

From here it's a straight shot back to the Zwinger along Annenstrasse, or you can take Ammonstrasse, parallel to the railway line, to the Hauptbahnhof, to continue with Walk 4.

WALK 4: UNIVERSITY AREA

From the east side of the Hauptbahnhof (main train station), the busy Löffler Strasse rises slightly to the south, so you could either take tram 8 to its Südvorstadt terminus, or walk through the Südvorstadt-West villa district, passing the Hübnerstrasse youth hostel and attractive Jugendstil houses at Hübnerstrasse 12 and 14, and apartment blocks at Nürnberger Strasse 32/34, 39–45 and 47.

Just south across Münchner Strasse is the **Technische Universität Dresden** or TUD (Dresden Technical University), founded in 1828, which now has around

35,000 students. Its main building, the Schumann-Bau on Münchner Platz, is an imposing block which housed the District Courts from 1907 to 1956. Entering the courtyard just to the left at Georg-Bähr-Strasse 7 you'll see in front of you a memorial wall erected in 1988 (with text in five languages) by a passage to the next court to the right, where over 2,000 people were executed by the Nazis between 1933 and 1945, including many from other jurisdictions (around two-thirds of those from the Czech 'Proctectorate of Bohemia and Moravia' executed by the Nazis were actually brought here to die). There's a sculpture group (by Arnd Wittig; 1962) representing resistance fighters awaiting execution, and indoors to the right are the offices of the **Gedenkstätte Münchner Platz** (Munich Square Memorial; ℡ 4633 1990; e gedenkstaette@mailbox.tu-dresden.de; www.stsg.de; ⏲10.00–16.00 Mon–Fri), with a room for temporary exhibitions and, upstairs, a library. It's also possible to visit the death cells and the former court room, now lecture hall 251 (⏲08.00–17.30 Mon–Fri). After World War II the building was used by the Soviet secret police as a transit detention centre and for trials of Nazis; after 1952 it was the central place of execution for the whole DDR.

In the Faculty of Electrotechnology and Information Technology at Helmholz Strasse 9 there's a permanent display of electrical equipment and temporary photographic exhibits in the gallery of the four-storey atrium, which are worth a look. Just to the east you'll pass the university's striking new Hörsaalzentrum (lecture theatre centre) at Bergstrasse 64 and opposite it at no 51 (across a new footbridge) the Mensa or university cafeteria (⏲08.00–20.00 Mon–Thu, 08.00–15.00 Fri, 11.00–14.00 Sat), well worth a visit for a coffee or more.

Just east at Zellescher Weg 18 is the modern **library** of the SLUB or Saxon State and University Libraries, which merged in 1996 and moved in here in 2003 (⏲ *09.00–22.00 Mon–Thu, 09.00–20.00 Fri/Sat*). There's a tour at 14.00 on Saturdays (✆ 467 7374; e *tour@slub-dresden.de; www.slub-dresden.de*) and upstairs (past a portrait of Elector August, who founded the library in 1556, and paintings by Anton Graff and Robert Sterl, among others) is the free museum (⏲ *10.00–17.00 Mon–Sat*). This puts on temporary shows, often excellent, displaying treasures from the collections, which date back to 1525 (a year after Duke Georg the Bearded set up a press in the Residenzschloss). In addition to early Lutheran Bibles and commentaries there's a Mayan Codex and a Dürer sketchbook, illuminated medieval manuscripts, the *Mainz Psalter* of 1457, scores by J S Bach, Vivaldi and Wagner, and prints by Carl August Richter. These are usually kept in the Schatzkammer (Treasure Room) which can be visited by appointment.

Returning north on Einstein Strasse towards the centre, you'll soon come to the **Lukaskirche** (Church of St Luke), built in 1899–1903 and without a steeple ever since 1945. It's a huge hall church with a fan vault which is used for concerts especially by the university orchestra and choirs. To the north are communist apartment blocks and student residences (with another Mensa cafeteria at Reichenbach Strasse 1), and by Löffler Strasse the Russian church, built in 1872–74 and visited by the likes of Dostoyevsky and Rachmaninov (⏲ *10.00–17.00 Tue–Sun, 13.00–17.00 Mon, with services 17.00 Wed & 10.00 Sun*). It's not very ornate but is recognisably Russian with its blue and gold domes, white marble iconostasis and many icons. From here you can stroll downhill to the Hauptbahnhof in five minutes.

From the university Nürnberger Strasse leads northwest to the Nossener Brücke over the railway (with the city's high-tech new power station on the far side). Down steps to the left is the Railway Museum (see page 213); heading south from here along Zwickauer Strasse, or taking Münchner Strasse and Nöthnitzer Strasse west from the university, you'll come to the station of Plauen (the first stop on S-Bahn line 3, and not to be confused with the town of Plauen far to the southwest). Just east of the station is the church of the Auferstehung (Resurrection) (⏱12.00–15.00 Mon–Fri), built in 1902; it's a fairly big neo-Renaissance hall church with a 49m tower. Plauen stands at the mouth of the Plauenscher Grund, a gorge where watermills provided the power for Dresden's first industries, including the Felsenkellerbrauerei (Cliff Cellar Brewery) and a glass-cutting and polishing mill established by Johann Friedrich Böttger in 1713. Saxon amethyst was also quarried from 1727 and polished here. The Reiche metal product factory (making moulds for chocolate machines, among other things) was famous across Europe. Maria Reiche (1903–88) was born in Dresden, studied at the Technical University, and left Germany to be a governess in Peru due partly to her disgust at German militarism, and from 1946 until her death she studied and protected the famous pre-Columbian Nasca lines.

The picturesque Grund also inspired many of the early Romantics including Kleist, Hans Christian Andersen, the painters Anton Graff, Caspar David Friedrich, Carl August Richter and his son Ludwig Richter. The Italian painter Giuseppe Grazzi, who taught at the Kunstakademie, had a summerhouse here from 1800, where artists gathered and the poet Wilhelm Müller wrote his cycle *Die Schöne Müllerin*, soon set to music by Schubert.

On the far side of the station a short path signed *Hohen Stein* leads to a viewpoint over the gorge of the Weisseritz (including a dramatic new autobahn bridge between two tunnels), and on to Coschütz. The railway also runs through the Grund; its next four stations serve the town of Freital, and from the first, Freital-Potschappel, it's a couple of hundred metres south to the factory of Meissen porcelain's less glamorous cousin, the Sächsische Porzellan-Manufaktur Dresden, better known as **Dresdner Porzellan**, at Carl-Thieme-Strasse 16 (✆ 647130; e *info@dresdner-porzellan.com; www.dresdner-porzellan.de;* ⏰ *09.00–17.00 Mon–Sat*). Founded in 1872, this produces a similar range to the Meissen factory but is less overwhelmed by coach parties. Tours in English start at 11.00 and 14.00 Monday to Friday (€7.50). Just southeast of Potschappel is the small mansion of **Schloss Burgk** (*Altburgkl 61;* ✆ *649 1562;* e *museum@freital.de; www.freital.de;* ⏰ *13.00–16.00 Tue–Fri, 10.00–17.00 Sat/Sun; €4*), where there's a mining exhibition, with a visitors' mine (⏰ *Apr–Oct 13.00–16.00 Tue/Thu, 10.00–16.00 first Sun in each month*) and an art collection.

You might wish to walk this far (6km from the Hauptbahnhof as the Krähe flies) but to reach Freital-Hainsberg (the fourth station) and Tharandt, the sixth and last (18mins from Dresden-Hauptbahnhof) you should take the S-Bahn. At Hainsberg you can change to the **Weisseritztalbahn**, a narrow-gauge steam railway (*www.weisseritztalbahn.de*) that usually runs to Kipsdorf, but is still recovering from 2002 flood damage. In Tharandt, 1km from the station, the

Forstbotanischer Garten (Forest-botanical Garden) is a lovely dendrological garden *(Am Forstgarten 1;* ℘ *035203 383 1258;* e *forstpark@forst-tu-dresden.de; www.forstbotanik.com;* ⊕ *Apr–Oct 08.00–17.00 Sat–Thu, museum 13.30–15.30 Sat–Thu; free)*. You can also walk to Tharandt Castle ruins (always open), 700m from the station, and on marked walks such as to Kurort Hartha (5km) or Grillenburg (10km).

WALK 6: GROSSER GARTEN AND STREHLEN

Opposite the Rathaus (City Hall) is the former Robotron computer factory, once the pride of the DDR and now an office centre; just beyond to the south, is the German Hygiene Museum (see page 211). Ahead on the left *(at Lenné Str 1, at the corner of Grunaer Str)* is Volkswagen's striking modern **Glaäserne Manufaktur** [map 2] (literally Glass Factory – but the term Transparent Factory

Transparent Factory

is preferred as it also refers to the visibility of the processes). Opened in 2002, at a cost of €186 million, it is clad with 27,500m² of glass, not just externally but also inside, so that visitors can watch the production line, and has a 40m-high circular glass tower where cars awaiting collection by their owners are parked. The metal-bashing is done elsewhere, with parts delivered by rail to VW's Logistics Centre in Friedrichstadt and brought by their distinctive blue CargoTram through the city centre to the factory on a just-in-time basis. Each tram carries the equivalent of three truckloads, or parts for six cars; the actual car bodies are brought by truck from Zwickau.

It's pretty much a boutique operation, with 800 staff (227 on the production line) producing a daily maximum of 150 Phaeton luxury sedans (some in fact Bentley Continentals), and more often only 40 or so (all cars are built to order, with a choice of colours and equipment). It's open for visits from 08.00 to 20.00 daily, although the production line works only Monday to Friday (so in winter it works only when the Palais im Grosser Garten is closed, requiring separate visits) and costs €4 with a leaflet in English or German; in season you'll need to book (✆ 01805 896268 – €0.24/min from a landline; e infoservices@glaesernemanufaktur.de; www.glaesernemanufaktur.de), and note that cameras are not allowed. Of course, there's no charge if you're thinking of buying a Phaeton.

There's a surprisingly good restaurant here (see page 109) and you can try a simulator for a virtual test drive of the Phaeton; it's definitely worth a visit to the toilets too.

Behind the Transparent Factory at Stübelallee 2 is the university's **Botanischer Garten** (Botanic Garden; ⊕Apr–Sep 10.00–18.00, Mar/Oct 10.00–17.00, Feb–Nov 10.00–16.00, Dec/Jan 10.00–15.30 all daily; free [map 2]). Established in 1815 by the Royal Saxon Surgical-Medical Academy as a garden for medicinal plants, it moved to this site in 1889–93; two gingkos planted in 1890 are now the oldest of its roughly 9,000 species and varieties. To the left as you enter are Asian plants then, in a glasshouse, orchids, succulents and carnivorous plants, then North American plants to the left with open-air succulents to the right. Further on to the right are pieces of petrified wood and fossils of plants that formed the brown coal deposits around Leipzig and Hoyerswerda, in front of the large Tropical House (with free toilets). Beyond this are the southern and eastern European and Caucasian plants and in the far right-hand corner native flora. To the east are alpines and more native flora, and in the southeastern arm of the garden shrubs and trees, and commercial plants with annuals beyond them. There are some good trees here, but they're not as mature as at Pillnitz.

To the south and east of the Transparent Factory and Botanic Garden is the **Grosser Garten** [map 2] or Great Garden (always open), best entered through the main gate facing the German Hygiene Museum. The garden (more of a park) was laid out for crown prince Johann Georg in 1676–83 by the court gardener Martin Göttler, and grew to cover an area of 2km x 2km. The **Palais im Grossen Garten** (*www.palais-grosser-garten.de* [map 2]) was built in 1680–91, the first Baroque palace in Dresden, with the pool to its east side added in 1715; August the Strong's collections of antiques and statues were installed from 1729. The Baroque garden, with copses and shelters for pheasants, was probably complete by 1718, and used for festivities until 1813, when it was devastated by the Napoleonic battles. From 1873 Johann Karl Friedrich Bouché was in charge of the gardens, creating the Carolasee (still popular for boating in summer and ice-skating in winter) and the Carolaschlösschen (now a restaurant), both named after King Albrecht's wife Carola. The palace was left roofless in 1945 and was only rebuilt in 1993–2002; it's still not finished, with bare walls awaiting plastering. On the ground floor there's a display (⏰*Apr–Oct 14.00–18.00 Tue–Sat, 11.00–18.00 Sun; Nov–Mar 11.00–18.00 Sat/Sun; adult €3, children €2*) of classical statuary by Balthasar Permoser and his pupils and successors, notably Benjamin Thomae and Gottfried Knöffler. The upper floors are currently used for concerts and can be visited on tours (⏰*14.30 summer Tue/winter Sat; €4*). There are also fine statues in the park, notably Pietro Balestra's allegorical statue *Time Steals Away Beauty*, about 100m west of the palace, in line with the gates and the German Hygiene Museum.

The communists' aim was to create a people's park, with the Pioneer Railway (operated by schoolchildren) opened in 1950, the Dahlia Garden in 1951 and the Sonnenhäusl puppet theatre in 1955. The **Parkeisenbahn** (Park Railway) [map 2], as it is now called (✆ *445 6795; e info-parkeisenbahn@schloesser.smf.sachsen.de; www.parkeisenbahn-dresden.de; ⏰mid Apr to early Oct 10.00–18.00 daily; to late Oct 13.00–17.00 Mon–Fri, 10.00–17.00 Sat/Sun & holidays, depending on the weather; adult €3.10, children €1.55*), is still operated by children, with a 5.6km circuit of 381mm-gauge track and six stations, including one at the zoo, with which there's a combined ticket (€8.50, children €4.60). The **Zoo** (*Tiergartenstr 1;* ✆ *478060; e info@zoo-dresden.de; www.zoo-dresden.de; ⏰08.30–16.30, last entry 15.45, daily, in summer to 18.30; adult €7, children aged 2–16 €4, family (2 adults and 4 children) €18* [map 2]) is the oldest in eastern Germany, founded in 1861, and is still going strong with 3,000 animals of about 400 species, and various new facilities opening, including an outdoor enclosure for the orang-utans, a new Africa house (with elephants, mandrills, chameleons and birds) and a tundra area (with Arctic foxes and snowy owls). There are also various apes, lions, pumas, deer, buffalo, zebras, chinchillas, dromedaries, kangaroos, snakes and birds such as eagles, vultures, parrots, penguins, spoonbills, pelicans, cranes, ibis, cormorants and ducks, not to mention the woodpeckers that move freely between the zoo and the Grosser Garten. The Streichelzoo or petting zoo has dwarf goats and sheep, and you can also watch the larger animals being fed between 12.00 and 15.00.

To the north of the Grosser Garten is an attractive area of suburban villas and then **Johannstadt** [map 2], notorious for its serried ranks of Plattenbau or communist tower blocks, but now in fact very nicely refurbished and prettified. At Pillnitzer Strasse 39 (on Güntzstr) the Sankt-Benno-Gymnasium is a new high school, built in 1996 by one of the grand old men of German architecture, Günther Behnisch. Opposite at Marschenerstrasse 15–27 the brightly coloured apartment block is now typical of the city's housing stock – all 48,000 apartments were sold in 2006 to a US equity firm for US\$1.2 billion, clearing all the city's debts, and are now being refurbished. Just north on Güntzplatz the very attractive Sparkasse (Savings Bank) was built in 1914 as the Stadthaus Johannstadt (city offices); opposite it is the weighty Landgericht or state courts. Gerokstrasse leads east to Fletscherstrasse, where the New Jewish Cemetery, established in 1867 on part of the Trinity cemetery, faces the university hospital.

From just east of the zoo, Oskarstrasse leads south (past Strehlen S-Bahn station) to **Wasaplatz**, where you'll find the Four Points Hotel Königshof facing Wasaplatz 1, a lovely Jugendstil house built in 1903 for the painter Gotthardt Kuehl and now a lovely bar-restaurant and Biergarten; other houses on the square date from 1902–05. There are also good examples at Gustav-Adolf-Strasse 13 (immediately west of Oskarstr) and Mockritzer Strasse 6 (four blocks southeast of Wasaplatz). About three blocks east of Wasaplatz is the big heavy Christuskirche, built of dark stone in 1903–05.

WALK 7: LOSCHWITZ AND PILLNITZ

From Albertplatz in the Neustadt, Bautzner Strasse leads east past Pfunds Molkerei and above the north bank of the Elbe. Tram 11 follows this road to Bühlau, from where bus 61 runs down to Loschwitz, Blasewitz and Strehlen. Taxis wait at the end of Diakonissenweg, which leads down to the ferry to Johannstadt. Beyond this are attractive villas built around a hundred years ago, such as Bautzner Strasse 82, 86 and 125; no 107 is the Kleine Szene, where Mary Wigman taught free dance. Bautzner Strasse climbs gently to the **Brauhaus am Waldschlösschen** (see page 126), also the venue for various gigs and clubs (see page 140). The 'Little Castle in the Forest' was a neo-Gothic hunting lodge built by the Elector's Head Chamberlain, Count Marcolini in 1790; by 1829 it had become a tavern serving the developing villa district and in 1836 Germany's first joint-stock brewery was founded here. Behind it at Waldschlösschen Strasse 6 is the private Uhrenmuseum (Clock Museum) (⏰ *10.00–13.00 & 14.00–18.00 Mon–Fri, 11.00–13.00 & 14.00–18.00 Sat/Sun; adult €2.70, children €1*), which is really a repair shop with an enthusiast's collection of odd timepieces.

Bautzner Strasse 171, 181 and 193 and Klarastrasse 2–8 are all lovely Jugendstil houses, beyond which Fischhausstrasse leads up to the Historisches Fischhaus (see page 121) on the edge of the König-Albert-Park, itself on the edge of the 50km² Dresdner Heide or Dresden Heath, a favourite spot for walking and cycling.

Facing the park on the south side of the road are the so-called **Elbe castles** [map 1], three palaces built in the 19th century with lovely connected parks that are open to the public. The first (*Bautzner Str 130*) is the **Schloss Albrechtsberg** (Albrechtsberg Castle), built in 1851–54 on the site of a house built in 1811 by James Ogilvy, Earl of Findlater and Seafield, who had left Britain because of his homosexuality and moved to Dresden to pursue his interest in Saxon wine, buying up many of the Loschwitzer vineyards. He died the same year that the house was completed, leaving it to his 'secretary' Johann Georg Fischer, whose wife promptly divorced him when the relationship came to light; Findlater and Fischer now lie in the same tomb in Loschwitz churchyard. The house was bought in 1821 by the hotelier Johann Gabriel Krebs and became a very popular excursion from the city; in 1850 it was sold to Prince Albrecht, the fifth son (and last of nine children) of King Friedrich Wilhelm III of Prussia. However, he continued to serve in the Prussian army and led the Prussian cavalry in the Franco–Prussian War, leading to his death from exhaustion in 1872. He commissioned Adolf Lohse (a pupil of Schinkel) to build a Tuscan Renaissance-style palace, with corner towers and a huge central gazebo. The most beautiful room is the magnificent Kronensaal (Hall of Crowns) which runs from front to rear of the house above the entry; its acoustics make this Dresden's finest chamber music venue (see page 131). The Turkish Bath is also a very beautiful room, and a popular setting for storytelling; in summer the Roman Bath, on the slope down to the river, is also used for concerts.

Guided tours take place at weekends (☎ 486 6666; *www.schloss-albrechtsberg.de; adult €4.50, children €3*).

Albrecht's wife and sons lived here until 1925 when they sold it to the city; in 1944 it was used by the staff of a Panzer division and survived the war undamaged, but in May 1945 was trashed by the Red Army before becoming the headquarters of the Soviet Military Administration of Germany, and in 1948 an Intourist hotel (run by the Soviet Foreign Trade Ministry). In 1951 it became the DDR's first Pioneer Palace, for communist youth activities, and since 1991 has been a catering school, with conferences, weddings and banquets hosted here.

Two large neo-Classical gatehouses stand on either side of the entrance, one housing the Prinzenkeller (see page 122) and the other a free exhibition (🕐 10.00–18.00), only in German, but with lots of information on the castle's history. The park is lovely, with fountains, a small lake with a Classical temple, and terrace on the slope down to the river; the Prussian landscaper Eduard Neide planted 1,664 mature trees and around 80,000 plants.

The park is common with the next of the Elbe castles, the **Lingnerschloss** (*Bautzner Str 132*), also built by Lohse in 1850–53, in a late neo-Classical style, for Baron von Stockhausen, Prince Albrecht's Chamberlain. In 1891 it was bought by the sewing-machine manufacturer Bruno Naumann, and in 1906 by Karl August Lingner (immensely rich thanks to Odol mouthwash, invented in 1893). The Dresden architect Wilhelm Kreis (who also built the German Hygiene Museum for Lingner) modernised the interior, with a few individual touches such as the three-manual organ on which Lingner played his own compositions on the phone to friends. You can also see the upper terminal of the cable-car which he used to drive up and down to the river. The Schloss passed to the city after Lingner's death in 1916 and the park was opened to the public in 1930 (with Lingner's neo-Classical mausoleum installed in 1920). It was used as a student residence after World War II then as an intellectuals' club; since 1993 it has been disused but is now being restored. There's a café on the terrace (⏰ 12.00–18.00 daily, in winter Fri–Sun), as well as a telescope (€0.50), and a shop selling books, cards, ornaments and souvenirs in the gatehouse (☎ 646 5382; www.lingnerschloss.de; ⏰09.00–19.00 Mon–Fri), where you can also book tours; the house is used for talks and readings (children's tales 15.00 Sun, adults 20.00 Fri).

There's a gate through to the park (⏰06.00–midnight) of the Hotel **Schloss Eckberg** (see page 95), which has an ugly modern annexe near the gatehouse and a spa, as well as a restaurant in the castle itself (see page 122). This was built by Christian Friedrich Arnold (a student of Semper) in 1859–61 in a Baronial Gothic Revival style for the Scottish merchant John Daniel Souchay. From the terrace (with a bronze statue by Sasha Schneider of an Egyptian boy worshipping the sun) there are great views of the Blue Wonder Bridge, meadows and villas opposite, and also tower blocks to the southwest.

A few hundred metres further east you should turn right down Schillerstrasse to reach the centre of **Loschwitz**, one of the original Sorb villages around Dresden (first recorded in 1315) and still very attractive, with the addition of the **Blaues Wunder** and the mountain railways (see page 69). The 1893 Blue Wonder's main span of 141m was an impressive length at the time although 160m spans had already been built in North America. Nevertheless Dresdeners are very attached to it. It was almost demolished by the German army at the end of World War II but two local residents (acting separately) cut the wires to the explosive charges. From here it's 4km to the Neustadt or 6km to the Altstadt along the meadows, making this a very popular cycle excursion.

Loschwitz, with the vineyards of the Loschwitzer Elbhang or Elbe slope, was popular with the early Romantics, such as Goethe and Kleist, and Schiller wrote most of *Don Carlos* here in 1785–87. There are still a few old half-timbered houses by the river but others were demolished during the construction of the bridge and replaced by four-storey red-brick apartment blocks. It's still pleasantly arty and a good place to live, with two arts centres, two bookshops and two bike shops. The most attractive part of town is Friedrich-Wieck-Strasse, just south of the bridge, but its centre is Körnerplatz, with the tiny Bräustübel bar facing the funicular terminal. A little way up Grundstrasse from here is the **Leonhardi Museum**, in a very ornate half-timbered building that was a mill until the landscape painter Eduard Leonhardi converted it to studios and a museum in the 1880s. At the top of the hill is the Villenviertel or villa quarter of Weisser Hirsch (White Stag) where the bourgeoisie built spacious new homes with fresh air and wide views at the start of the 20th century. The easiest way to visit is to take the funicular up and the monorail down, or vice versa, stopping at the Gaststätte Luisenhof (see page 121) for refreshment. The Ludwig Richter Weg is a walk of about an hour from the top of the monorail, looping down to the bottom via places where the painter lived and the Leonhardi Museum.

On the far side of the bridge is **Blasewitz**, another Sorb village (recorded in 1350) that is now less attractive than Loschwitz but which also has associations with the Romantics, as at the Schillergarten (see page 122). Just west, around the Waldpark (Dresden's second-largest park), are more Jugendstil villas such as Goetheallee 23, 24, 51 and 55, as well as some good late 20th-/early 21st-century infilling.

Immediately east of the monorail's lower terminal is a small octagonal Baroque church, built in 1705–08 by George Bähr and Johann Christian Fähre, with two galleries and a nice altar with red marble columns; destroyed in 1945, it was rebuilt in 1991–94. The Pillnitzer Landstrasse continues southeast by the river, passing the Loschwitz cemetery, where over 30 minor artists are buried, some with attractive tombs; opposite it, Pillnitzer Landstrasse 59 (built in 1897) is known as the Kunstlerhaus because of all the artists who lived there in the 1950s and 1960s.

Wachwitz and Niederpoyritz are pleasant riverside villages with pensions and pubs; entering **Hosterwitz** there are apple orchards opposite the waterworks (built by Hans Erlwein in 1907–08) and sculptures in the meadows. The Schifferkirche or Church of Maria am Wasser (St Mary's by the Water) was traditionally the church of the Elbe boatmen, built in 1497–1500 and rebuilt in 1704 in Baroque style. There's some fine 17th-century stone carving inside. The composer Carl Maria von Weber had a summerhouse on what is now Weberweg (leave bus 83 at Van-Gogh-Strasse, 10mins from Loschwitz) which is now a museum (see page 210). He spent the summers of 1818–19 and 1822–24 here with his wife, writing *Der Freischütz*, *Euryanthe*, *Oberon* and *The Invitation to the Dance*.

Just beyond are the only Dresden ferry that takes cars and the centre of the village, abutting the western end of the Pillnitz park. Just beyond the village, to the left on Bergweg, is the Weinbergkirche zum Heilige Geist (Vineyard Church of the Holy Ghost), a smallish Baroque hall built by Pöppelmann in 1723–25 (and restored in 1990–95) in a pretty isolated spot at the foot of the vine-covered slopes. It contains a large sandstone altar with a 17th-century relief of the Last Supper.

The road loops around to the east side of **Schloss Pillnitz**, the summer residence of the rulers of Saxony from 1765 to 1918 (☎ 261 3260; e pillnitz@ schloesser-dresden.de; www.schloesser-dresden.de).

The first castle was built here in 1420; in 1706 August the Strong gave it to his mistress Countess Cosel, and he took it back in 1718 when she fell from favour. He planned a grand expansion as a Lustschloss or pleasure palace and the Parisian-trained painter-architect Zacharias Longuelune produced a plan for a Temple of Bacchus in the shape of a wine cask. Sadly, perhaps, this was not built. Instead Matthäus Daniel Pöppelmann built the Wasserpalais (Water Palace) in 1720–21, in Baroque style with chinoiserie elements, followed by the Bergpalais (Hill Palace) and the Vineyard Church, with the riverside terrace and steps for boarding barges added by Longuelune in 1725. In 1788–91 the residential wings adjoining the two palaces were added by Christian Traugott Weinlig and after a fire in 1818 the palace to the east was rebuilt in neo-Classical style with new chapel and kitchen wings. The Heckengarten or Hedge Garden was planted by Cosel in 1712, followed by the English Garden in 1778 and the Chinese Garden in 1790, with a palm house being built in 1859–61. In 2006 the new Schlossmuseum opened in the New Palace, while the Bergpalais and Wasserpalais are home to the Museum of Decorative Arts (see page 216).

Entering from the east, there are toilets to the right before the Wache or watchhouse, which now houses a shop and visitor information (📞 261 3260; e info-pillnitz@schloesser.smf.sachsen.de; ⏰May–Oct 09.00–18.00, Nov–Apr 10.00–16.00, all daily). To the left is the Neues Palais, with new boutiques in the ground-floor passages, and to the right the Wasserpalais (especially lovely with its riverside terrace) and the Bergpalais (not noticeably higher than the Wasserpalais), both decorated with delightful chinoiserie murals on their exteriors. In the park just west of the Bergpalais a pavilion protects a gondola, ie: an eight-oared state barge. To the north are fine mature exotic trees such as Caucasian oak (*Quercus macranthera*), eastern hemlock (*Tsuga canadiensis*), Douglas fir (*Pseudotsuga menziesii*) and Japanese cedar (*Cryptomeria japonica*) as well as cedar, juniper, fir, yew, cypresses and pines.

Behind these is the orangery, built by August the Strong and greatly expanded at the end of the 19th century. Just west are gingko and magnolia trees, and the oldest and biggest Japanese camellia tree in Europe, 8.5m high, which produces up to 35,000 carmine red flowers between February and April. In 1776 four specimens of *Camellia japonica* were brought from Japan to Kew and one was planted here by 1801; it did well, with a wooden house built to protect it every winter. Since 1992 an electronically controlled glasshouse has been rolled over it from mid/late October until the end of April or early May; this can be visited (⏰10.00–17.00 daily) when the tree is in bloom. Tours of the park include the interiors of the English and Chinese pavilions, built in 1786 and 1804 respectively.

Born in 1872 in Bavaria, Hans Erlwein was the Dresden city architect from 1905 until 1914, when he left to become an ambulance driver on the Western Front. He was killed later that same year near Rheims, a terrible waste of an architect with a very light touch who in a few years did so much to establish the city's character. Working in something of a post-Jugendstil style, many of his buildings were also influenced by the Arts & Crafts or Garden City styles, with some traditional features such as oxeye windows as well. As city architect he had to turn his hand to bus garages, schools and apartment blocks as well as more attention-seeking projects such as the Italienisches Dörfchen, Artesian Well, Schlachthof, Hotel Maritim Congress and the Hosterwitz Waterworks, all described elsewhere in this chapter. The former include the Reick gas holders, the Striesen fire station, accommodation for staff of the city tramways (*Bühnaustrasse 4–8*), the Friedrichstadt Stadthaus (*Löbtauer Strasse 2*), and apartment blocks at Wilder-Mann-Strasse 6/8 (*on the corner of Industriestrasse*) and on Dölzschener Strasse. igeltour (see page 37) offer a walk around some of his buildings.

The 28ha park is open daily from 05.00 to dusk (*free*) and is a popular cycle route (continuing west, a new 5km cycle track runs alongside the Pillnitzer Landstr); the White Fleet's paddle-steamers dock just east of the castle, and the ferry just to the west links with bus 88 and tram 1. You can stay at the four-star Schloss-Hotel Pillnitz (see page 95), the Goldener Apfel Hotel & Vitalzentrum, Schulweg 3 (✆ 261660; www.goldener-apfel.de) or the pensions along the Pillnitzer Landstrasse to the west (see page 98).

WALK 8: HELLERAU

To the north of the city, just before the airport, Dresden-Hellerau was continental Europe's first garden city, founded in 1908 (*Garden Cities in Sight* by Ebenezer Howard, who had founded Letchworth Garden City in 1903, had been translated into German in 1907). It was begun by Hermann Muthesius, Richard Riemerschmid and Hans Erlwein, but it was the arrival of Karl Schmidt's **Deutsche Werkstätten** furniture factory in 1911 that galvanised the project – he had founded it in Dresden in 1898 and moved to Hellerau seeking a unity of nature, home life and work. A forerunner of the seminal post-World War I Bauhaus, it survived to be privatised in 1992, and still makes very good products; free tours are available of the factory at Moritzburger Weg 67 (✆ 838 8195). The **Festspielhaus** (Festival Hall) at Karl-Liebknecht-Strasse 56 was built in 1911–12 by Heinrich von Tessenow for Emile Jacques-Dalcroze, the teacher of dance and eurhythmics (see page 133); its most radical feature was a lack of separation between seating and stage. Free dance was developed here by Mary Wigman and Greta Palucca, and the tradition is being carried on by William Forsythe (see page 134).

In the 1930s army barracks were built in the Festspielhaus grounds and it was then taken over by the Red Army. In 2006 it reopened as the European Centre of

Arts (*www.kunstforumhellerau.de*), although the façade is still tatty; there are some Soviet murals by the stairs inside, including the Red Army's victory parade.

Tram 8 comes here from the Altstadt and Neustadt and along Moritzberger Weg; the Festspielhaus Hellerau stop is two stops before the terminus, on the far side of the autobahn which now bisects the suburb; see pages 96 and 122 for accommodation and a restaurant here.

WALK 9: PIESCHEN

Pieschen, the suburb immediately west of the Neustadt, is not particularly beautiful and is of no great historical importance but there are some attractive buildings. Heading northwest from the Neustädterbahnhof up Grossenhainer Strasse you'll soon come to the Petrikirche (Church of St Peter) on the right; built in 1888–90 it's a monumental red-brick neo-Gothic pile that was badly damaged in 1945 and rebuilt in 1950–55. Just beyond it at Grossenhainer Strasse 32 a splendid Jugendstil house (built in 1902) is now home to Jehmlich Orgelbau, Dresden's leading organ-builders since 1808. After passing under the railway you'll see good Jugendstil apartment blocks on the left side of Grossenhainer Strasse, and at no 203, on the west side of Trachenberger Platz, there's an attractive Jugendstil Apothek (chemist's shop; 1903–06). From here buses towards Moritzburg continue northwest (past the Wilder Mann terminal of tram 3) past more attractive villas. Alternatively it's under five minutes' walk south from Trachenberger Platz to the Pieschen S-Bahn station (on line S1 to Radebeul and Meissen), or the same distance west on Barbarastrasse to the Roman Catholic Church of St Joseph and its parish house, built in 1909–10 in neo-Romanesque style with Jugendstil elements.

Just south of the station is Altpieschen, with the Elbcenter shopping centre right by the river and the Watzke brewery just west (see page 126); Leipziger Strasse leads northwest, turning into Meissner Strasse, the main road through Radebeul (tram 4). There are fairly unexciting Jugendstil buildings at Leipziger Strasse 153/155 (just west of the Mickten tram stop), 218 and 230. Following the river downstream for a couple of kilometres brings you to **Übigau** (bus 70 and 80), where a Baroque mansion (built in 1724–26) became one of the key sites of Dresden's industrialisation, with a shipyard established in 1836–45 by Andreas Schubert that produced Saxony's first steamship and railway locomotive (the *Saxonia*). There are plans to restore the site and open it up (see *www.schloss-uebigau.de*).

10 Museums and Sightseeing

There are over 400 museums in Saxony, including community and private ones, seeing a total of over eight million visitors a year; of these, the 11 museums of the Dresden State Art Collections account for 1.5 million visitors a year. This is as it should be, for these are Dresden's most unmissable museums (see below).

A ticket for all the museums of the Dresden State Art Collections costs € 12 or € 7 for a child or € 25 for a family, while an annual ticket costs € 20; there's free entry (except for the Historisches Grünes Gewölbe) with the Dresden City-Card and Regio-Card (see page 72). There's also a two-day card for all the city's museums and galleries, costing € 10, or € 7 for a child; all city museums are free on Fridays from 14.00 (except holidays). Be sure to keep a € 1 coin handy as a deposit for the lockers in which you'll usually have to leave your hand baggage.

UNMISSABLES

The Altstadt or Old Town, on the south bank of the Elbe, is a Baroque jewel, with the superb state art galleries and museums, above all the Green Vault, displaying the fantastic treasures of August the Strong. The Neustadt, north of the river, is less picturesque but is a centre of bohemian art and culture and wild nightlife, with an amazing profusion of ethnic restaurants. You should be sure to see the Zwinger, a Baroque court housing some of the best museums, Volkswagen's Transparent Factory and the Yenidze building, a former tobacco factory built in the style of a mosque.

FRAUENKIRCHE (CHURCH OF OUR LADY) *An der Frauenkirche* [maps 2 & 3]

In 1722 George Bähr, the city's master carpenter, was asked to produce designs for a replacement for the old Frauenkirche, none of which found favour with Count von Wackerbarth, chief inspector of buildings; the chief state architect, Johann Christoph Knöffel, produced sketches that were more to the taste of the court, and his ideas for a circular cupola church with more massive pillars were taken up. The design was approved in 1726 and largely completed by 1736; by the time of Bähr's death in 1738 there were already cracks in the walls and leaks at the junction with the cupola, and there were calls for the cupola to be removed.

Nevertheless a lantern was added on top in 1740–43, and the building withstood the Prussian artillery in 1760. There were further repairs in 1820, 1864–65 and 1924, and the problem was at last solved in 1942. Just three years later the church was totally destroyed by the Allied air raids, when the heat of the firestorm led to the sandstone pillars cracking and then collapsing at about 10.00 on 15 February.

From 1958 there was widespread resistance to the city's plans to clear the rubble (especially any reusable masonry), and by 1962 there was a consensus that it should be left as a symbol of protest against war and destruction; from 1986 (when what is now the Hilton was under construction) there was pressure to allow clearing of the site, implying that rebuilding would never happen, but as soon as the changes of 1989 had happened the 'Appeal from Dresden' launched a rebuilding project. Reconstruction cost €131 million, including €6 million from the sale of Frauenkirche watches and €22.5 million from special DM10 coins. The crypt was reconsecrated in 1996, in 2004 a cross (by the son of one of the British bomber pilots and presented by the Duke of Kent) was placed on top of the so-called Stone Bell, and in 2005 the new organ (by Kern of Strasbourg) was consecrated. You'll pass the old Turmkreuz (Tower Cross) as you head for the exit.

Frauenkirche

The dome has again taken up its rightful place dominating the Neumarkt and the skyline of the Altstadt, but it does have a very odd patchwork exterior, with old blackened stones and new ones mixed up together. The interior is incredibly dramatic, and indeed shaped like a theatre, with one glassed-in gallery, two main ones above that and little ones higher up, and a huge and highly ornate altar/organ complex. There's a lot of gold and marbling, but also more subdued reds, greens, blues and yellows. In the crypt, the bare stone walls contrast with modern lighting, stairs and sculptures, especially in the side chapels (the Room of Destruction, Room of Hope, Room of Decision, etc).

There can be a substantial queue to enter the church, but there's plenty of room inside once you move away from the entry area. The main entry is by door E (exiting by door B on the south side), or for wheelchairs door A; for services you should enter the nave by door D or the galleries by doors C and E. The church is open (donations welcome) from 10.00 to 17.00 Monday to Saturday (Jan–Mar) or 18.00 (Apr–Dec), with variations at weekends; on Sunday services are at 11.00 and 18.00; there are organ prayers followed by a tour at noon Monday to Saturday and at 18.00 Monday to Friday, though on Thursday there is no tour, and on Friday there is also an ecumenical prayer in the crypt. There's an organ recital at 20.00 every third Wednesday, and concerts generally at 20.00 on Saturdays. Entry is free (if they charged €1 they'd be halfway to paying for the rebuilding already); photography isn't allowed inside but everyone is snapping away all the time. Audio-guides are available (in English, German, French, Italian and Japanese) for €2.50.

To visit the dome, head for door G (*to the northeast;* ⊕*Apr–Sep 10.00–13.00 & 14.00–18.00; Oct–Mar 14.00–16.00, all daily; adult €8, children/students €5, family €20, children under 6 are not admitted*). Visits outside regular hours can be arranged (✆ *498 1131;* e *fuehrungen@frauenkirche-dresden.org*).

Music has always been important here, with a Silbermann organ fitted in 1736 and concerts from the 1780s, although there was no permanent choir until 1897. In 1843 Wagner gave the premiere of his *Love Feast of the Apostles* here, with 1,200 singers and an orchestra of 100, and the church was the centre of the centenary celebrations for J S Bach in 1850 and Wagner in 1913. You'll find the concert programme at www.frauenkirche-dresden.org, featuring oratorios by Bach, Handel and Mendelssohn, and more modern works. Tickets can be booked at the Frauenkirche Information Centre (and souvenir shop) at Georg-Treu-Platz 3 (✆ 656 0680; e ticket@frauenkirche-dresden.de; ◷ 10.00–18.00 daily; Jan–Mar to 17.00) and in the Kulturpalast; there's also an Abendkasse (evening ticket office) at doors B and F an hour before concerts.

GALERIE NEUE MEISTER (NEW MASTERS PICTURE GALLERY) [maps 2 & 3]
Established in 1924, the collection of 19th- and 20th-century art was exhibited after World War II at Pillnitz and from 1965 in the Albertinum; this is now being refurbished (due to reopen in 2008) and the collection is being displayed in temporary shows in Dresden and elsewhere.

Artists represented include Manet, Monet, Degas, Van Gogh, Gauguin, Rodin, Paul Klee, and the Germans (many of whom lived and worked in the Dresden area) Caspar David Friedrich, Ludwig Richter, Ferdinand von Rayski, Gotthardt Kuehl, Lovis Corinth, Max Slevogt, Otto Dix, Wilhelm Trübner, Max Pietschmann and Robert Sterl (including a 1911 study of Karl August Lingner, founder of the German Hygiene Museum). There's also work by Dresden's own Die Brücke group, mainly Erich Heckel, Ernst Ludwig Kirchner and Karl Schmidt-Rottluff.

It's estimated that about 100,000 works in German museums were looted by the Nazis, almost all from Jews, and only a handful have so far been restituted. Because art prices are now so high, lawyers are scouring the archives to find cases and many top-quality Modern Movement pieces (worth millions of dollars each) are likely to be lost from public galleries such as this.

GEMÄLDEGALERIE DER ALTE MEISTER (OLD MASTERS PICTURE GALLERY) *Semperbau of the Zwinger;* ⊕ *10.00–18.00 Tue–Sun; adult €6, children €3.50, family €13* [maps 2 & 3]

The Electors' art collection (opened to the public in 1722, and from 1747 housed in the Johanneum) was moved in 1854 to the new neo-Renaissance gallery built by Gottfried Semper. The works were moved to safe storage in 1939 and then to Moscow and Kiev; in 1955 they were put on show in Moscow and handed over to a delegation from the DDR (to their great surprise), providing the impetus to rebuild the Zwinger. It reopened in 1956 and was thoroughly modernised in 1988–92.

The gallery isn't that huge (taking 60–90mins to visit) but it's stuffed with great works, notably from the Italian Renaissance. In the basement are the cashdesk, cloakroom and lockers, and the bookshop, where you can pay €28 for an exhaustive catalogue of the collection, or €15 for a good 168-page book in English; an audio-guide is also available in English or German.

You'll start in the Gobelinsaal, with two 16th-century tapestries from Brussels, and five from Raphael cartoons; there may be a temporary exhibition to the right, after which you should return to the main stairs (by the entry to the Gobelinsaal) and go up to the first floor, with two paintings by Jacopo Bassano among others on the stairs.

In Room 101 are two of Dresden's iconic Bellottos (see box, page 26), of the Frauenkirche and Kreuzkirche, and large portraits by Louis Silvestre of Elector Friedrich August (later August III of Poland) and his wife Maria Josepha and of August the Strong with Friedrich Wilhelm I of Prussia, and by Jean Marc Nattier of Graf Moritz von Sachsen (Marshal of France). In Room 102 (a side corridor) are five more big Bellottos of Dresden. In Room 104 are 17th-century Flemish works by Frans Snyders, Jacob Jordaens and Rubens, with more of the same in Room 105, including Rubens's visionary *Hero and Leander* and *Leda and the Swan*; there are also lots of Van Dycks, including St Jerome and portraits including Charles I and II of England. Room 106 houses 17th-century Dutch painters such as Aert de Gelder, Philips Koninck, and no fewer than ten Rembrandts (including a self-portrait as the prodigal son in a tavern with his wife Saskia). It's easy to miss Room 108, to the right from 106, with its German and Dutch Gothic art by Jan Gossaert, Jan Massys, Joos van Cleve, Jan Van Eyck, 11 by Cranach the Elder, four by Cranach the Younger, three by Dürer (including the *Dresden Altar*, c1496), and lovely pieces by Hans Maler and Hans Baldung Grien. In Room 107 there's more 17th-century Dutch art including Vermeer's *Matchmaker* and *Girl Reading a Letter at a Window*, plus small genre pieces by Metsu, Hobbema, Ruisdael et al.

In Rooms 109–110 (heading back along the other side of the building) there's even more 17th-century Dutch art, including Ferdinand Bol, Govaert Flinck, Frans Hals, ice scenes by Hendrik Avercamp, and two tiny works by Brueghel the Elder. In Room 111 there's 16th- and 17th-century Flemish art, including more work by Brueghel the Elder.

Room 112 houses 17th-century French art, including François Millet, Lorrain, Simon Vouet and lots by Poussin. There's 16th- and 17th-century Italian art in Room 113, including Bernardo Strozzi, Guercino, Agostino and Annibale Carracci, and in Room 114 lots by the little-known Roman Domenico Fetti, as well as Domenichino, Guido Reni and Carlo Dolci. Room 115 has rather better Italian work of the same period, notably two paintings by Sandro Botticelli (including a lovely *Virgin and Child with the infant John the Baptist*) and two by Lorenzo di Credi. Room 116 has earlier Italian art, including 14th–15th-century Siennese works under a cloth in a cabinet, Garofalo, and Battista Dossi both alone and with his brother Dosso Dossi.

From here return to Room 117 (in the centre), where there are big 16th-century paintings by Garofalo, Lorenzo di Credi, Andrea del Sarto, an excellent Correggio, a good tondo by Piero di Cosimo, and most famously Raphael's *Sistine Madonna*, which was commissioned by Pope Julius II in 1512 for the monastery of St Sixtus in Piacenza – *not* the Sistine Chapel – and bought by Friedrich August II. St Sixtus is on the left, St Barbara on the right; the Virgin seems to be floating down on a cloud between two gathered curtains, with her veil carried by the wind. The two bored angels at the bottom have been used as a separate image since 1804, and the pose was used for a portrait photo of Queen Victoria's son Prince Arthur in 1857; in 1955 it was used on a DDR stamp to commemorate the painting's return from the Soviet Union, and by 1997 it had appeared on 38 stamps in 29 countries. The dramatist Heinrich von Kleist loved the *Sistine Madonna*, seeing her as the apotheosis of human love, transcending itself and becoming divine.

Room 118 has lots more Italian art, including several Correggios and Palma il Vecchios, two each by Titian and Parmigianino, Giorgone's *Sleeping Venus*, finished by Titian after Giorgone's death in 1510, and single works by Leandro Bassano, Bernardino Licinio, Bartolomeo Veneto and others. Room 119 has no fewer than ten paintings by Veronese and five by Tintoretto, plus works by Annibale Carracci and Jacopo Bassano.

Take the steps up to the central Room 120, with yet more 16th- and 17th-century Italian art, by Anibale Carracci, Guercino and Guido Reni, and go on up to Room 209 for Spanish art of the same period, including El Greco, Luis de Morales, three by Velasquez and four by Murillo (including a lovely *Virgin and Child*). Beyond this, although they may be used for temporary exhibitions, there's usually several rooms of 17th- and 18th-century German, Swiss and English art, notably the wonderful Dresden collection of Cranachs, with 20 by Lucas Cranach the Elder and 14 by his studio, 18 by Lucas Cranach the Younger and one by his studio, plus one which could be by either of them. The elder Cranach was appointed court painter to Friedrich the Wise in Wittenberg in 1504, and remained there until 1550 when he followed Johann Friedrich, the last Ernestine Elector, into exile, dying two years later. The younger Cranach remained in Wittenberg until his death in 1586 and continued his father's successful painting business, becoming very wealthy and rising to be the city's Burgermeister; his style was very similar to his father's, and they're easily confused. Their portraits immortalised many of the Wettin Electors and their wives, as well as Martin Luther and his circle, and the elder Cranach also produced many fine nudes. You should also see works by Hans Holbein and Angelika Kauffmann, among others.

Returning through Room 208, with its Spanish art, you'll come to Rooms 207–203, full of 18th-century Italian art, of which the most notable examples are by Giuseppe Maria Crespi, Pompeo Batoni and Tiepolo, plus five good Canalettos in Room 204 with one Guardi, and a Bellotto of Verona in Room 203. In Room 202 there's soft-focus 18th-century French art by Louis de Silvestre, Nicolas Lancret and

Watteau, and in the dead-end Room 201 pastels by Maurice Quentin de la Tour, Jean Etienne Liotard and Rosalba Carriera.

HISTORISCHES AND NEUES GRÜNES GEWÖLBE (HISTORIC AND NEW GREEN VAULT)
Residenzschloss, Sophienstr; ✆ *4914 2000;* e *besucherservice@skd.smwk.sachsen.de; www.skd-dresden.de* [map 2]

In 1723–30 August the Strong, who had spent huge amounts of money building up fantastic collections of jewels, ornaments and other fine examples of the decorative arts, created a Kunstkammer or treasure chamber to beat all other Kunstkammers. He also created separate collections of paintings, porcelain, scientific instruments and so on, making him one of the first modern museologists. The Kunstkammer was to be an expression of his wealth and power, a Baroque synthesis of the arts. The contents of the Grünes Gewölbe were put into safe storage during World War II but were then seized by the Red Army and taken to Russia until 1958, after which a limited sample of the collection was displayed in the Albertinum. When the Residenzschloss was rebuilt, the Neues Grünes Gewölbe was created, using the best modern display technology; in September 2006 the original rooms on the ground floor of the castle's west wing were finally reopened. It cost a total of €41.6 million to create the two exhibition areas and display the collections.

The two displays have been kept separate, with the Neues Grünes Gewölbe upstairs functioning as a normal branch of the State Art Collections and the Historisches Grünes Gewölbe downstairs as a special spectacle, with a very limited number of more expensive tickets. Although the publicity and press coverage stress the stunning impact of the Historisches Grünes Gewölbe the Neues Grünes Gewölbe places more emphasis on the individual works, and it's easier to see the wealth of detail in each piece, thanks to the modern exhibition technology employed there.

The SKD (State Art Collections) Visitor Centre is on the corner of Schloss Strasse and Taschenberg (*diagonally opposite the Kulturpalast*; ⊕ *11.00–18.00 Mon–Fri, 10.00–18.00 Sat/Sun & holidays*). At the Sophienstrasse entrance to the Residenzschloss (at the west end of Taschenberg) there's often a long *Schlange* (queue), reaching back to the street by 10.00 (except on Tue). There are some staff outside but it's not that well organised. The line on the left is for the **Historisches Grünes Gewölbe** (Historic Green Vault), with people let through according to their timed tickets (⊕ *10.00–19.00 Wed–Mon*), which cost € 10 including an audio-guide (there are no reductions for the Dresden-Card and the like). As only 100 people per hour are allowed in, and only 200 tickets are available on the day, they're best bought in advance from Dresden-Werbung und Tourismus GmbH (*Ostra-Allee 11, Dresden-01067;* ℡ *0351 4919 2120;* f *4919 2146;* e *info@dresden-tourist.de; www.dresden-tourist.de*) or online at www.dresden.de/treasury (/schatzkammer in German), where you can buy up to ten tickets for each time slot (with a € 1.50 booking fee), and print them at home.

Perfectly reproducing the Historisches Grünes Gewölbe's original wall coverings cost € 12.3m alone, including 90 different shades of paint for the artificial marbling alone, and authentic metallic paints for the backing of the large crystal mirrors. Nearly 3,000 individual pieces are displayed in ten rooms, including fantastically set diamonds, sapphires, emeralds and rubies, figures of Moors sculpted by Balthasar Permoser and decorated by court jeweller Johann Melchior Dinglinger, *Autumn* from Arcimboldo's Four Seasons, and the jewel-studded obelisk known as the Obeliscus Augustalis. Turning left on the ground floor, you'll pass through a sort of airlock to remove dust and dirt from your shoes and clothes. Then you'll pass through the Amber Cabinet, Ivory Room, White Silver Room and Silver Gilt Room to the Hall of Precious Objects, where the individual items, including jewels, rock crystals, sea shells and ostrich eggs, all in rich and intricate settings, are overwhelmed by their sheer abundance, accentuated by mirrors. You can look through a wrought-iron gate to the Corner Cabinet, displaying more intimate smaller pieces, before continuing to the more restrained Heraldry Room and then the climax of the visit, the Jewel Room, with painted and gilt mirror walls and the jewelled garnitures of August the Strong and his son. The Bronze Room contains small bronze figures, mostly French, and finally the Room of Renaissance Bronzes contains wonderful larger sculptures by Adriaen de Vries and Giambologna (sent as a gift by Francesco I de' Medici in the 1570s, when there were strong links between Florence and Dresden).

The shorter queue to the right is for those without tickets for the Historisches Grünes Gewölbe, leading to the ticket desks, the cloakroom (generally overrun and without lockers) and the good bookshop. Stairs and a modern lift take you up to the **Neues Grünes Gewölbe** (New Green Vault; ⊕ *10.00–18.00 Wed–Mon; adult €6, children €3.50, €2 extra for an audio-guide*) on the first floor. Captions are well translated into English, and it takes about 90 minutes to go round. There are over a thousand items here, all intricately decorated and highly ornate.

The first room is the Saal der Kunststücke (Room of Artworks), where there's a lot of carved and lathe-turned ivory (a particular obsession of Christian I), as well as carved cherry stones, clocks, and superb carved glass and crystal panels from Saracchi of Milan as well as Prague and Dresden, and lovely reticulated glass from Venice. The highlight of this room is a carving of Daphne (made in Nürnberg in 1579–86) with red coral hair to show her turning into a tree as recounted in Ovid's *Metamorphoses*.

Next is the First Room of the Electors (as opposed to the Dukes who came before them), full of 17th-century silver including globes and automata, and Neptune supporting an ivory man-of-war, made by Jacob Zeller in Dresden in 1620. There's also Gujarati mother-of-pearl, and fine pieces by the brothers Hans (or Johann) and Daniel Kellerthaler, the first great Dresden goldsmiths.

The Second Room features ivory carvings by Melchior Barthel, court sculptor to 1672, and wood carvings by Johann Jacob Kretzschmer, who was court sculptor by 1728. There are also many pieces from Augsburg, and two English Garter medals.

The Raum der Königlichen Pretiosen (Room of Royal Valuables) contains gold and ivory perfume caskets made in the early 18th century, and lots of statuettes. The Dinglinger Saal (at the end, facing the Semperoper) shows work by court enameller Georg Friedrich Dinglinger (1666–1720), and his brother, court jeweller Johann Melchior (1664–1731) – highlights, modelled by Johann Melchior and enamelled by Georg Friedrich, are the Golden Coffee Service (1697–1701), and a fantastic huge model of the Court of Delhi on the Birthday of the Grand Moghul Aurangzeb (1701–08), with 132 gold-plated figurines decorated with no fewer than 4,909 diamonds, 160 rubies and 164 emeralds. There are also ivory and wood carvings by Balthasar Permoser (1651–1732), who spent years in Florence before becoming the Dresden court sculptor; he was clearly obsessed with Moors, oriental exoticism and the flagellated Christ. Benjamin Thomae (1682–1751), a pupil of Permoser, worked with Johann Melchior Dinglinger; there are additional pieces by the youngest Dinglinger brother, Georg Christoph (1668–1728), also a jeweller.

Returning by the Raum der Reisenden Pretiosen (Room of Travelling Valuables), there's a model for the *Golden Rider* statue (see page 162) and 400 leather cases for carrying valuables on journeys. There's also glassware – a glass factory was established in Dresden in 1700, and in 1713 Johann Friedrich Böttger, inventor of European porcelain, set up a mill for cutting and polishing glass and precious stones.

In the Neuber-Raum there's a fireplace made by Johann Christian Neuber, court jeweller from 1775, for the Grand Duke of Russia in 1782; there are also Russian medals and more ivory. The Spansel-Raum commemorates Jean Louis Spansel (1858–1930), who directed the Green Vault, History Museum and the Coin Cabinet from 1908 to 1923.

Above the Green Vaults, the **Kupferstich Kabinett** (Engravings Collection) houses over half a million pieces of graphic art created over a span of six centuries, from woodcuts and drawings to engravings, modern prints and photographs.

There's no permanent exhibition, but there's a regular succession of temporary shows (🕘10.00–18.00 Wed–Mon; €3, children €2). Art lovers and researchers can visit the Studiensaal or study room (✆ 4914 2000; 🕘10.00–13.00 & 14.00–16.00, Mon/Wed/Thu; 10.00–13.00 Fri; by reservation the first Sat of the month). In summer the Hausmannsturm (on the north side of the Residenzschloss, opposite the cathedral) is open as a viewpoint over the city, together with the Münz-Kabinett or Coin Collection, just a small selection from around 300,000 coins and medals (🕘10.00–18.00 Wed–Mon; adult €3, children €2).

HOFKIRCHE *Theaterplatz; 🕘09.00–17.00 Mon–Thu, 13.00–17.00 Fri, 10.30–17.00 Sat, 12.00–16.00 Sun; services 08.30 & 18.00 Mon–Fri, 18.00 Sat, 07.30, 09.00, 10.30, 16.30 (Polish) & 18.00 Sun* [map 2 & 3]
The cathedral of the Trinity was built in 1738–55 in late Roman-Baroque style. It was commissioned by Friedrich August II, who had converted to Catholicism in order to be elected King of Poland, from the Italian architect Gaetano Chiaveri, who resigned in 1748 and was replaced by Sebastian Wetzel, Johann Christoph Knöffel and Julius Schwarze. Destroyed in 1945, the left aisle was rebuilt as early as 1947, followed by the nave and right aisle in 1962 and the tower in 1991–97. In 1980 it became a cathedral and in 2002 the last of the 78 figures of saints on the exterior balustrade was replaced.

Hofkirche

It's a large basilica with double aisles on either side and a restrained interior of monochrome cream, except for the pale red and green marble on the altars. The altarpiece, painted in 1751 by Anton Raphael Mengs, is a large but not very striking Ascension, while the pulpit and statues of Church Fathers under the organ gallery are by Permoser; the modern glass altar and lectern were added in 1994–95. To the right of the door is the St Benno Chapel, dedicated to the 11th-century Bishop of Meissen whose mitre is here. In the crypt are the bodies of 49 Wettiner kings and princes plus the heart of August the Strong (the rest of whose body is with the other kings of Poland in Kraków).

The splendid organ is the last and largest built by Gottfried Silbermann with around 3,000 pipes; built in 1755, it was dismantled in 1944 and reinstalled in 1971. A wonderful instrument, it's used for recitals between 11.30 and noon on Wednesdays and Saturdays, as well as every third Wednesday at 20.00.

PORZELLANSAMMLUNG (PORCELAIN COLLECTION) *Zwinger;* ℡ *4914 2000;*
e *besucherservice@skd.smwk.sachsen.de; www.skd-dresden.de;* ⏰ *10.00–18.00 Tue–Sun; adult €5, children €3, family €11* [map 2 & 3]
Chinese porcelain first came into the Electoral collections in the 1590s, with gifts of Ming pieces from Ferdinando I de' Medici. However it was August the Strong who obsessively created what is now probably the world's third-biggest collection, after the Imperial Palace in Beijing and the Topkapı in Istanbul, buying over 20,000 pieces, as well as the Japanese Palace (see page 163) to display them in. The collection was opened to the public in 1717, and since 1962 has been in the southwest pavilion of

the Zwinger. The entrance is actually above the Glockenspiel Gate (with its 40 porcelain bells), on the east side of the Zwinger; go up the steps to either side, buy your ticket, then visit in turn the galleries on either side. There are English and German texts in the galleries.

Between 1602 and 1657 the VOC or Dutch United East India Company brought over two million pieces of blue-and-white Chinese Kraak porcelain to Europe; China then fell into chaos and the VOC looked to Japan instead, finding that the dense multi-coloured designs of Imari porcelain fitted the Baroque sensibility perfectly. There are excellent collections of both here, as well as cheaper Chinese imitations of Imari, and *famille verte*, of which August the Strong was very fond. There are also the famous 'Dragoon vases', 151 of which were sent by Friedrich Wilhelm I of Prussia in exchange for 600 dragoons from August the Strong (history does not record how many survived to see their families again).

In the ground floor of the corner pavilion are porcelain animal sculptures, made in Meissen from 1731, modelled by Gottlieb Kirchner to 1733, and then by Johann Joachim Kändler. In the southern galleries there's more 18th-century Meissen, including the first uniform dinner services, including the Red Dragon, the Yellow Lion, the Swan Service (designed by Kändler for Count Brühl) and others bearing the arms of Saxony and Poland. Johann Gregorius Höroldt, who worked at Meissen as a freelance painter from 1720 to 1765, created the European genre of porcelain painting, first in a chinoiserie style and then from 1730 in a more European style (featuring flowers, landscapes and hunting scenes). There are also moulded figurines by George Fritzsche, from 1723, followed by Kirchner and then Kändler, whose figures caught in movement were in tune with the Baroque spirit. August III's religiosity and his love of music and theatre provided inspiration for many figurines, as did the cult for exotic orientalism. Upstairs (in a pavilion on the terrace) is a historical display of early Meissen, including so-called Böttger stoneware and Böttger porcelain (see page 248).

August the Strong's porcelain collection continues on the south side of the Glockenspiel Gate (including Chinese goldfish bowls used for orange trees, with holes drilled in their bases in Dresden); at the far end is a very effective new display by New York architect Peter Marino, inspired by Zacharias Longuelune's design of 1735 for the Japanese Palace, showing blue-and-white Chinese porcelain symmetrically laid out on gilded consoles, mantelpieces and tables in front of silk-covered walls.

STADTMUSEUM UND STÄDTISCHE GALERIE DRESDEN (DRESDEN CITY MUSEUM AND CITY GALLERY) *Wilsdruffer Str 2;* ☎ *495 1288, 6564 8613;* e *presse@stmd.de; www.museen-dresden.de, http://stadtmuseum.dresden.de;* ⏱ *10.00–18.00 Tue–Thu & Sat/Sun, 12.00–20.00 Fri; adult €3, children €2, free on Fri after 14.00* [map 2 & 3]
The city museum is housed in the Landhaus, a stately Baroque mansion built in 1770–75 for the provincial legislature. The entry is now on the north side, although the very grand stairs are aligned with the south doors; however, you can go in and admire this without needing a ticket. One flight up is the City Gallery (☎ *6564 8611; www.galerie-dresden.de*), covered by the same tickets and opening hours as the museum, and with a guided tour on Fridays at 16.00. The city's collection of painting

and sculpture, amassed since 1869, includes just one work by every painter with any connection to Dresden, of which the Impressionists and post-Impressionists are possibly the best. The most notable are Gotthardt Kuehl (1850–1915), whose Impressionist view of the Augustusbrücke in winter is positively chilly; and Bernhard Kretzschmar (1889–1972), as well as Conrad Felixmüller and Otto Dix (see page 25). You can watch a choice of 16 videos including one on Dix in Dresden. On the other side of the main staircase are temporary art shows.

New displays on the history of the city are very well laid out, with summaries of information in English. The arrangement is a little odd, as you should start with Der Aufstieg Dresdens (The Rise of Dresden) on the third floor, then take internal stairs down to Die Stadt der Bürger (The City of Citizens), on the city's industrial development and the accompanying Lebensreform and Hygiene movements. Also on the second floor is the Democracy and Dictatorship display on 20th-century Dresden, while back on the third floor is Der Depot der Gegenwart (Depository of the Present), an offbeat look at various uncompleted projects. Also on the second floor is a superb exhibition, closing at the end of 2010, on the rebuilding of the Frauenkirche, with a very detailed booklet in English.

🏺 MUSEUMS AND GALLERIES

CARL-MARIA-VON-WEBER-MUSEUM *Dresdner Str 44, Hosterwitz; ☎ 261 8234; www.stmd.de; ⏰ 13.00–18.00 Wed–Sun; adult €2, children €1, free on Fri after 14.00*

In the summerhouse near Pillnitz (see page 185) where Weber spent the summers of 1818–19 and 1822–24 here with his wife, writing the operas *Der Freischütz*, *Euryanthe* and *Oberon*, as well as *The Invitation to the Dance*. In the living rooms and his workroom are notes and manuscripts as well as pictures and documents illustrating Weber's life, and recordings of his music are played.

DEUTSCHES HYGIENE-MUSEUM (GERMAN HYGIENE MUSEUM) *Lingnerplatz 1; ↩ 484 6670; e service@dhmd.de; www.dhmd.de; ⏱10.00–18.00 Tue–Sun; adult €6 for 2 days, Dresden-Card €4.50, children over 4, groups, students €3, family (2 adults & 4 children) €11* [map 2 & 3]

In 1893 Karl August Lingner invented Odol mouthwash, and, surfing the wave of a hygiene movement that encompassed the new science of bacteriology, body-building, nude bathing and Chlorodont toothpaste (invented in 1907, also in Dresden), became very rich. In 1911 he founded the German Hygiene Museum to spread the gospel of cleanliness and sanitation, and in 1927–30 Wilhelm Kreis (an architect later favoured by Hitler) built this fine Functionalist building. In 1911 the First International Hygiene Exhibition had been held in Dresden, and the second was also held here in 1930, with three million visitors. The museum unconditionally served the Nazi agenda of racial hygiene or eugenics, which encouraged the sterilisation or killing of 'inferior' races, and it did the same for the communist regime, pumping out teaching materials for the workers. The shell of the building, 80% destroyed in 1945, was rebuilt in 1946 (with halls for films, theatre and music), and was reconstructed to something closer to the original plans in 2001–05; alas,

Otto Dix's mural, destroyed by the Nazis in 1933, is missing, but the bronze figure of *Hygeia* (by Karl Albiker, 1931) has been restored to the courtyard.

As you might hope, access for the disabled is good. Tours of the permanent exhibition are given in German at 14.00 on weekends and holidays, and tours in English or French can be booked; there aren't many English captions, but audio tours are available in five languages.

Downstairs on the left side of the building is a Children's Museum, for four to 12 year olds, exploring the world of the senses in a fun way. To the right are the themed rooms of the permanent collection, starting with the famous Gläserne Mensch (Transparent Man), together with images of the human being in modern science. The first *Transparent Man* was made in 1925 in a shed at a jam factory and was a great success, becoming the symbol of the museum; since 1999 he has been a she, as the current model is female. It's followed by Leben und Sterben (From Conception to Death), with some huge and rather graphic models dating from 1900, illustrating foetal development and birth, as well as newer models of DNA/RNA, HIV and a huge fruitfly. There are also gadgets to allow visitors to experience what it's like for old folk to walk and hear. Essen und Trinken (Eating and Drinking) includes film taken inside the throat and stomach; and Sexualität (Love, Sex & Lifestyles in the Age of Reproductive Medical Science) covers the biological function of sexuality and hormones, and whether science is making sex superfluous. Then Erinnern, Denken, Lernen (Remembering, Thinking, Learning) asks how the brain works, what is consciousness, and whether computers will expand the brain's abilities; Bewegung (Motion) looks at co-ordination, with exercise equipment and videos of dance from across the world; and Hart und Haar (Beauty, Skin, Hair) looks at the boundaries between body and environment, and at our self-image, with lots of interactive terminals (in German or English). There's a good café-restaurant here (see page 109).

EISENBAHNMUSEUM (RAILWAY MUSEUM) *Zwickauer Str 86;* ☎ *461 3297, 0162 783 8603;* e *bwdresden@aol.com; www.igbwdresdenaltstadt.de;* ⊕ *May–Sep 10.00–14.00 first Sat of the month; adult €1.50, children €0.50* [map 1]
In a quarter-roundhouse, reached by steps from the southeast end of the Nossener Brücke (by bus 61's Zwickauer Str stop), is a small collection of steam and diesel locomotives tended by enthusiasts.

ERICH KÄSTNER MUSEUM *Villa Augustin am Albertplatz, Antonstr 1;* ☎ *804 5086; www.erick-kaestner-museum.de/english.htm;* ⊕ *10.00–18.00 Sun–Tue, 10.00–20.00 Wed, Thu for groups by reservation; adult €3, children €2, family €7* [map 2 & 3]
Erich Kästner (1899–1974) was born and brought up in the Aussere Neustadt close to this villa, then his uncle's home (300m from the Neustadt station), as described in his 1957 autobiography. He left the city to serve in the army and then to study in Leipzig, then lived in Berlin, where his satirical books were burnt by the Nazis. He's now mainly remembered for the children's novel *Emil and the Detectives* (1929); *Fabian* (1931) was his only major adult novel.
   Irish architect Ruairí O'Brien developed an interactive micromuseum that packs away into a wooden block 3m x 2m x 1.2m in size, or opens up into various modules

with lots of drawers, colour-coded by subject, that are quite fun to poke around in, although the cuttings and leaflets in them are all in German. Although portable, the micromuseum is now here permanently.

FESTUNG DRESDEN (DRESDEN FORTRESS) *Georg-Treu-Platz;* ↘ *491 4786;*
e *festung.dresden@schloesser-dresden.de; www.schloesser-dresden.de;* ⊕ *Apr–Oct 10.00–17.00, Nov–Mar 10.00–16.00, all daily; adult €3.10, children €2, family €8.20* [map 2 & 3]
Dresden's remaining fortifications, entered below the steps leading down to Georg-Treu-Platz, beside the Albertinum, are also where European porcelain was invented (see page 248). There's not a huge amount to see, but it's an atmospheric warren of chambers with the occasional view of the Elbe embankment.

Built in 1520–29 by Duke Georg the Bearded, they were extended in 1546–55 and in 1721. In 1748–49 Count Brühl laid out a garden on top of the riverside bastion and the cannon yards were filled in, and in 1809–29 the other fortifications were demolished. These northeastern casemates were used as a store for the White Fleet until 1990, when the remains of the city's oldest stone bridge were found amid the stonework above the moat. In 1991 two courtyards were opened up, and since 1993 the state has owned the Festung and opened it up for visits.

GALERIE NEUE MEISTER See page 196.

GEMÄLDEGALERIE DER ALTE MEISTER See page 197.

HISTORISCHES AND NEUES GRÜNES GEWÖLBE See page 201.

KRAFTWERK (POWER STATION) *Wettiner Platz 7;* \ *860 4180; www.drewag.de;* ⊕ *10.00–17.00 Wed; free* [map 2 & 3]
Drewag (Dresden Wasser und Gass, the city's main utility) opens up its former power station once a week, when quite a few engineering students come in to examine the kit (mainly electrical) displayed on the ground floor. Visits start upstairs with good audio-visual shows (in German) on the history of gas and water provision, starting with gas lights in Theaterplatz in 1828 (remembered as the first gas lighting in Germany without British help). There was a gasworks right next to the Zwinger until 1843.

KRASZEWSKI MUSEUM *Nordstr 28, Neustadt;* \ *804 4450;* e *presse@stmd.de; www.museen-dresden.de;* ⊕ *10.00–18.00 Wed–Sun; adult €2, children €1* [map 4]
Jósef Ignacy Kraszewski (1812–87) was one of the leading Polish writers of the 19th century and a political activist who was expelled from his country by its Russian rulers. He lived in Dresden from 1863–84 and became the hub of Polish exile life; in 1884 he was jailed for three-and-a-half years for allegedly spying for the French. He went to Italy to recover his health and then died in Geneva.

There's a permanent exhibition on Saxon–Polish relations, plus temporary exhibitions on contemporary Poland; there's a café and a library with Polish newspapers and magazines.

KÜGELGENHAUS (MUSEUM DER DRESDNER ROMANTIK) (MUSEUM OF ROMANTICISM IN DRESDEN) *Hauptstr 13;* ☏ *804 4760;* e *presse@stmd.de; www.museen-dresden.de;* ⊕ *10.00–18.00 Wed–Sun & holidays; adult €2, children €1, free on Fri after 14.00* [map 4]

The Museum of Romanticism is on the second floor of this historic building (built in 1697–99), in the homely apartment of the painter Gerhard von Kügelgen (1772–1820), who moved here with his family in 1808 and entertained many of the great figures in the development of German Romanticism (see page 25). He taught painting at the Dresden Kunstakademie and was a friend and teacher of Caspar David Friedrich; he was killed by a robber while travelling from his studio in Loschwitz to Dresden. His son Wilhelm (1802–67) is remembered for his memoirs *Jugend-Erinnerungen eines Altes Mannes* (An Old Man's Memories of Youth).

There's also coverage of his friend Christian Körner, whose home (see page 163) was visited by the dramatists Johann Wolfgang von Goethe, Friedrich Schiller and Heinrich von Kleist, as well as Mozart, the scientist Wilhelm von Humboldt and the philosophers Friedrich von Schlegel and Johann Gottfried von Herder (who was the first to call Dresden 'Elbforenz' or the 'Florence of the Elbe').

The flat has painted ceilings and some period furniture, and paintings by Anton Graff (see page 25) and Dorothea Stock (Körner's sister-in-law), who painted many of their friends.

KUNSTGEWERBEMUSEUM (MUSEUM OF DECORATIVE ARTS) *Schloss Pillnitz;* ☏ *4914 2000;* e *besucherservice@skd.smwk.sachsen.de; www.skd-dresden.de;* ⊕ *May–Oct*

Bergpalais 10.00–18.00 Tue–Sun, Wasserpalais 10.00–18.00 Wed–Mon; adult €3, children €2, family €7

Pillnitz's Wasserpalais and Bergpalais (not to be confused with the Schlossmuseum) have been home since 1963 to a collection of furniture and furnishings, well worth a visit simply as a means to see the delightful chinoiserie décor of the palaces themselves. Here are August the Strong's throne, his unique silver furniture from Augsburg, furniture by the royal lacquerer Martin Schnell (in chinoiserie-style) and from the Deutsche Werkstätten Hellerau, as well as glassware, textiles (lace, embroideries, damask and tapestries), Italian majolica, Delftware, English stoneware, French bronzes and Japanese lacquerware. The collection also includes contemporary pieces by the American glass artist Dale Chihuli, Ron Arad and Japanese craftsmen.

The Weinlig-Zimmer (where Emperor Leopold II stayed during the 1791 Pillnitz Convention with Elector Friedrich August III, the King of Prussia and the brother of the King of France to discuss the French Revolution) is in its original state, with woodcarvings from 1790.

MATHEMATISCH-PHYSIKALISCHER SALON (MATHEMATICAL AND PHYSICAL SALON)
Zwinger; ☎ 4914 2000; www.skd-dresden.de; ⏱ 10.00–18.00 Tue–Sun; adult €3, children €2, family €5 [map 2 & 3]

Founded as part of the Elector's Kunstkammer or art collection around 1560, there were nearly 1,000 instruments by 1587, and the Mathematical-Physical Salon moved to the Zwinger's southwestern pavilion in 1746. The instruments were used for astronomical observations and from 1783 the city council's clockmaker took the time from here by pocket watch to set the city's clocks; from 1839 it was taken to the railway station by portable clock, then from 1889 by telegraph. Now observations here are used only to set the clock on the Zwinger's Kronentur.

Captions are almost all in German, but audio-guides, in all major languages, are available for €1.50; there's a tour on Saturdays at 15.00.

Highlights of the first room include globes from 1515, an astrological compass made in Dresden in 1561, a globe of the heavens made in 1643 by Willem Jansz Blaeu in Amsterdam, a model of the solar system made around 1800 in London (a gift of Wilhelm Herschel) and theodolites from 1820 on. In the second ground-floor room there are huge 17th-century nautical telescopes and 18th-century reflecting telescopes on mounts, including one made by Herschel in 1781 (similar to that he used to discover Uranus) and a couple more made in London, huge burning mirrors, a vacuum pump made in Leipzig in 1709, adding machines from around 1781 to 1915, the oldest surviving metal thermometer (c1747, with four lead bars registering degrees Delisle, which worked backwards with water boiling at 0°C and freezing at 150°!) and mercury thermometer (1760), and weights and measures.

You have to go outside and up to the terrace for the clocks pavilion (with captions in German and English), where the centrepiece is an astronomical clock made in 1563–68 in central Germany). There are also automata from the 1580s, a merry-go-round automaton clock made in Augsburg around 1590, horizontal table clocks from c1600, 16th- and 17th-century astrolabes, an alarm clock (with a drumming bear to wake you) from c1625, three pendant (fob) watches from the 1630s, rolling-ball clocks (which were expected to be the basis of the most accurate clocks), an early pendulum clock made in 1674 in The Hague, pocket watches (some with fine enamels) from 1670 and the late 18th century, and a wide range of other timepieces. None, alas, is working, but they are things of great beauty as well as good examples of technical ingenuity.

MILITÄRHISTORISCHES MUSEUM DER BUNDESWEHR (MILITARY HISTORY MUSEUM OF THE FEDERAL ARMY) *Friedrich-Olbricht-Platz 2;* ✆ *823 2803;* e *milhistmuseumbweingang@bundeswehr.org; www.mhm-dresden.de;* ⏱*09.00–17.00 Tue–Sun; free* [map 1]

The former arsenal, a hugely imposing building built in 1873–76 on the ridge above the Neustadt (at the southern edge of a huge military area), has housed a military museum since 1897, but is closed until early 2009 for modernisation, with Daniel Libeskind and Hans-Günter Merz adding a glass wedge breaking out of the building's Classicist façade, a €35 million project that has generated some controversy as it is a protected monument. The new glass façade naturally stands for transparency, against the weight and impenetrability of the old regime. In the meantime there's a sizeable temporary display in a former factory at the rear (around the right/east side of the main building). From the Stauffenbergallee stop (trams 7 and 8), follow the oak-lined alleys west through the park, past the Red Army war memorial, and turn left on Hans-Oster-Strasse (named after a Dresden-born artillery general tortured and executed in 1945 as an opponent of the Nazi regime); the museum is ahead on the square named after Friedrich Olbricht, another general also executed in 1945.

Captions are in German only but an English leaflet is available. The first part of the temporary show displays medals, uniforms and a bit of armour, and the *Brandtaucher* (Fire-diver), the first German submarine (built in 1850–51) and the world's oldest surviving sub, which sank in Kiel harbour in 1851. There's also a display on the fighter ace Max Immelmann, born in Dresden in 1890, who developed the famous Immelmann Turn, a climbing stall turn that allows a plane to quickly make a second attack on another plane. After shooting down 17 planes, he was himself shot down and killed in June 1916.

The section on German Military History 1945–70 displays all kinds of hardware, including an early Enigma code machine and a superb model of the *Bismarck* (about 5m long), an 80cm-diameter shell for a 1930s' rail-mounted cannon, a V1 flying bomb, Patton, T54 and Leopard tanks, Yak 18, MiG-21, Frog 7 and Starfighter planes, an Alouette helicopter, a 40mm Breda-Bofors anti-aircraft gun and an Honest John tactical nuclear missile, as well as miscellanea from both the DDR and NATO. Outside there are more planes and helicopters, and if you go around to the western end of the complex you'll see naval gun turrets and a torpedo-boat, plus a V2 rocket. Although obviously a temporary show, there's plenty of space and lots of kit to keep boys of all ages happy; the permanent show will have to cover peacekeeping and Germany's role with NATO in Kosovo, Afghanistan and elsewhere. Apparently the theme will be that war stands for violence, death, hatred, fear and human behaviour in extreme situations, so it could be very different from other military museums. The museum also has displays in the fortress of Königstein (see page 271).

MUSEUM FÜR MINERALOGIE UND GEOLOGIE (MUSEUM OF MINERALOGY AND GEOLOGY) *Zwinger;* ☏ *892 6403; www.snsd.de;* ⏲ *10.00–18.00 Tue–Sun; adult* €3, *children* €1.50 [map 2 & 3]

The mineralogical and geological collection, started in 1650, now numbers around 300,000 objects, a fraction of which are displayed here, in the Long Gallery, on the left as you enter the Zwinger under the Kronentor.

MUSEUM FÜR SACHSISCHE VOLKSKUNST MIT PUPPENTHEATERSAMMLUNG (MUSEUM OF SAXON FOLKLORE WITH PUPPET THEATRE COLLECTION) *Jägerhof, Köpckestr 1;* ☏ *4914 2000; www.skd-dresden.de;* ⏲ *10.00–18.00 Tue–Sun; adult* €3, *children* €2, *family* €7 [map 4]

The Folklore Museum – where information is in German only – was founded in 1897 and moved in 1913 to the Jägerhof, Dresden's oldest surviving Renaissance building, a wing of what used to be the Princely Hunters' Court. In the low-vaulted ground-floor corridor of this long, thin building with three stair-towers are displays of stoves, looms (with examples of *Blaudruck* printing on cloth) and furniture, as well as earthenware and stoneware (including big Biersteins of course), glassware, both Passion and Nativity cribs, and both butter and Lebkuchen (chocolate-coated ginger biscuits) moulds. Upstairs is a wonderful display of toys, including trains, mini merry-go-rounds, a working model of a coal mine, lovely wooden chandeliers, Noah's Arks, a parade of carved miners in ceremonial gear (used as candleholders) and miners' ceremonial axes and Sorb costumes with splendid trimmings. There are Erzegbirge Christmas pyramids up to 1.5m high (see page 147), all with vanes on top turned by an oil lamp. There are boxes of toys for kids to rummage in, and benches with multi-media terminals showing historic photos and films with background texts.

On the floor above is a collection of puppets in a variety of costumes and settings, mostly from traditional stories presented at the Puppen Theatre (see page 136). Incidentally, a new Doll Museum is due to open in 2007 at Königsbrücker Strasse 53, with around 500 dolls and 30 doll's houses from 1850–1950.

MUSEUM FÜR TIERKUNDE (NATURAL HISTORY MUSEUM) *Palaisplatz 11;* ⟍ *892 6326; www.snsd.de;* ⊕ *10.00–18.00 Tue–Sun; adult €3, children €1.50, family €7* [map 4]
On the first floor of the Japanese Palace, this mainly puts on temporary shows, although major items such as the mammoth are probably there most of the time. There is text in English. The collection was founded in 1560 and set up as a separate museum in 1728 by August the Strong; it now holds around 6.5 million pieces.

MUSEUM FÜR VÖLKERKUNDE (MUSEUM OF ETHNOGRAPHY) *Palaisplatz 11;* ⟍ *892 6202, 814 4841;* e *info@mvd.smwk.sachsen.de; www.voelkerkunde-dresden.de;* ⊕ *10.00–18.00 Tue–Sun; adult €4, children, & all on first Tue of the month, €2* [map 4]
On the first floor of the Japanese Palace, this is the third-oldest ethnographic museum in Germany, having been set up as a separate department of the natural history collection in 1875 and as a museum in 1878. Of the 35,000 objects, around a third came as gifts to the Electors. By the late 16th century the Electors were collecting ivory spoons from west Africa and Javanese daggers, as well as African lances and ivory knives, for instance, in the 18th century. One of the most

spectacular and valuable items is a feather cape made by the Penuti people in California, given in 1854 by the Mexican diplomat General José López Uraga.

English leaflets are available, although you may find them only at the end of the exhibition.

NEUE SÄCHSISCHE KUNSTVEREIN GALERIE (GALLERY OF THE NEW SAXON ARTISTS' UNION) *St Petersburger Str 2;* ✎ *4382 2310; e kv@saechsischer-kunstverein.de; www.saechsischer-kunstverein.de;* ⊕ *15.00–19.00 Tue–Fri, 10.00–14.00 Sat; free* [map 2 & 3]
Temporary shows of modern art by members of the New Saxon Artists' Union.

RUSTKAMMER (ARMOURY COLLECTION) *Zwinger;* ✎ *4914 2000; e besucherservice@skd.smwk.service.de; www.skd-dresden.de;* ⊕ *10.00–18.00 Tue–Sun; adult €3, children €2, family €7* [map 2 & 3]
In the Semperbau, across the entry passage from the Old Masters Gallery, is a display of 1,320 weapons from a collection of around 10,000. It is to move in the next couple of years to the Residenzschloss, where a separate Costume Collection, Gun Gallery and Turkish Chamber will be set up.

Only the admission prices are in English, but you should be able to appreciate the splendid workmanship of the collection without translation. The displays include three Saxon electoral swords, matching armour for man and horse made by the Antwerp goldsmith Eliseus Libaerts for King Erik XIV of Sweden, gold-mounted sets of weapons by Pere Juan Poch of Barcelona, tournament armour by the Augsburg armourer Anton Peffenhauser, very ornate 18th-century crossbows and hunting guns, ivory pistols made in Maastricht in 1660, lots of 17th-century Turkish weapons and mail. The central aisle is lined with impressive suits of 16th–17th-century ceremonial armour; at the rear there's miniature armour made for the royal children, 16th-century Italian daggers that spring open to leave a very nasty wound, and tournament gear including ring-lances used by ladies in carriages to spear rings.

SCHLOSS UND PARK PILLNITZ (PILLNITZ CASTLE AND PARK) *August-Böckstiegel-Str 2;* ☎ *261 3260;* e *info-pillnitz@schloesser.smf.sachsen.de; www.schloesser-dresden.de;* ✆*late Mar–early Nov 10.00–18.00 daily; tours hourly 11.00–14.00 Sat/Sun in winter; adult €3, children €2*
The new Schlossmuseum (Castle Museum) in the Neues Palais should not be confused with the Museum of Decorative Arts (in the Wasserpalais and Bergpalais). Opened in June 2006 it has a permanent exhibition on the history of the palace and its residents, the Baroque festivals and also religious life here.

SKULPTURENSAMMLUNG (SCULPTURE COLLECTION) *French Pavilion, Zwinger;* ☎ *4914 2000;* e *besucherservice@skd.smwk.service.de; www.skd-dresden.de;* ✆*10.00–18.00 Tue–Sun; adult €2.50, children €1.50* [map 2 & 3]
In 2008 this will move back to the Albertinum, but for the time being it's in this pleasant sunlit gallery. August the Strong began the antiques collection, and by 1784 there were over 800 plaster casts of Classical sculptures for artists to study. They were displayed in this same gallery from 1879 to 1890 then moved to the

Albertinum while the medieval sculptures went to the Albrechtsburg in Meissen. There's a good English-language text, and a tour on Sundays at 14.00.

In the anteroom you can see Permoser's *Apollo and Minerva* without paying; in the gallery proper are Roman busts (c AD140–160) including those of the emperors Marcus Aurelius and Antoninus Pius, with his wife Faustina, and from the same period Roman stone copies of Greek bronzes, including the so-called *Dresden Youth*, after the School of Polykleitos (c430BC), long judged to be the perfect model of a Classical statue. There are two 16th-century bronzes and 17th-century casts of Giambologna's *Abduction of Dejanira by the Centaur Nessus* and of Baccio Bandinelli's *St Jerome*. From the early 20th century there are modern works by Georg Kolbe, Ernesto de Fiori, Wilhelm Lehmbruck, Bernhard Hoetger, and from the post-war years pieces by Emil Cimiotti and Wieland Förster.

STADTMUSEUM UND STÄDTISCHE GALERIE DRESDEN See page 209.

TECHNISCHE SAMMLUNGEN DRESDEN (DRESDEN TECHNICAL COLLECTIONS)
Junghansstr 1, Striesen; ✎ *488 7201; www.tsd.de;* ⊕ *09.00–17.00 Tue–Fri, 10.00–18.00 Sat/Sun & hols; adult €3, children €2, family €8* [map 1]
The city's own technology collection is open most days, but it's inconvenient to reach and you have to pay. It's in the former Ernemann camera factory (later Zeiss-Ikon and VEB Pentacon), with a viewing platform in the 48m-high Ernemann Tower, and lots of East German cameras, typewriters, sewing machines, radios, TVs, calculators, computers and domestic machines.

VERKEHRSMUSEUM (TRANSPORT MUSEUM) *Neumarkt;* ✆ *86440;*
e *info@verkehrsmuseum.sachsen.de; www.verkehrsmuseum-dresden.de;*
🕐 *10.00–17.00 Tue–Sun & hols; adult €3, children €1.50, family €8* [map 2 & 3]
The transport museum is housed, appropriately enough, in the Renaissance stables
built by Christian I in 1586–91 and converted into an art gallery by August the Strong
in 1729–30, when the present façade and 'English' steps were added. Partition walls
had to be added in 1831, with more alterations in 1876 when it was renamed the
Johanneum, after the late king. Information is in German only, but that shouldn't
matter much.

In the vaulted former stables around the central hall are preserved locomotives,
including the *Muldenthal*, the oldest original steam locomotive in eastern Germany,
built in Chemnitz in 1861; a 750mm-gauge 0-4-4-0 tank engine, built in Chemnitz in
1898; an experimental electric locomotive built by Siemens in Berlin in 1899; a 1916
Baldwin (a 600mm-gauge war design built in the US for use in France); an electric
loco built by Hennigsdorf in Berlin in 1931; and the cab end of SVT 137-155, a diesel
railcar that achieved a world-record speed of 215km/h (134mph) in 1939. On the
other side of the building are trams, relics of a system that operated in Dresden with
horses from 1872 to 1900 and with electric trams since 1893.

In the double-height central hall (with two reproduction planes overhead) are old
cars, including reproductions of three 1886 Benzes, an 1885 Daimler motorbike
(with a wooden frame), a 1904 Excelsior (made in Zurich), a 1904 Wanderer (made
in Chemnitz), a 1911 Benz Phaeton, and a 1926 Pilot (made in Dresden and capable
of 95km/h). From the communist era there's a 1968 prototype of a Wartburg, and

a couple of Melkus sports cars, made in Dresden using Wartburg engines and other parts from Trabants and Wartburgs.

Going up to the first floor, start to the left, past one of August the Strong's mileposts, with a display of early bicycles, starting in 1817 with a model without pedals; another from 1868 had the pedals driving the front wheel. There are also motorbikes, starting with a Czech design made in 1899, and photos and models of communist German trucks and buses. On the other side is a large display on railway history, with original maps, prints and models, notably of the immense Elstertal and Göltzschtal viaducts built in 1846–51; the latter, at 567m in length and 78m in height, was the world's highest railway bridge and its largest brick bridge, containing 20 million bricks.

There's a room full of planes above the museum entry, and on the next floor up an O-gauge model railway system, set up in 1971, that covers 325m^2 and uses over 600m of track; it runs on Wednesdays at 11.00, 14.00 and 15.30, and daily in December. In 2007 a new shipping display is opening, starting with the first steamships on the Elbe in the 1830s. Also on the second floor you can see the 40-minute film *Dresden Wie Es Einst War* (*Dresden As It Once Was*; 10.45, 12.00, 13.15 & 14.30, 15.45 Tue–Sun), shot in the 1930s.

✝ CHURCHES

DREIKÖNIGSKIRCHE (THREE KINGS CHURCH) *Hauptstr, Neustadt* [map 4]
An Augustinian monastery was established here in 1481, becoming a Lutheran church in 1539 and burning down in 1685; a temporary church was built in 1688,

replaced in 1736–39 by the imposing new building designed by Pöppelmann and Bähr, with its 86m-high tower added in 1854–59. It was destroyed in 1945 and rebuilt in 1984–89 but now only the west end is used as a church, the rest being the Haus der Kirche, with meeting rooms, exhibitions, a cafeteria and a shop selling Third-World crafts. In the church itself, the largely unrestored altar is by Thomae, with the five wise and five foolish virgins sculpted between the Evangelists Matthew and John. Above the entry (beneath the organ loft, with a new Eule organ installed in 1992) is a 1721 copy of the famous *Dresdner Totentanz* or *Dance of Death* – a graphically detailed procession of all social types, classes and ages – carved in 1535 by Christoph Walter. The church tower (⊕*Mar–Oct 11.00–16.00 Tue, 11.00–17.00 Wed–Sat, 11.30–17.00 Sun & hols; Nov–Feb 12.00–16.00 Wed, 10.00–16.00 Thu–Fri, 10.00–17.00 Sat, 11.30–16.30 Sun & hols; adult €1.50, children €1, under-10s free*) offers the best viewpoint in the Neustadt; entry is by Door D outside.

FRAUENKIRCHE See page 193.

HOFKIRCHE See page 206.

KREUZKIRCHE (CHURCH OF THE CROSS) *Altmarkt* [map 3]
There was a Romanesque basilica of St Nicholas on this site by 1215 and a splinter of the True Cross was given to the church in 1234 by Margrave Heinrich, but in 1491 both church and relic were destroyed by fire. In 1499 a new vaulted Gothic church was completed, where in 1539 the first Lutheran service in Dresden was held. This

was destroyed by fire in 1699 and by Prussian artillery in 1760, and rebuilt in 1766–92 as a Baroque structure; after another fire in 1897 it was given a Jugendstil interior that was largely destroyed in 1945, although the tower and walls were largely intact. It was again rebuilt and reconsecrated in 1955; the Baroque chancel and organ gallery were battered but can still be seen (with a new Jehmlich organ installed in 1963), while the rest of the interior is very bare plaster. The Jugendstil painting (1900) above the altar survived the bombing but lost its bright colours; below the altar is a bronze relief showing the first Lutheran service here. In the porch is an early Baroque *Ecce Homo* statue (c1603, probably by Melchior Barthel), as well as Jugendstil grilles.

The entry to the tower is in the Schütz chapel (commemorating the Kapellmeister from 1615–72 – see page 20), which has a cross of nails, given by Coventry Cathedral, and stone epitaphs from the time of Schütz. The spire is 92m high with a lookout platform at 54m (☉Apr–Oct 10.00–17.30 Mon–Fri, 10.00–16.30 Sat, 12.00–17.30 Sun; Nov–Mar 10.00–15.30 Mon–Sat, 12.00–16.30 Sun; during Striezelmarkt to 20.00; adult €2, children €1, family €5). The tower also contains the second-largest peal of bells in Germany, the largest weighing 11.5 tonnes and the four others a total of 28.45 tonnes.

You can hear the church choir, which has been famous for 800 years, at the Sunday services (09.30); there are also organ prayers on Wednesdays at 17.00.

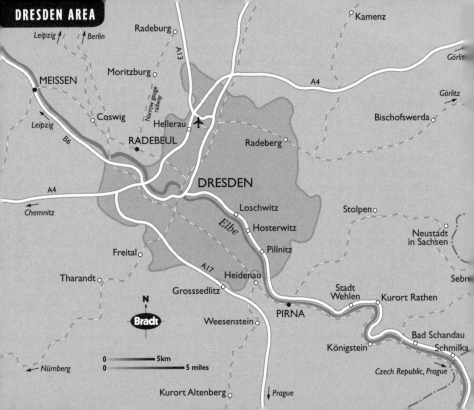

11 Beyond the City

MORITZBURG

Moritzburg, just 25km northwest of the city, is dominated by the beautiful castle established, naturally, by Elector Moritz in 1546. Built as a moated hunting lodge, it was one of the first Renaissance buildings in Saxony before August the Strong commissioned Matthias Daniel Pöppelmann in 1730 to rebuild it as a Baroque summer residence and a setting for glamorous parties. It's now owned by Prince Rudiger von Sachsen, great-grandson of the last king, who caused a stir in 2005 when he placed an advert for a princess to share his estates with him.

GETTING HERE AND AWAY Without a car or bike, it's most easily reached by bus 362 from the Neustadt Bahnhof, which on weekdays leaves at 15 and 45 minutes past the hour (taking 40mins), the latter continuing to Radeburg (16mins further); at weekends they leave on the hour (mostly continuing to Radeburg on the even hours). Tickets can be bought from the VVO machine inside the station or from the driver. You can also take the S-Bahn or tram 4 to Radebeul-Ost then the occasional narrow-gauge steam train (see below). Bike rental is available through Bike & Fun Fahrradpool (0172 790 2480; Apr–Oct) at the Moritzburg tourist office. There are also various hiking trails passing through Moritzburg, all well signed, including one marked with an Indian head leading to the Karl May Museum in Radebeul (see page 238). Cycle routes include the Moritzburgerweg to Kleinzadel and Nieschütz (west of Meissen) and others to Coswig and Radebeul (both by the Elbe, about 10km away).

WHERE TO STAY AND EAT On the central Käthe-Kollwitz-Platz, the **Café zur Erholung** is a friendly smoke-free café open from 08.00 (09.00 at w/ends) which also has rooms (↘ 035207 82183). The **Gasthof 'Goldener Brezel'**, just north at Schlossallee 24 (↘ 035207 89798) which opened in 1740, has a modern extension with rooms. The **Gasthof Forsthaus** at Schlossallee 11 (↘ 035207 81500; e forsthaus-moritzburg@ t-online-de) has an excellent restaurant specialising in local fish and game. The **Churfuerstliche Waldschaenke Moritzburg**, just north by the lake on Grosse Fasanenstrasse (↘ 035027 8600; e info@waldschaenke-moritzburg.de; www.waldschaenkemoritzburg.de), is a four-star hotel and restaurant with 33 rooms. On Rossmarkt, just south of Käthe-Kollwitz-Platz, are two pensions and a café. Heading north from the train station, on the south side of the village, you'll pass a couple of pleasant pensions and then a grander inn on the main square, Käthe-Kollwitz-Platz, opposite a monument to the artist (see page 235) and the Haus des Pferdes (House of the Horse).

WHAT TO SEE AND DO Moritzburg is a great centre of equestrianism, known for its stud farm and the Parade of Stallions on the first weekend of September, which ends with a 16-in-hand performing before an audience of tens of thousands (also in the autumn is the Moritzburg fish harvest, when the ponds are emptied of carp).

Horseriding and trips in horse-drawn carriages are available. Schlossallee, the tree-lined main street, leads to the right past the Haus des Gastes (tourist office) at Schlossallee 3B (✆ 035207 8540; e *moritzburgtouristeninfo@web.de, moritzburg-touristinfo@t-online.de; www.moritzburg.de;* ⏲*Nov–Mar 09.00–17.00 only Mon–Fri*), with an electronic room availability indicator and free phone.

Ahead, reached by a causeway across the lake, is the **castle** (✆ *035207 87318;* e *moritzburg@schloesserland-sachsen.de; www.schlossmoritzburg.de;* ⏲*Apr–Oct 10.00–17.30 daily; Nov/Dec/Feb/Mar 10.00–16.00 Tue–Sun; Jan 10.00–16.00 Sat/Sun; adult €6, student €4, children €1, family €10*). Hourly tours cost €2, an audio-guide costs €2 (and €10 deposit), and a leaflet in French or English costs €0.50. Under the vault of the rear entry hall is an 18th-century carriage, and to the left a history display (in English and German). Beyond this is a recreation of August the Strong's Feather Room, with a bed, canopy and wall hangings made of over two million exotic feathers (an 18th-century craze), now displayed behind a glass screen after a 19-year restoration, along with Chinese celadon vases (1662–1722). On the other side of the hall is a display on food and drink at court (where 600–700 people had to be taken care of), with pots and pans, some discovered when the lake was dredged in 1992. There's also a restaurant-café (from 10.00).

Upstairs, you'll find antlers everywhere, mainly from the red deer that have been enthusiastically hunted here for centuries and which still feature on the menus of many Dresden restaurants. Most rooms are also furnished with 18th-century leather and gold wall coverings, Saxon and French furniture (mostly original to the castle), oriental and Meissen porcelain, and 17th- and 18th-century paintings. In the

Moritzgalerie are portraits of Moritz (possibly by the younger Cranach), Christian II and Johann Georg I. In the Billiard Room is a billiard table made in Saxony c1700, one of the oldest in Germany, and on the leather wall coverings hunting scenes painted in 1730 perhaps by the Venetian Lorenzo Rossi. The Second Guest Chamber has 18th-century portraits, of Countess Cosel and Philip V of Spain, and a couple by Louis de Silvestre. In the anteroom of Queen Maria Josepha, wife of August the Strong, are scenes of boating and hunting (or rather massacres). A corridor passes above the chapel; to the right of the altar is a Permoser marble sculpture (1725) of Christ at the Pillar. In the Second Electors' Chamber are portraits of the Prime Minister Count Brühl and his wife, a Louis de Silvestre (1732) of Frau von Carlowitz, and a large peacock and two eagles, modelled in porcelain by Kändler in 1731–34.

The First Electors' Chamber has a copy of Hyacinthe Rigaud's portrait of Friedrich August II, and Imari porcelain jars. The Monströsensaal or Hall of Monstrosities is so called because of the four dozen-odd sets of misformed antlers; there are also Gobelin-like leather tapestries and porcelain models of birds by Kändler. The central Stone Hall (the original entry hall) has four welcoming fires lit in winter, and more racks of antlers. The First August Chamber houses portraits of August the Strong (by the studio of Louis de Silvestre, c1718) and of his wife, and of Johann Georg III and his wife; the Second Chamber has a Silvestre of Field Marshal Count Flemming (c1728) and Imari jars, as also in the Chamber with Chinese Wall Coverings.

The 1,200ha deer park and forest are open for walking, with marked paths. One objective would be the **Fasanenschlösschen** (Little Pheasant Castle), 2.5km north, a Rococo gem (built in 1782, with a fascinating chinoiserie interior) where August the Strong met his mistresses. It opened in early 2007 as a museum of Late Baroque Court Culture; it has its own harbour on the lake, with a lighthouse overlooking the scene of miniature sea battles.

Nearby on the Radeburg road is the **Wildgehege** or Game Enclosure (*Fasanerie 4;* ✆ *035207 81488; www.smul.sachsen.de;* ⏰ *Mar–Oct 10.00–18.00; Nov/Dec 09.00–16.00; Jan/Feb 09.00–16.00 Sat/Sun; adult €2.50, children €1.50*), a wildlife park with roe and red deer, elk, wolf, otter, nutria, moufflon, boar, dwarf goats and pigs, American silver fox, Arctic fox, wild cat, lynx, rabbit, hare, mink, owls and pheasants, etc; feeding time is 14.30.

It's 300m south (to the right leaving the castle) to the **Käthe Kollwitz Haus**, Meissner Strasse 7 (*Rüdenhof, just south of the Kalkreuther Str bus stop;* ✆ *82818;* e *info@kollwitz-moritzburg.de; www.kollwitz-moritzburg.de;* ⏰ *Apr–Oct 11.00–17.00 Mon–Fri, 10.00–17.00 Sat/Sun; Nov–Mar 12.00–16.00 Tue–Fri, 11.00–16.00 Sat/Sun; adult €2, children €1*). This is the only surviving home of perhaps the finest German artist of the mid 20th century, although in fact she lived here for less than a year and made no art here. Born in 1867, she spent her working life in Berlin, was widowed in 1940, and was evacuated in 1943. In July 1944 she was invited here by Prince Heinrich von Sachsen, which must have been hard for a lifelong leftist to take, and died here on 22 April 1945. She was buried in Moritzburg, then exhumed, cremated in Meissen and reburied in Berlin. There are prints and a couple of her sculptures here, and selections in German from her memoirs. The two upstairs rooms in which she lived are unfurnished.

Radeburg (not to be confused with Radeberg with its brewery – see below) is the terminus of the Lössnitzgrund railway, the most accessible of Saxony's famous narrow-gauge lines.

GETTING THERE AND AWAY The 750mm-gauge railway runs from Radebeul (see below) and along the Lössnitz Valley through Moritzburg, and like the other lines still operates a regular all-year steam-hauled service rather than just a summer tourist operation. Opened in 1884, it's operated by five locomotives built in Chemnitz in 1953–54 (the most powerful 750mm-gauge locomotives built, although with a maximum speed of just 30km/h); there's another built in Chemnitz in 1899 and a Henschel loco from the 1920s, as well as four historic carriages (dating from 1913–32) and more recent open and covered carriages.

Fares are €2 to go to the next station, €4 for two to three stops, €5.80 for four to six stops, €6.40 for seven to ten stops (double for returns); a bike or dog costs €2 and a family ticket €9–15 one-way. There are eight trains a day between Radebeul and Moritzburg, and only four continuing to Radeburg, so the easiest option is to take a bus from Dresden to Moritzburg, then a train to Radebeul and tram or S-Bahn back to Dresden; if you choose to go to Radeburg there are buses back to Dresden. The Traditionsbahn Radebeul also operates a few special excursions (€6 to Moritzburg or €8 to Radeburg). For information contact the Lössnitzgrundbahn (*Am Bahnhof 1, 01468 Moritzburg;* ✎ *035207 89290;* e *loessnitzgrundbahn@bvo.de; www.loessnitzgrundbahn.de*).

There's a nice streamside path from the Bahnhof to the small bus station, from where there are hourly buses to Dresden Neustadt via Moritzburg, and to Radeberg via Klotzsche (near Dresden Airport).

WHAT TO SEE AND DO Radeburg was the birthplace of the folk artist Heinrich Zille, featured in the museum at Heinrich-Zille-Strasse 9 (↘ *035208 4341;* ⊕ *10.00–16.00 Tue/Thu/Fri & the 1st & 3rd Sat of each month; adult* €*2, children* €*1*).

RADEBEUL

A 1923 amalgamation of nine small villages that's now a suburb of Dresden, Radebeul is worth a stop *en route* to Meissen, particularly if you're on the wine trail. The Dresden-Card is valid on tram 4 into Radebeul, also served by four stations on the S1 S-Bahn line to Meissen. All phone numbers use the Dresden code (0351).

 WHERE TO STAY See page 96. There's also a **youth hostel** at Weintraubenstrasse 12 (↘ *838 2880; www.djh-sachsen.de*).

PRACTICALITIES There is **tourist information** available at Meissner Strasse 152 (↘ *19433;* e *tourismus@radebeul.de; www.radebeul.de*). See page 81 for bike rental.

WHAT TO SEE AND DO Radebeul-Ost station is the starting point for the steam-hauled narrow-gauge railway to Moritzburg and Radeburg (see above); 700m west at Karl-May-Strasse (a block south of the Schildenstrasse tram stop) is the **Karl-May-Museum** (✆ 837 3010/3031; e info@karl-may-museum.de; www.karl-may-museum.de; ⊕ Mar–Oct 09.00–18.00 Tue–Sun & hols; Nov–Feb 10.00–16.00 Tue–Sun & hols; adult €6, children €4), in the home of the writer of Wild West tales apparently beloved by all German children. Born in 1842, May bought the large plain building he named Villa Shatterhand in 1895 and lived here until his death in 1912. You should start at the rear with the Villa Bärenfett (Bear's Foot), a log cabin added in 1928, with a display on the native peoples of North America; in the main house are mementoes of May's life, including relics from Palestine and first editions with Sasha Schneider's clearly homoerotic illustrations, and one room furnished as it was in his time.

Just to the west in a communist office block at Wasastrasse 50 (on the main Meissner Strasse at the Wasastrasse tram stop) is **Zeitreise** (✆ 835 1780; e mail@wasapark-austellungsgesellchaft.de; www.zeitreise-ddr.de; ⊕ 10.00–18.00 Tue–Sun; adult €6, children €4.50), a tongue-in-cheek evocation of communist times. On the ground floor are cars, including lots of Trabants in various forms, made in Zwickau between 1957 and 1991, and Wartburgs, tiny caravans and motorbikes; on the first floor there's just a small model railway. On the second are workshops (with authentic pin-ups), offices (with typewriters and stamps, and just a few Robotron computers), a room of watches and clocks and a room of bikes. On the third floor there's a reading area with books and magazines published in the DDR, and various rooms of period clothes to put on for photos; accordions and electronic keyboards; skis, skates, a scull and a windsurfer;

camping gear; photographic kit; model yachts, cars and planes; TVs, radios, tape recorders and record players; top-loader washing machines; Deutsche Werkstätte Hellerau furnishings; kitchen equipment and vacuum cleaners; a bathroom, bedrooms; and a big room of prams, dolls and toys. It's an amazing collection of junk.

To the north (1.5km up Eduard-Bilz-Strasse, or 10 mins from Weisses Ross on the narrow-gauge line) is the **Hoflössnitz** vineyard, where Elector Johann Georg I built a Renaissance summer home that's now a museum, the Weingutmuseum Hoflössnitz (*Knohllweg 37;* ✆ *839 8333;* e *info@hofloessnitz.de; www.hofloessnitz.de;* ⏱ *10.00–13.00 & 14.00–18.00 Tue–Fri, 10.00–18.00 Sat/Sun & hols; adult* € *2.30, children* € *1.50*). The 390 steps of the Himmelsleiter (Ladder of Heaven) lead up to the Bismarck Tower and the Spitzhaus restaurant (*Spitzhausstr 36;* ✆ *830 9305;* e *restaurant@spitzhaus-radebeul.de; www.spitzhaus-radebeul.de*). Just to the east on Weinbergstrasse are smaller private vineyards, such as the Retzsch-Gut at no 20 (✆ *836 0400*), founded in 1649 and now named after the painter Friedrich August Retzsch (1779–1857) who lived here, illustrating Goethe, Schiller and Shakespeare and also making wine; and also Weingut Friedrich Aust, no 10 (✆ *893 90100*). You can also taste wine nearby at the Alte Weinkeller Oberlössnitz, Weinbergstrasse 16 (✆ *836 4821*); Weinkeller am Goldenen Wagen, Hoflössnitzstr 62 (✆ *836 2553; www.goldenerwagen.de*); and the Weinstube in der Hoflössnitz (✆ *836 4170*). Continuing west from the Hoflössnitz on Obere Burgstrasse, there's the Winzerei und Weinhaus Förster at no 21 (✆ *930 6207*).

The **Landesbühnen Sachsen**, immediately north of the Radebeul-Weintrauben station (Landesbühnen Sachsen tram stop) is home to Germany's second-largest subsidised repertory theatre (see page 135); a new town centre is being developed around its modern Stammhaus venue. At the Radebeul-West station (Moritzburger Str tram stop) is the world's smallest cinema (with just nine seats), the Palast Kino, Bahnhofstrasse 10 (✆ 0351 656 3419; e info@palastkino.de; www.palastkino.de; adult €3, or €25 to rent the whole cinema). Immediately south is **Altkötzschenbroda**, the oldest and most charming part of Radebeul (first recorded as Coschebrode in 1271), a tree-lined square by the Elbe with Weinkellers, galleries and craft shops.

The best sight in Radebeul, however, is to the west on Mittlere Bergstrasse (1.5km east of Radebeul-Zitzschweig station), where **Schloss Wackerbarth** (✆ 89550; e kontakt@schloss-wackerbarth.de; www.schloss-wackerbarth.de) houses the Sächsisches Staatsweingut (Saxon State Winery). Built in 1727–29 by Count von Wackerbath as his retirement home, it's a fine Baroque mansion with beautiful gardens and an octagonal pavilion, the belvedere, at the top of a staircase through the terraces. The vineyard is Germany's third-oldest sparkling wine producer, having produced its Sekt (fermented in the bottle) for almost 200 years (⏰ from 10.00 daily, there's a wine tour at 14.00 and a Sekt tour at 17.00; at w/ends they run on alternate hours; adult €9). There's a good restaurant (⏰ 12.00–22.00 Mon–Fri, 10.00–22.00 Sat/Sun).

There are various **wine festivals**: the Weinfest Hoflössnitz at the end of August, two at Schloss Wackerbarth in mid June and mid September, and also in September in Altkötzschenbroda.

Although the coach parties that flood into Meissen just stop at the porcelain factory and then head for the autobahn, it is in fact centuries older than Dresden and has the region's cathedral plus a fine castle, dramatically set together on a hill above the Elbe. It was founded in 929, when King Henry the Fowler established a castle here and established a margravate to rule the territories he had annexed, and the bishopric was founded in 963. St Benno, Bishop of Meissen, did much for his diocese before dying in 1106 at the high altar; he was canonised in 1523, the so-called 'last canonisation of the Middle Ages' which infuriated Luther and impelled him towards a break with the Catholic Church. The Wettins moved their capital to Dresden in 1485, followed by the bishopric in 1581; little happened here (other than being badly damaged during the Thirty Years War) until the opening of Europe's first porcelain factory in 1710 in the Albrechtsburg Castle. In 1861 this was moved to its present site on the edge of the town.

GETTING THERE The easiest way to get here from Dresden is by the S-Bahn, leaving the Hauptbahnhof on the hour and half hour (line S1; 50mins). At the moment there are stations only in Vorbrücke, on the right bank of the Elbe, and at Meissen-Triebischtal, near the porcelain factory, but the Meissen-Altstadt station, on the left bank near the Old Town, will open at the end of 2008, making access much easier for tourists. This is also the start of a scenic back route to Leipzig (RB 110, every 2hrs), although it's about 20 minutes faster to take the S-Bahn to Coswig and change

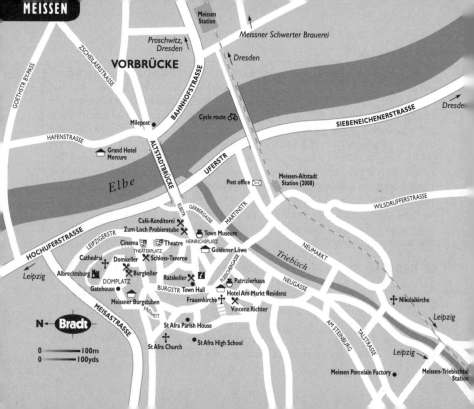

MEISSEN

Meissen Station

Meissner Schwerter Brauerei

Proschwitz, Dresden

VORBRÜCKE

Dresden

ZSCHEILAERSTRASSE

BAHNHOFSTRASSE

GOETHESTR BYPASS

Cycle route

SIEBENEICHENERSTRASSE

Dresde

HAFENSTRASSE

Milepost

ALTSTADTBRÜCKE

Grand Hotel Mercure

UFERSTR

Post office ✉

Meissen-Altstadt Station (2008)

WILSDRUFFERSTRASSE

Elbe

ELBSTR

GERBERGASSE

MARTINSTR

Triebisch

NEUMARKT

HOCHUFERSTRASSE

Café-Konditorei Zum Loch Probierstube

Town Museum

LEIPZIGERSTR

Cinema

Theatre

HEINRICHSPLATZ

Goldener Löwe

Leipzig

THEATERPLATZ

Schloss-Taverne

Cathedral

Domkeller

BLEISCHERGASSE

NEUGASSE

Albrechtsburg

Burgkeller

Ratskeller

Patrizierhaus

DOMPLATZ

Town Hall

Nikolaikirche

Gatehouse

BURGSTR

Hotel Am Markt Residenz

Meissner Burgstuben

Frauenkirche

AM STEINBURG

Leipzig

FREIHEIT

Vincenz Richter

TALSTRASSE

N **Bradt**

St Afra Parish House

St Afra Church

St Afra High School

Leipzig

MEISASTRASSE

0 ——— 100m
0 ——— 100yds

Meissen Porcelain Factory

Meissen-Triebischtal Station

there for a mainline train to Leipzig. Road traffic is dreadfully congested, although a second road bridge opened in 1997. In fact the most pleasant way to get here, if you have time, is by bicycle along the riverside Elberadweg.

WHERE TO STAY AND EAT Meissen Tourist, Gerbergasse 4 (✆ *03521 459950;* e *incoming@meissentourist.de; www.meissen-tourist.de*) can book you into **hotels**, **pensions or private rooms**; they also offer bed and breakfast packages with entry to the porcelain factory, the Albrechtsburg and the Dom. Towards the porcelain factory are some handy **pensions**, at Neugasse 22 (✆ *03521 452561;* e *kontakt@schoenitzmeissen.de*), no 29 (✆ *03521 401203*) and no 54, and Talstrasse 5 (✆ *03521 452397;* e *info@pension-manu.de*) and no 60 (✆ *03521 453806; www.pensiontriebischtal.de*).

Hotel Goldener Löwe Heinrichsplatz 6; ✆ 03521 41110; e goldener-loewe@meissen-hotel.com; www.meissen-hotel.com. In the heart of the Altstadt this is a lovely place, parts of which date from 1457; it also has a grand dining room & a Weinstube. $$$$

Grand Hotel Mercure Hafenstr 27; ✆ 03521 72250; e h1699@accor.com; www.dresden-hotel-meissen.de. Just northeast of the bridge, this is the best place to stay: a small Schloss with AC rooms & a gym. $$$

Hotel Am Markt Residenz An Der Frauenkirche 1 at the corner of Fleischergasse; ✆ 03521 41510; e residenz@meissen-hotel.com; www.meissen-hotel.com. A homely place above a café. $$$

There are quite a few generic Asian **restaurants** as well as kebab and pizza joints, notably on Theaterplatz, where the Goldener Ring at no 9 serves Greek food; Café Wehnert at no 6 is a good bakery; and there's a Dürüm Kebap Haus at no 4.

✘ **Burgkeller** Domplatz 11; ☏ 03521 41400; e burgkeller@meissen-hotel.de; www.meissen-hotel.de. A café (⏲ 14.30–18.00), the Böttgerstube restaurant (⏲ 11.30–22.00) & also skittles (⏲ 10.00–23.00). $$$

✘ **Café-Konditorei Schreiber** Elbstr 31. Serving coffee & fine pastries since 1867. $

✘ **Domkeller** Domplatz 9; ☏ 03521 457676; e info@domkeller.com; www.domkeller.com. A terrace-café (⏲ 10.00–18.00 Mon–Fri, 10.00–19.00 Sat/Sun) & restaurant (⏲ 11.00–22.00 Sun–Fri, to 23.00 Sat). $$$

⌂ **Meissner Burgstuben** Freiheit 3; ☏ 03521 453685; e meissner-burgstuben@t-online.de; www.meissnerburgstuben.de; ⏲ 10.00–18.00 Tue–Sun. On the way to the Domplatz, this is a café which also has 6 pleasant rooms. $

✘ **Ratskeller** Markt 1; ☏ 03521 459393; e bierlaterne@t-online.de; www.ratskeller-meissen.de; ⏲ Apr–Oct 11.00–22.00 daily, Nov–Mar 11.00–19.00. This has an English menu & serves soups, salads, fish & German dishes, as well as beer. $$$

✘ **Schloss-Taverne** Schlossstufen 1; ☏ 03521 402409; e schloss-taverne@t-online.de; www.schloss-taverne.de. Just off Schlossberg in a typical Meissen inner court, this serves French & German food. $$$

✘ **Zum Loch Probierstube** Elbstr 27; ☏ 03521 452028. A good little pub, with food & beer. $

Meissen boasts Saxony's oldest private **brewery**, the Meissner Schwerter Brauerei (*Ziegelstr 6*; ☏ *03521 731443*; e *mail@schwerter-brauerei.de*; www.schwerterbrauerei.de; ⏲ *09.00–15.00 & from 17.00 Mon–Fri, from 11.00 Sat/Sun*), founded in 1460, before the purity law of 1516. Unfortunately it's now in an industrial area a couple of kilometres to the southeast on the Coswig road, but you can visit to taste the pils, lager, porter and dark St Afra Dunkel. You can take a one-hour visit without tasting (€4), a two-hour visit with tasting (€6), or a three-hour visit with tasting and a meal (€22.40); bottles can be bought (⏰07.00–12.30 & 13.00–15.00 Mon–Fri).

Wine is important here too: just across the river is Schloss Proschwitz (*01665 Zadel über Meissen, Dorfanger 19*; ✆ *03521 76760*; e *weingut@schloss-proschwitz.de*; *www.schloss-proschwitz.de*), one of the largest and oldest vineyards in Saxony, returned in 1990 to Prince Georg zu Lippe, who has rapidly turned it into one of the best of the local producers. You can visit (⏰10.00–18.00 daily) to taste wines (including sparkling Sekt) and spirits. The other leading local wine-maker is Vincenz Richter, whose produce can be tasted at his restaurant in Meissen at An der Frauenkirche 12 (✆ *03521 453285*; e *restaurant@vincenz-richter.de*; *www.vincenz-richter.de*; ⏰*from 12.00 Tue–Sun*).

There's a good paved cycle route on the right/east bank of the Elbe through Meissen, and in Winkwitz, immediately beyond Proschwitz, a couple of places ideal for combining accommodation, easy riverside cycling and wine-tasting.

🏠 **Hotel Knorre** Elbtalstr 3; ✆ 03521 72810; ⏰11.00–22.00 daily. $$$
🏠 **Weinstube Erste Weinkönigin** Elbtalstr 5; ✆ 03521 739601; e weinstube-weisflug@web.de; www.weinstubeweisflug.de; ⏰from 11.00 Wed–Sun. The home of the region's first Wine Queen (in 1987) & also her daughter, the 16th.
🏠 **Weinterrassen Kämpfe** Elbtalstr 28; ✆ 03521 738461; e weinterrassen.kaempfe@t-online.de; www.weinterrassen.de; ⏰May–Oct from 18.00 Mon–Fri, from 12.00 Sat/Sun & holidays; Nov–Apr by appointment

PRACTICALITIES AND VISITS City-Bus is Meissen's **transit system** including, from April to October, the minibus route E which leaves on the hour and half hour from the porcelain factory to the Marktplatz, Albrechtsburg and the Dom (€2.55, €3.60 return, €1.75/2.50 children, or €10.50/9 for day tickets).

WHAT TO SEE AND DO Heading left out of the main station, in Vorbrücke, Bahnhofstrasse leads to the Altstadtbrücke, with a 4m-high milepost, erected in 1722, at the east end of the bridge. It gives the distance to Dresden as 5³/₈ hours, ie: 24.4km. Across the river, Elbstrasse leads into the Old Town, to Heinrichsplatz where to the left you'll see the **Stadtmuseum** (↝ 03521 458857; ⊕ 11.00–17.00 daily; adult €3, children €2, family €8) in the 13th–15th-century former Franciscan church. The nave is used for temporary shows and modern galleries for the historic exhibits, starting with Neolithic stone tools from c4600BC and ceramics from c2400BC, then Roman coins, Slavic ceramics (9th–12th centuries), church carvings (c1240), a small winged altar (1518), and in a room off the east end of the south gallery more recent artefacts such as a fishtrap and nets, lacemaking equipment, pewter tankards, armour and cannonballs, and 18th-century paintings. Off the upper gallery another room covers the 19th century, with exhibits such as a shooting target, a helmet from Germany's first volunteer fire brigade, model boats and porcelain. Above this is an exhibition on Samuel Hahnemann (1755–1843), the son of a porcelain painter, who founded homoeopathic medicine. In the former cloister (at the foot of the stairs) are funerary memorials, four by Kändler.

Continuing west of Elbstrasse, the next square is the Markt, with the Rathaus (Town Hall; 1480) on the right, its windows used as an Advent calendar in December.

To the left is the tourist office (*Markt 3; ☏ 41940; e service@touristinfomeissen.de; www.touristinfo-meissen.de*) and opposite at Markt 9 the site where Germany's first volunteer fire brigade was formed in 1841, now Huth's Wein-und-Tee Haus. Just to the left, Rosengasse runs past the **Frauenkirche** (*⊕May–Oct 10.00–12.00 & 14.00–16.00 daily*), a late Gothic hall church, rebuilt after a fire in 1447 by the same masons and architect who built the Albrechtsberg, the Rathaus and some townhouses. There's a great carved altar (c1500) depicting the coronation of Mary, with the Nativity and the death of Mary to the left, the Last Supper and Christ on the Via Dolorosa on the right, and the burial of Jesus on the predella (base). The 13th-century tower was damaged by lightning in 1547 and made higher, with stairs for the town's fire watchman (who kept guard here until 1907); you can ask to climb it, although the view from the Schlossberg are similar. In 1929 a chime of 37 porcelain bells (visible from the lower town) was fitted in the tower, playing hymns six times a day as well as striking the hours.

Just above the Frauenkirche (in addition to public toilets) are the remains of the Tuchmachertor (built as the cemetery gate in 1600) and the Altes Brauhaus, a gabled Renaissance house (c1569–74) with a relief of Samson's fight with the lion. Just west of the church at Webergasse 1, the **Museum Patrizierhaus** (*☏ 409090; www.patrizierhaus-meissen.de; ⊕10.00–17.00 Sat/Sun, Tue–Thu by reservation on ☏ 03521 731235; adult €3.50, children €2.50*) is a museum of 17th-century home life in a Renaissance townhouse built in 1557–58.

To the right from the church steps (marked with discreet copper signs to the cathedral) lead up to a street called Freiheit (Freedom); to the right you'll pass the

THE HISTORY OF MEISSEN PORCELAIN

The 2008–10 period will see the celebration of the 300th anniversary of the creation of European hard porcelain. This is generally credited to Johann Friedrich Böttger (1682–1719), although this now seems to be not altogether the case. A Berlin chemist's apprentice, he turned to alchemy and shut himself away trying to make gold. Rumours spread that he was close to finding the secret and King Friedrich I was getting interested, and Böttger, fearing failure, fled in 1701 to Saxony. He was imprisoned by August the Strong and ordered to make gold while being held prisoner in the Albrechtsburg in 1705–06. He failed, but from late 1707 worked with the polymath Ehrenfried Walter von Tschirnhaus in the Dresden Festung, and in 1708 they made a kind of hard stoneware known as Böttgersteinzeug, which was ideal for carving and polishing. Tschirnhaus died of dysentery in 1708, but Böttger worked on and in 1709–10 produced white porcelain (although possibly only after being given a formula found in Tschirnhaus's papers). Porcelain had been created in China around 200BC and in Europe it was known as 'white gold', as the manufacturing process was secret and it was immensely rare and valuable.

The mixture is half kaolin (a type of clay, from near Meissen), a quarter quartz and a

St Afra Gymnasium (high school; 1877–79) and Pfarrhaus (parish house; 1535), to reach the **church of St Afra**, consecrated in 1064 and rebuilt in 1240 and in the 15th century in late Gothic style, with a Baroque tower added in 1765. The chancel quarter feldspar (which replaced alabaster after 1724); it's mixed with water, poured into moulds and biscuit-fired (at 950°C), then the crossed swords are added and it's glazed and fired again (at 1,400°C), shrinking by 16% in size. Enamels fuse with the glaze at 900°C, but temperatures over 1,350°C are needed to make it truly translucent. After painting there's a final firing at about 820°C.

In 1710 August set up the first European porcelain factory in the Albrechtsburg; in 1717 a version of the Chinese cobalt blue underglaze was developed, although it was only really attractive after 1733, after Böttger's death in 1719, at just 37. From 1722 every piece was marked with the crossed blue swords that became the world's first trademark, evolving over the years until it took its current form in 1946.

Johann Joachim Kändler (1706–75) trained with Benjamin Thomae, and became court sculptor in 1730. The next year August the Strong sent him to the Meissen factory to create a menagerie of porcelain animal sculptures (with Gottlieb Kirchner, who left in 1733); he created the art of European porcelain sculpture, and then in 1736–41 produced the first uniform dinner services, for the king and for Count Brühl. However, the animal sculptures were so big and complex that the project was called off in 1739.

is particularly light, all plain white and red-painted columns and arches, and there's a fairly simple winged altar (1503) in the left aisle, and lots of good stone-carving, starting with the 1670s' Saxon coat of arms over the entry, as well as memorials

(1435–1594) in the Grabkapelle at the rear of the right aisle. There's also an early Baroque altar and a lovely black wood pulpit.

Continuing north, you'll soon turn right to the castle hill, passing a Renaissance gateway and tower (1609–10) and the Burglehenhaus, home of the Romantic painter Ludwig Richter from 1828 to 1836, when he was a drawing teacher at the porcelain factory, then in the Albrechtsberg. Crossing the Schlossbrücke (Castle Bridge; 1221–27) you'll pass under the Torhaus (gatehouse), built at the same time and modified in neo-Gothic style in 1874–75; it's a museum, furnished as in Richter's time.

Entering the **Domplatz** (Cathedral Square), you see a path leading right around the north and east sides of the Albrechtsburg and the cathedral, past small lawns and viewpoints, with steps either down to the riverside or to Schlossberg, south of the hill. To the right, as you enter the square, are the Burgkeller and Domkeller cafés, the houses at Domplatz 10, home to the painter Georg Freidrich Kersting (1818–47), and Domplatz 8, home to Kändler (1740–75), and the Dompropstei or presbytery at Domplatz 7, where it's worth looking into the courtyard. At the far end, through the cloister, is the entry to the **Dom**, perhaps Germany's purest Gothic cathedral (✆ 03521 452490; www.dom-zu-meissen.de; ⏰Apr–Oct 09.00–18.00, Nov–Mar 10.00–16.00, all daily; adult €2.50, children/students €1.50, family €6.50; combined ticket with Albrechtsberg €5.50/3.50/14.50). A guide costs €1.50, or there are tours hourly from 10.00 (the last at 16.30) and tower visits (⏰Apr–Oct 13.00–16.00 hourly). From May to October there are organ recitals at noon (Mon–Sat) and concerts at 18.00 on Saturdays.

Built between c1250 and 1410, it feels cold and unlike a living church (although there are services: ⊕ 12.00 Sun, 09.00 Wed). You enter under the rood screen into the high Gothic nave, with an altarpiece by the studio of the younger Cranach and a porcelain crucifix by Kändler. At the far end is the 15th-century Furstenkapelle (Princes' Chapel), full of tombs and grave brasses (some by Dürer and the older Cranach); go to the far end to look back at the carvings over the entry, of Christ, the Virgin and the Apostles.

On the south side is the tomb-chapel of Duke Georg, built in the 1520s with a fine Renaissance portal, an altar designed by the older Cranach, and a very Baroque plaster ceiling (1670–76). At the west end of the south aisle steps lead up to the 14th-century Marienkapelle, with a small display on the life of St Benno, including the very worn ivory tip of his bishop's stave. At the east end of the same aisle spiral stairs lead up to the Johanniskapelle (1291) and a gallery high above the altar and pulpit. In the chancel there are fine statues by the Naumburg Master, a winged altarpiece and simple choirstalls. To the left is the Great Sacristy, between the Dom and the Albrechtsburg, with portraits by Cranach the Younger of Luther, Philip Melanchthon and Hans von Lindenau. The Choir Passage leads to the right around the apse to the Chapterhouse, where you can see drawings and models of the cathedral and wooden figures. Coming out into the cloister, you can go down to the Dom-Museum under the Chapterhouse, with an old font and other bits and pieces; the All Saints Chapel (1296) is a simple Gothic space with a stone altarpiece (c1400), now lined with gravestones.

Turning left out of the cathedral, you can go on under an arch to the Bischofssitz (1476–1518), once the seat of the bishop, and a dead-end terrace looking over the Elbe.

You have to back right around the Dom to enter the **Albrechtsburg** (*Domplatz 1;* ☎ *03521 47070;* e *albrechtsburg@schloesserland-sachsen.de; www.albrechtsburgmeissen.de;* ⊕ *Mar–Oct 10.00–18.00, Nov–Feb 10.00–17.00, all daily; adult* €3.50, *children* €2.50, *family* €9, *combined tickets with Dom as above*). A tour costs €1.50, or there's a new audio-guide for €2. Arnold von Westfalen began building a new castle in 1470, creating the German 'Schloss' style of residential castle; but after the Wettin territories split in 1485 work ground to a halt. It was completed in 1521–24 by Duke Georg the Bearded but was largely unused. Rebuilt after the Thirty Years War by Johann Georg II and renamed the Albrechtsburg, it was used by August the Strong in 1710 for Europe's first porcelain factory. In 1873–75 it was decorated with murals by 11 artists, and in 1881 it opened to the public as a memorial to Saxon history. The introductory display is in English, but most information is in German.

From outside you'll see the spiral stair-tower of the Grosse Wendelstein (1477–83), based on a French model; going in and upstairs by older spiral stairs you'll come to the Great Hall, with portraits of Wettin rulers in a tapestry-like style. To the right in a room leading to the Grosse Wendelstein is a display (in German) on the castle's construction. To the east the Kurfürstenzimmern (Electors' Rooms), have more impressionistic paintings on the military adventures of Duke Albrecht; the chapel has ornate 19th-century decorations and stained glass. To the north the Great Court Chamber is also very ornate, with a vault rebuilt in the 19th century and limewood sculptures of rulers from the same time. Beyond is the Small Dining Room (possibly the original living room), with furnishings installed in 1878 as a silver wedding gift for King Albrecht and Queen Carola.

Up the spiral stairs to the second floor, the North Wing was the realm of the courts' ladies with their sons and their tutors; the first room to the right is the neo-Gothic Great Chamber of Appeal, with a reproduction of a 15th-century stove and paintings by James Marshall (1838–1902). Beyond the Small Chamber of Appeal is the Böttger Room, with paintings of Böttger conducting the experiments that would lead to European production of porcelain while a prisoner in the Albechtsburg. Loop back past the door to the Grosse Wendelstein and through the Great Chamber of Appeal and go right to the asymmetrical Elector August Room and the Chamber of the Old Duchess, with windows on three sides and a lovely cellular vault (with no ribs), and 15th- and 16th-century statues of Christ and various saints.

Back in the Old Town, a block south of the Stadtmuseum and the Frauenkirche, the main shopping street, Neugasse, leads southwest to the Triebisch Valley and, in under ten minutes, the porcelain factory; across the river at the start of the one-way system is the Romanesque **Nikolaikirche** (*Church of St Nicholas*; ⊕*May–Sep 14.00–16.00 Wed/Thu/Sun*), Meissen's oldest, dating from the 12th century. The remains of late Romanesque paintings survive on the west side of the choir, and there's an early Gothic triple window in the east apse and a 13th-century bell.

Destroyed by the Hussites in 1429, it was rebuilt, and with the Reformation became the cemetery chapel of the Afrakirche; in the 1920s it became a memorial for the dead of World War I, with porcelain sculptures 2.5m high.

The **Porzellan-Manufaktur** (Porcelain Factory), Talstrasse 9 (✆ *468208;* e *besucherbuero@meissen.com; www.meissen.com;* ⊕*May–Oct 09.00–18.00,*

Nov–Apr 09.00–17.00, all daily; adult €8, children/students €4, family €18) is now very much a tourist attraction, with a modern entry wing added in 2005. Here you can rent an audio-guide in any of 14 languages (€8), snack at the Café Meissen (⊕*09.00–18.00 daily*), or eat at the Restaurant M upstairs (☏ *468730; www.gastronomie-meissen.de;* ⊕*from 11.00 daily*).

Tickets cost €6 (children €3) to visit the permanent and special exhibitions, or €8/4 with a 35-minute workshop demonstration as well. This basically consists of watching a craftsman painting porcelain, with a commentary in various languages. You can also take a full tour for €45 in German or €60 in English. There are also courses on porcelain painting, for instance, costing €343 for 15 hours over three days, or €533 for 30 hours over five days. To be honest, you need do little more than visit the big shop (⊕*May–Oct 09.00–18.00, Nov–Apr 09.00–17.00*): the cheapest items are salt and pepper shakers for €28/45, the most expensive a full-colour Virgin and Child for €6,923.

Turning left from the porcelain factory and left again to cross the Triebisch, you'll find Meissen-Triebischtal station on your right, for trains back to Dresden.

RADEBERG

Radeberg, 15km northeast of Dresden (and not to be confused with Radeburg), is famous for its brewery, the first in Germany to brew Czech-style pilsner in 1870 (followed by the first German Camembert cheese in 1884), but it also has a fine castle.

GETTING THERE AND AWAY It's most easily reached by trains on lines RE1/2 and RB34/60/61, towards Kamenz, Bischofswerda, Bautzen and Görlitz, taking 18 minutes from Dresden-Neustadt, although there are also buses from the northern suburbs.

 WHERE TO STAY There is accommodation at the **Ratskeller**, Am Markt 1 (↺ *03528 416560;* e *info@ratskeller-radeberg.de*), and at the four-star **Hotel Sportwelt**, Am Sandeberg 2 (↺ *03528 48800;* e *gast@hotel-sportwelt.de; www.hotel-sportwelt.de*), which has tennis, badminton and squash facilities, and a sauna.

WHAT TO SEE AND DO From the station it's a couple of minutes down Bahnhof Strasse to the **Radeberger Exportbierbrauerei** at Dresdner Strasse 2, which can be visited only by appointment (↺ *03528 454880;* e *brauereibesichtigung@ radeberger.de; www.radeberger.de;* ⊕ *10.00–17.30 Mon–Fri, 10.00–15.00 Sat/Sun; adult €6 inc samples*). Turning right on Dresdner Strasse (keep to the right side) to cross the bridge, you'll come to the **Kaiserhof Brauereiausschank** at Hauptstrasse 62 (↺ *03528 40970;* e *gast@kaiserhof-radeberg.de; www.kaiserhof-radeberg.de;* ⊕ *11.00–midnight Mon–Fri, from 07.00 Sat/Sun*), the brewery tap where you can sample its products, especially the unfiltered Zwickel, available only here and at the Radeberger Spezialausschank on the Brühl Terrace in Dresden.

Continuing up the hill you'll pass the **Radeberger Destillation und Liqueurfabrik** at Hauptstrasse 44 (↺ *03528 418918; www.radeberger-likoerfabrik.de*), selling

Radeberger Bitter since 1877, and come to the Markt at the top of the hill. **Tourist information** is available in the Rathaus (built in 1769) to the left at Am Markt 18 (✆ 450213; *www.radeberg.de*); it's worth looking in at the Jugendstil **Ratsaal** (council chamber) too.

Going to the right from the square and then left on Schlossstrasse (where there are more Baroque houses from the 1740s) it's not far to the charming little **Schloss Klippenstein** (✆ 03528 442600; e *schloss@stadt-radeberg.de*; *www.schlossklippenstein.de*; ⊕09.00–12.00 & 13.00–16.00 Tue–Fri, 11.00–17.00 Sat/Sun & hols; adult €2, children €1, family €5). Look first at the scale model of the solar system, starting with the sun by the gate, Mercury 17m away by the stream and Mars at the far end of the castle opposite another gate. The castle on its granite spur was first recorded in 1289 and was transformed by Elector Moritz into a Renaissance hunting lodge; the poet August Friedrich Ernst Langbein was born here in 1757. Now it's an enjoyable mixture of neo-Classical, Renaissance and Gothic styles. Refurbishment will continue here until 2012.

After passing through the lower court you'll come to the open rooms around the upper court, filled with odds and ends of furnishings, plus a room of televisions produced in Radeberg between 1952 and 1990.

Returning down Hauptstrasse, it's worth turning right to the **Church of the Holy Name of God**, built in 1486 and rebuilt in 1730 after a fire. It now has a 61m-high Baroque tower and a pulpit, font and other furnishings by the Dresden sculptor Johann Christoph Feige. There are views from its terrace over the town to the brewery.

From the station of Heidenau, in Dresden's eastern suburbs, the Müglitztalbahn branch runs south to Kurort Altenberg, a mountain resort near the Czech border. Trains run hourly Monday to Friday and two-hourly at weekends and holidays (on Sat/Sun from 18 Nov there are also two fast trains from Dresden Hauptbahnhof, as well as WintersportExpress buses). The third stop is Weesenstein, where **Schloss Weesenstein** is 800m from the station at Am Schlossberg 1 (☏ 035207 6260; e _weesentein@schloesserland-sachsen.de; www.schloss-weesenstein.de;_ ⊕Apr–Oct 09.00–18.00 daily, Nov–Mar 10.00–17.00 daily). It's a big, topsy-turvy place, with the banqueting hall in the attic and the stables on the fifth floor above the cellar vaults, which are above the royal living quarters. It's 700 years old and covers all styles from Gothic to neo-Classical, with a Baroque chapel and park, and a restaurant in the former kitchen.

From **Kurort Altenberg** station (where there's a tourist information centre; ☏ 035056 23993; e _infoaltenberg@t-online.de; www.altenberg.de_) it's 500m to the start of the ski-runs, where you can rent bikes in summer from Fahhrad Kohl (☏ 035056 35253). There's also cross-country skiing, a bobsled run, horse-sleighs and snowshoe rental; for lift and snow information call ☏ 035056 34239.

Two stops east of Heidenau on the S-Bahn is Heidenau-Grosssedlitz, a minor halt from which a path marked with red dots leads to August the Strong's Baroque gardens at **Grosssedlitz**, 20–30 minutes' walk to the left/south. After crossing a busy main road there's a choice between the Lovers' Walk to the left (25mins) and the more direct Old

Married Couples' Walk straight ahead, starting up a wooded valley on a gravel track then through fields to the park gate (20mins). Begun by Count Christoph August von Wackerbarth and sold half-finished to the king, Grosssedlitz, at Parkstrasse 85, Heidenau (✆ 03529 56390; e grosssedlitz@schloesserland-sachsen.de; www.barockgarten-grosssedlitz.de; ⊕ mid Mar–Sep 08.00–20.00, Oct 08.00–18.00, Nov–mid-Mar 08.00–16.00 (depending on weather), all daily, Dec–mid Mar 08.00–16.00 Sat/Sun & hols; adult €2.60, children €1.50, free Nov–mid Mar, tour €2.60/2.10 pp) was to have been the Saxon Versailles, but even August ran out of money after three years and only the orangeries were completed as planned, in addition to the mansarded little yellow ochre Baroque Schloss. It's still a 'masterpiece of silent music', with its beautifully curved flight of steps and orangery set into the terraced bowl, hardly noticeable until you come to its edge. The gardens are in the French style with Italian influence, with orangery parterres, fountains and sculptures of classical deities. From mid March to the end of October there's a shop in the Upper Orangery (✆ 03529 563919) and a café.

Leaving by the same gate, there's a junction a minute to the right, from where the Lovers' Walk leads to the left and down to the main road in just ten minutes; to the right it's only 2km to Pirna; alternatively, just north of the station the riverside path also leads east to Pirna.

PIRNA

Like Meissen, Pirna is as old or older than Dresden; founded by 1269, it is still an attractive historic town, with a pedestrianised centre, just beyond Dresden's suburbs.

GETTING THERE AND AWAY It's reached by up to four S-Bahn trains per hour on lines S-1 and S-2, from Meissen, Dresden Airport and city-centre stations (23mins from the Hauptbahnhof); the White Fleet paddle-steamers also call here, and it's on the riverside cycle route.

GETTING AROUND Local **buses** are run by the Verkehrsgesellschaft Sächsische Schweiz (*VSS; Bahnhofstr 16;* ↖ *781010;* e *service@vss-pirna.de; www.vss-pirna.de*), including routes to Graupa, Pillnitz, Stolpen and Königstein. The Elberadweg runs along the left/south bank of the Elbe, and pedestrians and cycles can cross by the rail bridge, as well as the busy road bridges. **Bikes** can be rented from Fahrradhaus Bieberstein, Clare-Zetkin-Strasse 14 (↖ *03501 781574*), opposite the Bike & Snow shop.

 WHERE TO STAY Hotels include:

🏠 **Romantik Hotel Deutsches Haus** Niedere Burgstr 1; ↖ 03501 46880; e deutsches-haus@romantikhotels.de; www.romantikhotel-pirna.de. Something of a boutique hotel in a historic house right by the Markt. $$$
🏠 **aktiv-hotel** Clara-Zetkin-Str 56B; ↖ 03501 79000; www.sporthotel-pirna.de. A 3-star hotel in the southern outskirts, with sports facilities including tennis courts, massages & solarium. $$
🏠 **Gasthaus Weisses Ross** Königsteiner Str 3; ↖ 03501 447409; www.weisses-ross-pirna.de. Pirna's oldest inn (first recorded in 1550), where Tsar Alexander & Goethe slept, this is now mainly a pub-restaurant (11.00–22.00 Mon–Sat, to 20.00 Sun) but it has 3 apts for rent. $$
🏠 **Hotel Bernardo Bellotto** Lange Str 29; ↖ 03501 46040; www.hotel-bellotto.de/en. Just north of the Markt, a historic house without a restaurant. $$

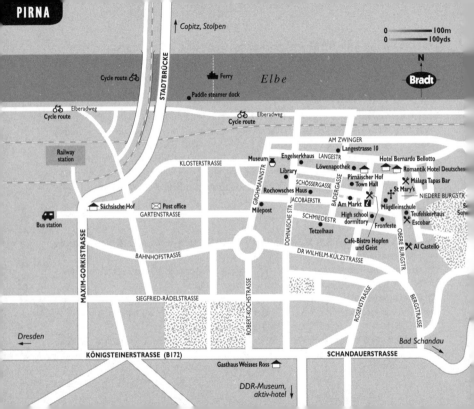

🏠 **Hotel Pirnäischer Hof** Am Markt 4; 📞 03501 44380; www.pirnascher-hof.de. Right in the centre, in a historic building on the Markt. $$

🏠 **Sächsische Hof** Gartenstr 21; 📞 03501 447551. An unexciting but adequate place opposite the station. $$

There's a **youth hostel** across the river in Copitz (*Zum Wesenitzbogen;* 📞 *03501 445601; www.djh-sachsen.de*). Likewise there's **camping** across the river at Waldcamping am Natursee (*Aussere Pillnitzer Str 19;* 📞 *03501 523773;* ✉ *waldcamping@stadtwerke-pirna.de; www.waldcamping-pirna.com*). Some 3km from Copitz-Nord station, it has space for 97 caravans and 24 tents, plus five four-person bungalows.

✗ **WHERE TO EAT AND DRINK** There are some pretty trendy new places to eat, such as:

✗ **Café-Bistro Hopfen und Geist** Am Markt 5; 📞 03501 467152; 🕐11.00–midnight. $$

✗ **Escobar restaurant-café-bar** Teufelserkerhaus, Obere Burgstr 1; 📞 03501 582773; www.esco-bar.com; 🕐17.00–10.00 Mon–Sat, 10.00–01.00 Sun. $$

✗ **Málaga Tapas Bar** Niedere Burgstr 61; 📞 03501 442341; www.esco-bar.com; 🕐from 16.00 daily. $

✗ **Ristorante Al Castello** Obere Burgstr 3; 📞 03501 466690; 🕐from 17.00 Tue–Sun. $$

Across the river in Copitz, the Brauhaus Pirna 'Zum Giesser' at Basteistrasse 60 (📞 *03501 464646; www.brauhaus-pirna.de;* 🕐*from 11.00 daily*) is a classy brewpub with good filling food too. The beers include Pils and Dunkel (Dark) as well as seasonal brews.

PRACTICALITIES For tourist information, visit **Tourist Service Pirna** in the Canalettohaus (↘ *03501 46570;* e *touristservice@pirna.de; www.pirna.de;* ⊕ *09.00–18.00 Mon–Fri, 09.30–13.00 Sat; plus Apr–Oct 09.30–14.00 Sat, 11.00–14.00 Sun/hols*). They will book rooms and sell tickets, books and souvenirs. There are useful lockers (€ 1 deposit) by the bike racks outside; tourist information is also available at the museum.

WHAT TO SEE AND DO From the train and bus station cross the ring road and go east on Gartenstrasse (its west end lined with fine Jugendstil villas) past the Filmpalast and post office, then go left on Grohmannstrasse and at once right on Jacobäerstrasse, crossing what was clearly the site of the city wall. Here stands a 4.5m-high *Postdistanzsäule* or Post Distance Sleeve (ie: milepost), erected in 1722 by August the Strong on the main square. Two blocks further east is the Market Square, with the **Rathaus** in the centre. Built in 1396, it was rebuilt in 1555–56 by Wolf Blechschmidt, and modified in 1822 and 1878. On the east gable is a splendid clock showing the phases of the moon and below the clockface are the town's arms. There's also a fine sundial on the south wall.

At the east end of the square in Am Markt 7, the **Canalettohaus** (so called not because Bellotto stayed there but because it's in the centre of his painting *Marktplatz zu Pirna* of 1752–54). In its present form the Canalettohaus dates from 1520–25 (marking the transition from Gothic to Renaissance); the ground floor has a cassette ceiling fitted in 1630. To its north the Peter Ulrich Haus, Am Markt 3, is a late Gothic corner house (1506) with a fine doorway. On the square's north side no 20 is the Marienhaus (where Napoleon stayed), so called due to the 1.5m statue of the Virgin and Child (1514) high on the corner. Am Markt 19 was once the White Swan Inn, as indicated by the swan over the door. Nos 17 and 18 were the Löwenapotheke (Lion Apothecary; 1578), with a carved golden lion and mortar on the façade; it served as a pharmacy for over 400 years, and has a two-storey wooden gallery in the courtyard. Am Markt 14, south of Schössergasse, is a late Gothic merchant's house with a Baroque portal added in 1743. On the square's south side no 12 (c1548) served as the electoral administration from 1648 to 1854; no 11, built in 1527 and modified in 1900, has an interesting cellular vault on the ground floor (visible inside the shop).

Just east of the square is the **Marienkirche** (Church of St Mary; ⊕ 11.00–17.00, winter to 15.00, Mon–Sat, 15.00–17.00 Sun), a three-naved late Gothic church built in 1502–46 with an older tower (1466–79) with a steeple added in the 18th century. The spacious interior has a tightly woven late Gothic fan vault on 12 columns, plus murals (1544–46), a big ornate sandstone altar and a font carved with 26 children showing the day's activities.

The Blechshmidthaus, just north of the church at Niedere Burgstrasse 1, was the home of the mason Wolf Blechschmidt, built by 1544 with a fine staircase tower and a painted Renaissance ceiling on the first floor; it's now a hotel (see page 259). Just beyond is the Quartier 1 project, Baroque townhouses being rebuilt as apartments and restaurants.

Just south of the church at Kirchplatz 10 the Mägdleinschule (girls' school), in use by 1555, now houses the Kuratorium Altstadt (Old Town curatorship) and you can visit a classroom. Just south at Obere Burgstrasse 1 the Teufelserkerhaus, built at the end of the 16th century and the beginning of the 17th, takes its name from the two-storey bay window (1622) supported by three devilish figures. Behind it an alley leads up to Schloss Sonnenstein, overlooking the town to the east; recorded by 1269, in 1811 the castle became Germany's first psychological hospital, and under the Nazis around 15,000 mentally ill people were 'euthanised' here. It was used to treat the survivors of the Dresden firestorm, and is now a high school.

At Obere Burgstrasse 14 the Alte Knabenschule or former boys' school was built in 1583 with a second floor added in 1720; the Erlpeterbrunnen fountain was recorded by 1384, with the statue of a boy added in 1908. Turning right onto Schlossstrasse, at no 8 (and Schmiedestrasse 55) the massive Fronfeste (first recorded in 1572) was the town prison until 1949 and is now a cultural centre with regular art exhibitions. At Schlossstrasse 13 (facing the Canalettohaus) a late Gothic merchant's house (c1500), with a Renaissance façade and a beautiful bay window (1630), now houses the high school dormitory, with pupils from the Czech Republic as well as Saxony living here.

A block south of the Markt, Schmiedestrasse 22 dates from the second half of the 17th century. No 19, the Tetzelhaus, was the birthplace in about 1465 of Johann Tetzel (see page 3), who became a notorious indulgence preacher and one of Luther's chief opponents. Just west of the Markt at Schössergasse 3 the Rochowsches Haus (by 1608) was rebuilt from 1756 by Baron Rochow, commandant of Sonnenstein

Castle, as a Baroque townhouse with his coat of arms on the façade. Across the road to the west at Dohnaische Strasse 76 the Stadtbibliothek (town library) has a richly decorated Renaissance sandstone doorway and huge 18th-century gullwing doors; it's worth going inside to see the wooden galleries and parts of the city wall at the rear. Just north, the Engelserkerhaus, at the corner of Barbiergasse, was built by 1479; note the angel in the centre console of the bay window and the portal with a lion's head. Just east at Lange Strasse 10 (on the corner of Badergasse) is another late Gothic merchant's house, rebuilt in Baroque style around 1719 for Friedrich August and his bride Maria Josepha, who spent their first night together in Saxony here; it has a fine portal and a wood-beamed ceiling.

To the rear of the library the Klosterhof or former Dominican monastery (founded c1300) now houses the **town museum** (✆ 03501 527985; e stadtmuseum@pirna.de; ⊕May–Oct 10.00–18.00 Tue–Sun; Nov–Apr 10.00–17.00 Tue–Sun; adult €3, children €1.50). The well-presented displays include stone tools, ceramics and ancient coins, church carvings, silver and pewter and a copy of Bellotto's painting of the Markt. Temporary exhibits are on the second floor, and you can also see the monastery's chapterhouse.

The **DDR-Museum** (Rottwerndorfer Str 56; ✆ 03501 774842; www.ddr-museumpirna.de; ⊕Apr–early Oct 10.00–18.00 Tue–Sun; early Oct–Mar 10.00–17.00 Tue–Thu, Sat/Sun; adult €2.50, children €2), about 2km south of the centre down Clara-Zetkin-Strasse (bus N or the rare 209, 216 or 218) is well hidden 100m down a lane beyond the swimming pool and sports centre, where you'll find a shed full of communist trivia, including radio technology, the Pioneers, and a complete home.

From Pirna the Elbe and accompanying road and railway are soon hemmed in by sandstone cliffs as they approach the Sächsishe Schweiz or Saxon Switzerland, part of the mountains along the Czech border. The railway (the Dresden–Prague main line) stays on the left/south side while the road follows the other bank, and ferries (see page 75) and the very occasional bridge link the two.

It was the Swiss painters Anton Graff (1736–1813) and Adrian Zingg (1734–1816) who dubbed the area the Saxon Switzerland; Caspar David Friedrich was drawn to Dresden by its art treasures but became a landscapist. He and Ludwig Richter hiked and painted here, and some of the paths they took have been linked as the Malerweg (Painters' Way), a loop from Pirna via Königstein, Schöna and Wehlen.

One hundred million years ago this area was a sea in which Cretaceous deposits were laid down and later compacted, deformed then eroded, forming what is known as the Quader sandstone; there are also some intrusions of basalt and granite. Thus there are tablelands or mesas and deep-cut gullies between them. These have microclimates, often inverted so that the higher land is warmer while the gorges, which often only have water after heavy rain or snowmelt, are cold and dark. These are largely filled with beech trees as well as oak, fir, birch and pine, and 27 species of fern; wildlife includes otter, shrew and salamander, owls, black storks, kingfishers and dippers. On the rock reefs there's heather, bilberry, red whortleberry and crowberry, with peregrines, kestrels and swifts. Altitudes range from 110m (by the Elbe at Pirna) to 723m (Hoher Schneeberg).

Conservation efforts began in 1877 but the 93km² national park was created only in 1990. For information contact the Nationalparkverwaltung Sächsische Schweiz, Schandauer Strasse 36, 01824 Königstein (✆ 035021 68229; www.nationalparksaechsische-schweiz.de). The park information centre is the Nationalparkhaus in Bad Schandau (Dresdner Str 2B; ✆ 035022 50240; e nationalparkhaus@lanu.de; www.lanu.de/nationalparkzentrum.html; ⊕ Apr–Oct 09.00–18.00 daily; Nov–Mar 09.00–17.00 Tue–Sun, Jan closed; adult €4, children, disabled, public transport users €3, family €7.50), and the Tourismusverband Sächsische Schweiz (Saxon Switzerland Tourism Association) is across the river (Am Bahnhof 6, 01814 Bad Schandau; ✆ 035022 4950; e info@saechsische-schweiz.de; www.saechsische-schweiz.de). There's also a protected area on the Czech side of the border, with an information centre in Krásna Lípa (Křinické Námešti 5; ✆ +42 413 99413).

WEHLEN AND RATHEN S-Bahn trains run once or twice an hour all the way to Schöna, right on the Czech border. The second stop after Pirna is Stadt Wehlen, across the river from the actual village (reached by ferry); the home of the post-Impressionist painter Robert Sterl (1867–1932) is 400m from the station at Robert-Sterl-Strasse 30 (✆ 035020 70216; e kontakt@robert-sterl-haus.de; www.robert-sterl-haus.de; ⊕ May–Oct 10.00–17.00 Thu–Sun & hols; adult €2.50, children €1.50). Also in Wehlen, Spasstours Stadt Wehlen at Mennickestrasse 29 (✆ 03524 71084; e info@elbeerleben.de) rent boats (€25–40/day) and will transport them to Dresden or Bad Schandau, as well as combining with Peers Bike-Adventures (Am Kronenhügel 5, Dohna 03529; ✆ 518853; www.peers-touren.de). There's a hotel and pensions here.

The next station is Kurort Rathen, again across the river from the resort, famed for its open-air theatre (see page 136), where in summer you can see dramatisations of Karl May's Wild West tales, as well as opera, musicals and concerts. A bit further west on the north bank is the **Bastei** or bastion, the classic viewpoint of Saxon Switzerland, as seen in all the tourist leaflets, where a bridge was built by 1826 purely for the use of tourists, and replaced in stone in 1851. There's a large restaurant and hotel here, strangely absent from the leaflets: the Berghotel und Panoramarestaurant Bastei (↘ *035204 7790;* e *info@bastei-berghotel.de; www.basteiberghotel.de;* $$), 194m above the river. Festung Express in Königstein (see below) runs an antique bus via Bad Schandau to the town and fortress of Königstein.

KÖNIGSTEIN The railway continues around a huge S-bend to the next station, at Königstein, this time on the right side of the river to visit the fortress. There's a ferry from the main road (accessible from the station's westbound platform, or follow signs from the road), and the paddle-steamers also call here.

Where to stay and eat

🏠 **Amtshof** Pirnaer Str 30; ↘ 68511. Restaurant with simple rooms.

🏠 **Gaststätte und Pension Sachsenstub'l** Amtsgasse 16; ↘ 035201 68332; www.sachsenstuebel.de. A nice townhouse. $$

🏠 **Hotel Lindenhof Königstein** Gohrischer Str 2; ↘ 035201 68243; e lindenhof@t-online.de; www.lindenhofkoenigstein.de. 3-star. $$

🏠 **Hotel-Pension Vogelsberg** Elbhäuserweg 20; ↘ 035201 7650. $$

There's also **Camping Königstein** (*Schandauer Str 25;* `035201 68224;` e *info@camping-koenigstein.de; www.camping-koenigstein.de;* ⏲*Apr–Oct*). Just north of Königstein in a loop of the Elbe, is the Lilienstein, a 415m-high mesa (table mountain) with a microwave tower and the three-star **Panorama Hotel Lilienstein** on top.

Practicalities You can rent inflatable boats from **Kanu Aktiv Tours** (*Schandauer Str 17;* `035021 599960;` e *info@kanu-aktiv-tours.de; www.kanu-aktiv-tours.de*) for €27 per day (or €22 for the Königstein–Pirna run); they also have an indoor climbing wall (*www.outdoor-inside.de;* ⏲*Apr–Oct 14.00–18.00 Tue–Sun;* €12 for 2hrs) – Saxon Switzerland is Germany's rock-climbing mecca, with 14,000 routes on 1,100 cliffs.

What to see and do This is a nice little town, with lots of facilities (including three tourist offices); heading downhill from the station it won't be long before you come to the Tourismusverein Elbsandsteingebirge (*Bahnhofstr 1;* `03501 599699;` e *sandsteinregion@aol.com; www.tourismusverein-elbsandsteingebirge.de;* ⏲*09.00–17.30 Mon–Fri, 09.00–15.00 Sat/Sun*). Just beyond is the main roundabout and a bridge over a stream, beyond which is the rival Haus des Gastes (*Scheiberberg 2;* `035021 68261;` e *touristinfo@koenigstein-sachsen.de; www.koenigsteinsachsen.de*) by a bakery-café and Festung Express (*Dresdner Str 1;* `67614`) which runs the bus to the Bastei (see above) and a roadtrain up to the fortress half-hourly in summer and for the Advent market.

To the west Amtsgasse and Goethestrasse lead to the half-timbered Haus des Gastes, the official tourist office, with the library and post office. From here a path to the fortress, marked with a blue stripe, starts up some stone flags and into a beech wood; after ten minutes turn right at a field and again after a couple of houses. A level gravel track leads below the fortress; after five minutes take a path up to the right, reaching the entrance in another five minutes. To the right, before the ticket office, is the Panoramaaufzug, a glass lift built in 2006, used mainly in summer and weekends (€1.50, free for disabled, buggies & under 16s). In summer there's a separate ticket office, further on, for the pedestrian route under the Torhaus; otherwise access is by a lift inside the walls, built in 1970 to carry small trucks.

The **Festung Königstein** (Königstein Fortress; ☏ 035021 64607; e *info@festungkoenigstein.de; www.festung-koenigstein.de;* ⏰*Apr–Sep 09.00–20.00, Oct 09.00–18.00, Nov–Mar 09.00–17.00, all daily; adult €5, children €3, family €12*) consists of over 30 buildings scattered across a 9.5ha plateau where a chapel had been built by the end of the 12th century and a castle by 1241. In the second half of the 15th century this was rebuilt and by 1589 was a full-blown fortress, with the Georgenburg added in the next century and rebuilt in 1816.

Audio-guides are available in any of eight languages for €2.50, or tours from €1.50 per person; but, loosely speaking, you should go around to the left from the lift. You'll pass the officers' mess, built in 1897 and now a restaurant; a barracks block built in 1589–90 and rebuilt in 1715–16 by Pöppelmann, and a wooden barracks block built in 1899; the guardhouse (with cells), built in 1883; stables, built in 1828; and the Gatehouse or Commandant's Residence, with a sitting room and kitchen nicely furnished as in 1900. Attached to it is the Georgenburg, where you may find an art exhibition, and on the first floor an exhibition from the Military History Museum (see page 219; ⏀*summer only*). Going around to the rear of the Torhaus and upstairs, you'll find a similar exhibition on the Saxon Artillery (⏀*Apr–Sep 10.00–17.30, Oct 10.00–16.30, Nov–Mar 09.00–15.45, all daily*). Carrying on along the walls, above the Elbe, at the rear of the Georgenburg you'll find the state prison museum, with information (mostly in German) on the notable people held here, including Böttger in 1706–07, before developing European porcelain; Mikhail Bakunin after the uprising of 1849, before being sent to Siberia; the social democrat leader August Bebel in 1872–74; and playwright Frank Wedekind in 1898 for satirising King Wilhelm II.

Going to the right on the walls, with some 18th-century cannon dotted around, you'll come to a lovely ochre-yellow Baroque pavilion, a Renaissance structure rebuilt in 1731 by August the Strong (with a sort of dumb waiter to raise a fully laid table from the kitchen below) and renamed the Friedrichsburg in honour of the Prussian king and crown prince.

Immediately beyond is the Blitzeichenplateau or Lightning Oak Plateau, where a 300-year-old oak stood until 1972, often being struck by lightning (three people were killed in 1925). To the right are 19th-century casemates for artillery shells and the Pestkasemate, made in an 8m-deep rock crack to isolate plague victims.

Heading back to the right you'll come to the Garrison church, on the site of the 13th-century chapel, rebuilt in 1676 with a tower added in 1681 (⏀*May–Oct daily & w/ends in Advent; live music at 15.00 on 3rd Sun of the month May–Oct & every Sun in*

Advent). The Magdalenburg, built in 1621–22, was rebuilt by Pöppelmann in 1725 to house August the Strong's 250,000-litre wine store; in summer there are exhibitions on the upper floor. The Brunnenhaus (wellhouse) houses an information centre and shop in summer and an exhibition on the fortress waterworks, a well dug by Saxon miners in 1563–69 and now restored, with a 'wellcam' giving a view of the water 152m below. At the rear is the Schatzhaus (treasure house), built in 1854–55 with walls 1.7m thick – up to two million thaler were kept here.

In addition to the restaurant in the officers' mess, there's the better Erlebnis restaurant In Den Kasematten (\ *035021 64444;* e *info@festung.com; www.kasematten.de*), below the lift, which opens for brunch (⊕*11.00–15.00 daily; adult* €*16, children* €*9*), with costumes and entertainment relating to the years 1700 or 1900.

Leaving the lift to the right, there's another path down to the town, marked with red dots, which drops gradually around the other side of the fortress and on down a flagged road to meet the main road above the Edeka supermarket; it's best to go on through Königstein village for the station, as there's no pavement on the main road.

BAD SCHANDAU The next station to the east, **Bad Schandau**, is opposite the town (the largest on the Upper Elbe) but for once linked by a bridge as well as a ferry.

Practicalities There's a tourist information centre (⊕*08.00–17.00 daily, winter Mon–Fri only*) at the station, which is served by six EuroCity trains a day and one night train, in addition to the S-Bahn. The road bridge is not far west of the station and the town, or there's a ferry every 30 minutes (see page 75).

Where to stay and eat

⌂ **Parkhotel Bad Schandau** Rudolf-Sendig-Str 12; ☎ 035022 520; e info@parkhotel-bad-schandau.de; www.parkhotel-bad-schandau.de. The best (4-star) hotel, opposite the elevator, in the beautiful Villa Sendig (1880) & Königsvilla (1887) with modern wings housing a spa & beauty centre & another Mediterranean restaurant. $$$

⌂ **Apparthotel Am Schlossberg** Elbstr 6, by the national park ☎ 035022 925100; e mail@apparthotel-amschlossberg; www.apparthotel-am-schlossberg. Has plenty of good disabled-accessible rooms. $$

⌂ **Gasthaus Zum Roten Haus** Marktstr 10; ☎ 035022 42343; e hotel_zumrotenhaus@web.de; www.hotel-zum-roten-haus.de; $$. A nice hotel-restaurant.

⌂ **Sigl's Hotel-Bistro-Bierbar** Kirnitzschtalstr 17; ☎ 035022 40702; e sigls@weka-touristik.de. A stylish little place on the west side of the park. $$

✕ **Konditorei-Café Stammler** Opposite the tourist office.

In **Ostrau** there are more **spa resorts**, the Campingplatz-Pension Ostrauer Mühle (☎ 035022 42742; e info@ostrauermuehle.de; www.ostrauermuehle.de), which charges €4.75 per person from 15 June to 15 September (€4.25 in low season; children €3/2.75) plus €2.75–4.50 for a tent and €1.75 for a car; there are also rooms ($$) and Wanderquartier (Hikers' Quarters, 34 bunks in 8 rooms) at €7.50 per person. There's also a **youth hostel** here at Dorfstrasse 14 (☎ 035022 42408; www.djh-sachsen.de), and pensions (and a Chinese restaurant) along the road east from Bad Schandau.

At the Nationalparkhaus there's the **Restaurant der Jahrezeiten** (☎ 035022 50783; ⏱11.00–21.00) which offers an organic breakfast buffet (⏱07.30–10.00). On

11

Kirchstrasse, the pedestrian alley opposite the church, are the Kaisergarten (Chinese) and Kreta (Greek) restaurants, and the Mario Gelato Eiscafé.

What to see and do From the bridge, you'll come first to the Nationalpark Haus (see above), then at the west end of Marktplatz the Haus des Gastes (*Markt 12;* \ *035022 90030/33;* e *info@bad-schandau.de; www.bad-schandau.de;* ⊕*mid Mar–Oct 09.00–21.00 daily; winter 09.00–18.00 Mon–Fri, 09.00–13.00 Sat/Sun & hols*), supplies tourist information in a former Renaissance brewery (there's access to the main room, with leaflets, when the office is closed).

To the east the Jugendstil Sendig Fountain, built in 1896, was destroyed in 1945, rebuilt then damaged by flooding and is being refurbished again. Behind it a whole block is being rebuilt as a five-star Medical Wellness Hotel. At the far end of Marktplatz the **Johanniskirche** (always open, via the Pfarrhaus courtyard) probably dates from the 14th century, with its tower added in 1645 by a priest from Transylvania and the nave rebuilt in 1671. It was burnt down and rebuilt in 1709–10, and refitted internally in 1876–77 with a cassette ceiling and stained glass. In 1927 an altar originally in Dresden's Kreuzkirche was installed, with splendid reliefs (1574–79) of the Passover meal and the Last Supper. There are striking photos of the flood of 2002 (marginally lower than the record flood of 1845) which reached the ground-floor ceiling of the Pfarrhaus; that of 2006 only reached a foot above the floor.

A little further east, at the Hotel Lindenhof, you can turn inland to the Kirnitzsch Valley, with the Kurpark (spa park) leading to the town museum (closed due to flood damage, but with a few millstones and stone moulds outside) to the right, and the terminal of the **Kirnitzschtalbahn**, a rural tramway opened in 1898 that runs up the valley to the Lichtenhainer Waterfall (⊕Apr–Oct every 30mins 08.15–19.45; Nov–Mar roughly every 70mins 09.50–16.15; adult €3 sgl, €4 return, children/bikes €1.50/2, day €5/2.50). Historic trams are used on May Day, the last full weekend of July (the Kirnitzschtalfest) and 3 October (German Reunification Day). The trip takes 25–30 minutes, and walking back will take 2½ hours. It's 1.5km up the valley to the Pflanzengarten (Flower Garden; ⊕Mar–Oct 08.00–19.00) and another 1.5km to the Fortshaus (Forest House), where you'll see one of the largest spruce trees in Europe, 54m high and around 360 years old. From the Kurpark a path also leads up to the east to Ostrau, a hilltop area of sanatoria; there's a network of marked paths linking Ostrau, the waterfall and through the hills to the east to Schmilka (7km by the most direct path).

Just east by the river the **Toskana Therme** is a very modern spa (Rudolf-Sendig-Str 8A; ☎ 035022 54610; e badschandau@toskana-therme.de; www.toskanatherme.de; ⊕10.00–22.00 Sun–Thu, 10.00–midnight Fri/Sat, full moon nights to 02.00; €11 2hrs, €18 day, children €5.50/10.50), with pools, saunas, treatments and a good Mediterranean restaurant. Just beyond is an elevator, opened in 1905, that rises 50m to the Ostrau Plateau (⊕Apr–Oct 09.00–18.00 daily, May–Sep 09.00–19.00 daily, Nov–Mar 09.00–17.00 Tue–Sun; adult €1.50, €2.50 return, children, disabled, bikes €1/1.50, family €4/6.50).

SCHMILKA From Bad Schandau you can follow the riverside cycle path east to Schmilka (5km), on the Czech border. The S-Bahn trains turn around here, with a connecting ferry (see page 75), as well as four buses a day. At weekends, in addition to the many hikers, Dresdeners come here to walk across the border for cheap beer and shopping.

Opposite the ferry a side road leads past the **Pension Rauschenstein** (✆ *035022 40900;* e *info@schmilka.de; www.pension-rauschenstein.de*), **Pension Elb-Café** (✆ *035022 42398*), **Haus Alpenrose** (✆ *035022 41976*), and a couple of lovely old pensions booked through the Pension Rauchenstein. At the top is a **Bistro-Imbiss** to grab a snack before you head on; the road leads 6.5km to the **Berghotel Grosserwinterberg** (✆ *035022 40050;* e *hotelgwb@aol.com; www.elbsandstein.de*), with a popular mountaintop restaurant. Trails lead through the hills to Ostrau, Lichterhainer Waterfall and other points in the Krinitzschtal; overnight camping is not allowed but hikers can sleep in Boofen or bivouac shelters.

SEBNITZ AND STOLPEN From Bad Schandau a scenic railway crosses the river and follows the lovely Sebnitz Valley; trains on route RB71 run every two hours, taking 25 minutes to the town of **Sebnitz**, straddling the Czech border, which is famed for the manufacture of silk flowers, as shown in both the Kunstblumen-und-Heimat-museum (*Hertigswalder Str 12;* ◷ *10.00–17.00 Tue–Sun*), and the Deutsche Kunstblumen Zentrum (*Neustädter Weg 10;* ✆ *035971 53181;* ◷ *10.00–17.00 Tue–Sun*), both 1.5km from the station. Tourist information is available at Schillerstrasse 3 (✆ *035971 53079;* e *fvb_sebnitz@t-online.de; www.sebnitz.de*).

Trains continue for 14 minutes to Neustadt, beyond which there's an hourly service (Mon–Fri) to Pirna. Twelve minutes from Neustadt (28mins from Pirna) is the station of **Stolpen**, 2km south of the small town and castle (*Schlossstr 10;* ☏ *035973 23410;* e *burg.stolpen@t-online.de; www.burg.stolpen.de;* ⊕*Apr–Oct 09.00–18.00, Nov–Mar 10.00–16.00, all daily; adult €3, children €2.50, tour €30*), famed as the place where August the Strong's discarded mistress **Countess Cosel** (1680–1765) was imprisoned for the last 49 years of her life. She divorced Count Hoym, one of August's ministers, in 1699 to become the king's mistress, bearing him three children. However, her jealousy of his Polish mistresses led to her being imprisoned here from 1716; even though August died in 1733 she was unable to persuade his son to release her and remained here longing for death. Her tomb is in the chapel, and of course there's a very popular exhibition in the Cosel (or Johannis) Tower on the whole sorry story. You can also visit medieval torture chambers, the Bishop's Court or administrative centre, and the well buildings, with models illustrating the castle's water supply.

The castle was founded in 1222 and was attacked in the Hussite wars, the Thirty Years War, the Seven Years War and by the French in 1813; from 1859 it was restored by King Johann. Below in the attractive Baroque town the Stolpen information office is at Schlossstrasse 14A (☏ *035973 19433;* e *stolpeninformation@t-online.de; www.stolpen-info.de*).

12 Language

GRAMMAR AND PRONUNCIATION

The German language is part of the Indo-European family, its vocabulary incorporating some Latin-/French-based words, and more recently English words. It's an inflected language, with three genders in the singular (which are all the same in the plural). The initial letters of nouns are capitalised; verbs always come at the end of a sentence, and there are lots of compound nouns (without hyphens to help foreigners). All in all, it's a very distinctive language, which can be learnt fairly easily if you're willing to absorb and stick to its strict rules.

The *Umlaut* (two dots above an a, i or u) is an accent that shows the 'fronting' of that vowel (ie: being pronounced with the tongue at the front of the mouth and rounder lips) due to the influence of a 'front' vowel in the next syllable; so an 'a' becomes like 'eh', an 'o' like 'ur' and a 'u' like 'ew'. This is common in plurals (*Mann/Männer* – man/men) and comparatives (*lang/länger* – long/longer). In email addresses, for instance, these can be spelt ae, ie and ue; in an index you may find words with umlauts listed as if the umlaut is not there, or following the umlaut-free letters.

Another peculiarity is the *Eszett* (ß), representing a double-s, which is on its way out in the modern online/anglicised world, and is not used in this book, or in Switzerland.

Be aware of the German method of telling the time – *Halb sechs* (literally half-six) means half an hour before six o'clock, ie: 5.30. not 6.30, and so on.

Saxony (and Upper Thuringia) do have a pretty thick accent but this is not really a problem in the city. However rural bus drivers can be a bit hard to follow. In Lusatia (northeast of Dresden) the Sorbian minority speak their own Slavic language, and the local Germans also have a Lusatian dialect.

USEFUL WORDS AND PHRASES

Phonetic guides to pronunciation are given in parentheses for the following German words and phrases:

THE BASICS

Good morning	*Guten Morgen* [Gooten morgen]
Good afternoon	*Guten Nachmittag* [Gooten nachmittarg]
Good evening	*Guten Abend* [Gooten arbent]
Hello	*Guten Tag* [Gooten targ]
Goodbye	*Auf wiedersehen* [Owf veederzeyen]
My name is …	*Ich heisse …* [Ik hysser]
What is your name?	*Wie heissen Sie?* (formal) [vee hyssen zee]
	Wie heisst Du? (informal) [vee hysst doo]
I am from …	*Ich komme aus …* [Ik comma ows]
England/America/Australia	*England/Amerika/Australien*

How are you?	*Wie geht's?* [Vee gates]
Pleased to meet you	*Angenehm* (formal) [Ann-ge-name]
	Freut mich (less formal) [Froit mick]
Please	*Bitte* [bitter]
There you are (when giving something to someone)	*Bitte schön* [bitter shern]
Thank you	*Danke* [danker]
	(Careful! This does mean 'thank you' if you say it *after* you have accepted and received something. However, if you anticipate being given something and say it before the action is completed, for example if someone offers you a cup of tea, it means 'No thank you' and you won't get that cuppa!)
Excuse me	*Entschuldigen Sie* [Entshooldigen zee]
Don't mention it	*Bitte schön* [bitter shern]
Cheers!	*Prost!* [prrowst]
yes	*Ja* [yah]
no	*Nein* [nine]
I don't understand	*Ich verstehe nicht* [Ik vershtayer nikt]
Please would you speak more slowly	*Können Sie bitte ganz langsam sprechen* [Kernen zee gans langsaam sprrecken]
Do you understand?	*Verstehen Sie?* [vershtayen zee]

QUESTIONS

how?	*Wie?* [Vee]	which?	*Welche?* [Velcher]
what?	*Was?* [Vas]	when?	*Wann?* [Van]
where?	*Wo?* [Vo]	why?	*Warum?* [Varoom]
what is it?	*Was ist das?* [Vas isst dass]	who?	*Wer?* [Ver]
		how much?	*Wieviel?* [Veefeel]

NUMBERS

1	*eins* [eynz]	16	*sechzehn* [zeckzayn]
2	*zwei* [zwy]	17	*siebzehn* [zeezayn]
3	*drei* [dry]	18	*achtzehn* [ucktzayn]
4	*vier* [fear]	19	*neunzehn* [noynzayn]
5	*fünf* [foonf]	20	*zwanzig* [zwansigg]
6	*sechs* [zex]	21	*einundzwanzig* [eyn-unt-zwansigg]
7	*sieben* [zeeben]	30	*dreissig* [drysigg]
8	*acht* [akt]	40	*vierzig* [fearsigg]
9	*neun* [noyn]	50	*fünfzig* [foonfsigg]
10	*zehn* [zain]	60	*sechszig* [zecksigg]
11	*elf* [elf]	70	*siebszig* [zeebsigg]
12	*zwölf* [zwurlf]	80	*achtzig* [uchtsigg]
13	*dreizehn* [dryzayn]	90	*neunzig* [noynsigg]
14	*vierzehn* [fearzayn]	100	*hundert* [hun-dirt]
15	*fünfzehn* [foonfzayn]	1,000	*tausend* [tau-sent]

TIME

What time is it?	*Wie spät ist es?* [Vee shpate isst ess]
It's ... am	*Es ist ... Uhr morgens* [Ess isst... oower more-genz]
afternoon	*Es ist ... Uhr nachmittags* [Ess isst... oower nuck-mittargs]
evening	*Es ist ... Uhr nachts* [Ess isst... oower nuckts]
today	*Heute* [hoyter]
tonight	*Heute Nacht* [hoyter nuckt]
tomorrow	*Morgen* [morgan]
yesterday	*Gestern* [gestern]
morning	*Morgen* [morgan]
evening	*Abend* [are-bent]

Days

Monday	*Montag* [monn-targ]
Tuesday	*Dienstag* [deens-targ]
Wednesday	*Mittwoch* [mitt-vock]
Thursday	*Donnerstag* [donners-targ]
Friday	*Freitag* [fry-targ]
Saturday	*Samstag/Sonnabend* [zams-targ/zonare-bent]
Sunday	*Sonntag* [zon-targ]

Months

January	*Januar* [yanwar]
February	*Februar* [febwar]
March	*März* [merz]
April	*April* [appril]
May	*Mai* [my]
June	*Juni* [yoonee]
July	*Juli* [yoolee]
August	*August* [owgust]
September	*September* [september]
October	*Oktober* [ocktoowber]
November	*November* [november]
December	*Dezember* [deezember]

GETTING AROUND
Public transport

I'd like ...	*Ich möchte* [Ik merckter]
... a ticket	*eine Fahrkarte* [ayna farkarte]
there and back	*hin und zurück* [hin unt zoorook]
one-way	*einzel* [aynsell]
... a return ticket	*... eine Rückfahrkarte* [ayna rruk-far-karter]
I want to go to ...	*Ich will nach ... reisen* [Ik vil nack wrysen]
How much is it?	*Wieviel kostet es?* [vee feel costet ess]

What time does the train/ the bus leave?	*Wann fährt der Zug/der Bus ab?* [van fert der tsoog/der boos ab]
What time is it now?	*Wie spät ist es?* [Vee shpate isst ess]
The train has been ...	*Der Zug ...* [der tsoog]
...delayed	*... hat Verspätung* [hat fershpaytung]
...cancelled	*... annulliert* [a-null-eert]
first class	*Erste Klasse* [ersta klasser]
second class	*Zweite Klasse* [zwyter klasser]
sleeping car	*Schlafwagen* [schlaaff-wargen]
platform	*Gleis* [glyss]
ticket office	*Fahrkartenschalter* [far-carrten-shalter]
timetable	*Fahrplan* [far-plan]
supplementary charge	*Zuschlag* [tsoo-shlarg]
from	*von* [fon]
to	*nach* [nack]
bus station	*Busbahnhof* [boos-barn-hohwf]
railway station	*Bahnhof* [barn-hohwf]
airport	*Flughafen* [floog-haff-en]
port	*Hafen* [haff-en]
bus	*Bus* [boos]
train	*Zug* [tsoog]
plane	*Flugzeug* [floowg-tsoyg]
boat	*Schiff* [shiff]

ferry	*Fähre* [fairer]
car	*Auto* [ow-tow]
4x4	*4x4/Allradantrieb* [fear mall fear]/[all-rart-ann-treeb]
taxi	*Taxi* [taxi]
motorbike/moped	*Motorrad/Moped* [mow-torr-rart/mow-pedd]
bicycle	*Fahrrad* [far-rart]
arrival/departure	*Ankunft/Abfahrt* [ann-koonft/abb-fart]
here	*hier* [heer]
there	*da* [dar]
bon voyage!	*Gute Reise!* [gooter rye-ser]

Private transport

Is this the road to…?	*Ist diese die Strasse nach…?*
	[Isst dee-ser dee strrasser nack]
Where is the service station?	*Wo ist der nächste Tankstelle?*
	[Vo isst der neckste tank-shteller]
Please fill it up	*Volltanken, bitte* [voll-tank-ken bitter]
I'd like … litres of [ ]	[Number] *Liter* … [leeter] [Type], *bitte!* [bitter]
diesel	*Diesel* [dees-sel]
petrol	*Benzin* [benn-tzeen]
I have broken down	*Ich habe eine Panne* [Ik harbour ayna panner]

Road signs

give way	*Vorfahrt beachten* [four-fart bee-uckt-ten]
danger	*Gefahrstelle* [ge-far-shteller]
no entry	*Keine Einfahrt* [kiner ayn-fart]
detour	*Umleitung* [oom-ligh-tung]
one-way	*Einbahnstrasse* [ayn-barn-shteller]
toll	*Gebühr* [ge-bure]
entry	*Einfahrt* [ayn-fart]
exit	*Ausfahrt* [ows-far]
keep clear	*frei halten* [fry-hal-ten]

Directions

Where is it?	*Wo ist es?* [vo isst ess]
Go straight ahead	*geradeaus* [ge-rad-e-ows]
turn left	*nach links abbiegen* [nack links ab-bee-gen]
turn right	*nach rechts abbiegen* [nack reckts ab-bee-gen]
...at the traffic lights	*... an der Ampel* [ann dare am-pel]
...at the roundabout	*... an dem Kreisverkehr* [ann daym crise-ferr-kerr]
north	*Nord* [nort]
south	*Süd* [zooed]
east	*Ost* [osst]
west	*West* [vest]
behind	*hinter* [hint-err]

286

in front of	*Vor/gegenüber* [for/gay-gen-oober]
near/far	*nah/weit* [naa/vite]
opposite	*gegenüber* [gay-gen-oober]

Street signs

entrance	*Eingang* [ayn-gang]
exit	*Ausgang* [ows-gang]
open	*geöffnet* [ge-erff-net]
closed	*geschlossen* [ge-shloss-en]
toilets – men/women	*Toiletten – Herren/Damen*
	[toy-let-ten – hair-en/dar-men]
information	*Auskunft* [ows-koonft]

Tourist information

| tourist information office | *Fremdenverkehrsamt* [fremt-enn-fer-kers-ampt] |
| calendar of events | *Veranstaltungskalender* [fer-an-stal-tungs-kal-en-der] |

ACCOMMODATION

| Where is a cheap/ comfortable hotel? | *Wo gibt es ein billiges/bequemes Hotel* [vo gibt ess ayn bill-ig-ess/bee-kwem-ez hoe-tell] |
| hostel/guesthouse/homestay | *Jugendherberge/Pension/Ferienwohnung* [you-gend-her-burger/ponsee-on/ferry-envohnung] |

Could you please write the address?	*Bitte schreiben Sie die Adresse* [bitter shryben zee dee add-re-sser owf]
Do you have any rooms available?	*Haben Sie freie Zimmer?* [har-ben zee fry-er zimm-er]
I'd like ...	*Ich möchte ...* [Ik merckte]
... a single room	... *ein Einzelzimmer* [ayn ayn-zell-zimm-er]
... a double room	... *ein Doppelzimmer* (ie: with one double bed) [ayn do-pell-zimm-er]
... a room with two beds	... *ein zwei-bett Zimmer* [ayn zwy-bet-zimm-er]
with a bathroom	*mit Bad* [mitt bart]
to share a dorm	*ein Platz in ein Mehrbettzimmer* [ayn plats in ayn mare-bet zimm-er]
How much is it per night/ person?	*Was kostest es pro Nacht/pro Person?* [vas kostet ess pro nackt/pro per-zone]
Where is the toilet?	*Wo sind die Toiletten?* [vo sint dee toy-let-ten]
Where is the bathroom?	*Wo ist das Badezimmer?* [vo isst dass barda-zimm-er]
Is there hot water?	*Gibt es heisses Wasser?* [gibt ess heysses wass-er]
Is there electricity?	*Gibt es Ström?* [gibt ess shtrome]
Is breakfast included?	*Ist Frühstück inbegriffen?* [isst frew-shtook in-be-griff-enn]
I am leaving today	*Ich reise heute ab* [Ik rey-ser hoy-ter ab]

FOOD

Do you have a table for ... people?	*Haben Sie einen Tisch für ... Personen?* [hab-en zee ayn-en tish fuwer ... per-zone-en]
dishes/a menu for children?	*Gerichte/eine Speisekarte für Kinder?* [ge-rick-te/ayna shpy-zer-carr-terr fuwer kinn-der]
I am a vegetarian	*Ich bin Vegetarier* [Ik binn vague-a-tair-ree-er]
Do you have any vegetarian dishes?	*Haben Sie vegetarische Gerichte?* [har-ben zee vague-a-tair-ish-e ge-rick-te]
Please bring me ... a fork/knife/spoon	*Bitte bringen Sir mir ...* [bitter bring-en zee meer] *eine Gabel/ein Messer/einen Löffel* [ayna gar-bel/ayn messa/ayn-en ler-fell]
Please may I have the bill?	*Die Rechnung bitte?* [dee reck-nung bitter]
Keep the change	*Stimmt so!* [shtimpt zo]
tip	*Trinkgeld* [trink-gelt]

Basics

bread	*Brot* [brr + oe [as in hoe] + t]
butter	*Butter* [butter] [the u is like the oom in oomph]
cheese	*Käse* [kay-zerr]
olive oil	*Olivenöl* [o-leave-en-erl]
pepper	*Pfeffer* [pfe-fer]
salt	*Salz* [zalz]
mustard	*Senf* [zenf]

| vinegar | *Essig* [ess-ig] |
| sugar | *Zucker* [zuu-ker] |

Vegetables
cauliflower	*Blumenkohl* [blue-men-coal]
carrots	*Mohrrüben/Karotten* [more-rewb-en/carr-ott-en]
garlic	*Knoblauch* [knoh-blowwk]
onion	*Zwiebel* [zwee-bell]
asparagus	*Spargel* [sparr-gell]
potato	*Kartoffel* [car-toff-ell]
chips	*Pommes frites/Pommes* [pom-ess freetz/pomm-ess]

Meat
beef	*Rindfleisch* [rint-flysh]
chicken	*Hähnchen* [hen-cken]
pork	*Kalbfleisch* [calp-flysh]
lamb	*Lammfleisch* [Lamb-flysh]
sausage	*Wurst* [voo-erst]

DRINKS
beer	*Bier* [beer]
coffee	*Kaffee* [café]
fruit juice	*Obstsaft* [ob-st-zafft]
milk	*Milch* [millck]

tea	*Tee* [tay]
water	*Wasser* [vasser]
sparkling or still	*Mit Kohlensäure oder ohne Kohlensäure?*
	[Mitt coal-en-zoy-rer odour owner coal-en-zoy-rer]
wine	*Wein* [vine]

SHOPPING

I'd like to buy...	*Ich möchte .... kaufen* [Ik merckter cow-fen]
How much is it?	*Was kostet es?* [vas koss-tet ess]
I don't like it	*Es gefällt mir nicht* [ess ge-fellt meer nickt]
I'm just looking	*Ich möchte mich nur umsehen*
	[Ik merchter mick noower um- (u as in oomph) zeh-en]
It's too expensive	*Es ist zu teuer* [ess isst tsoo toy-er]
I'll take it	*Ich neheme es* [Ik name-er ess]
Do you accept … ?	*Nehmen Sie … ?* [neigh-men zee]
credit cards	*Kreditkarten?* [credeet-carton]
travellers' cheques	*Reiseschecks* [rey-ser shex]
receipt	*Quittung* [qwvit-tung]
more	*mehr* [mare]
less	*weniger* [venig-ga]
a bit smaller	*etwas kleine* [et-vas kligh-ner]
a bit bigger	*etwas grösser* [et-vas grow-ser]

COMMUNICATIONS

I am looking for…	*Ich suche...* [Ik zoocke]
bank	*eine Bank* [ayna bank]
post office	*Postamt* [posst-ampt]
church	*Kirche* [kirr-cker]
embassy	*Botschaft* [bowt-shafft]
exchange office	*Wechselstube* [veck-sel stoober]

EMERGENCY

Help!	*Hilfe!* [hill-ferr]
Call a doctor!	*Rufen Sie einen Arzt!* [roofen zee ayn-en artst]
There's been an accident	*Es ist ein Unfall geschehen* [ess isst ayn un-fall ge-shay-en]
I'm lost	*Ich habe mich verlaufen* [Ik harbour mick fer-lowf-fen]
Leave me in peace/Go away!	*Lass mich in Ruhe!/Geh weg!* [Lass mick in roower/Gay vek]
police	*Polizei* [pol-iz-eye]
fire	*Feuer* [foy-er]
ambulance	*Krankenwagen* [crank-en-var-gen]
thief/theft	*Dieb/Diebstahl* [deeb/deeb-shtarl]
hospital	*Krankenhaus* [crank-en-house]
I am ill	Ich *bin* krank [Ik bin crank]

HEALTH

diarrhoea	*Durchfall* [doo-erck-fall]
nausea	*Übelkeit* [oo-bell-kite]
doctor	*Arzt* [artst]
prescription	*Rezept* [re-zept]
pharmacy	*Apoteke* [ap-oh-take-er]
headache tablets	*Tabletten gegen Kopfschmerzen* [tab-let-en]
antibiotics	*Antibiotikum* [an-tee-bee-ott-ee-come]
antiseptic	*Antiseptikum* [an-tee-sep-tee-come]
tampon	*Tampon* [tam-ponn]
condom	*Kondom/Präservativ* [con-dom/pres-erv-a-teev]
contraceptive	*empfängnisverhütungs Mittel* [emp-feng-nis-fer-hoot-ungs-mittell]
sunblock	*Sonnenschutzcreme* [zon-en-shutz-cray-mer]
I am …	*Ich bin …* [Ik bin]
… asthmatic	*… asthmatisch* [ass-mat-tish]
… epileptic	*… epileptisch/fallsüchtig* [eppy-lepp-tish/fall-zoock-tig]
… diabetic	*… zuckerkrank* [soo-ker-crank]
I'm allergic to …	*Ich bin allergisch gegen …* [Ik bin al-er-gish gay-gen …]
… penicillin	*… Penizillin* [pen-its-ill-en]
… nuts	*… Nüsse* [nusser]
… bees	*… Bienen* [been-en]

TRAVEL WITH CHILDREN

Is there a … ?	*Gibt es … ?* [gibbed ess]
somewhere I can change my baby?	*irgendwo Ich meinem Baby die Windein wechseln kann?* [irr-gend-vo ik mine-en bay-bee dee vin-deln veck-seln can]
a children's menu?	*eine Speisekarte für Kinder* [ayna shpi-ser-carter fuwer kind-err]
Do you have … ?	*Haben Sie … ?* [har-ben zee]
baby milk/baby food	*Babymilch/Babynahrung* [bay-bee-millck/bay-bee ner-rung]
nappies	*Windeln* [vin-deln]
potty	*Töpfchen* [terpf-cken]
babysitting service	*einen Babysitter-Service* [ayn-en bay-bee-sitt-er servees]
highchair	*einein Hochstuhl* [ayn-en hock-shtool]
Are children allowed?	*Sind Kinder wilkommen?* [zint kind-err vil-kom-men]

OTHER

my/mine/ours/yours	*meine/meins/unsere/euer/* [miner/mynz/oy-er]
and/some/but	*und/manche/aber* [und/man-cker/arb-er]
this/that	*dies/das* [deez/dass]
expensive/cheap	*teuer/billig* [toy-er/bill-ig]
beautiful/ugly	*schön/hässlich* [shern/hess-lick]

294

old/new	*alt/neu* [alt/noy]
good/bad	*gut/schlecht* [goot/shleckt]
early/late	*früh/spät* [froo/shpate]
hot/cold	*heiss/kalt* [heyss/calt]
difficult/easy	*schwierig/leicht* [shweerrig/lie-ckt]
boring/interesting	*langweilig/interessant* [lang-vy-lig/in-ter-ress-ant]

FCO TRAVEL ADVICE
know before you go
fco.gov.uk/travel

Bradt Travel Guides is a partner to the 'know before you go' campaign, masterminded by the UK Foreign and Commonwealth Office to promote the importance of finding out about a destination before you travel. By combining the up-to-date advice of the FCO with the in-depth knowledge of Bradt authors, you'll ensure that your trip will be as trouble-free as possible.

www.fco.gov.uk/travel

12

13 Further Information

BOOKS

Clayton, Anthony and Russell, Alan (eds) *Dresden: A City Reborn* Berg, 2001. A celebration of Dresden's cultural greatness in the past, its destruction and its recreation.

McLachlan, Gordon *Rough Guide to Germany* 6th edn, Rough Guides, 2004

Ritter, Maria *Return to Dresden* University Press of Mississippi, 2004. A Californian psychologist returns to the scenes of her wartime childhood and attempts to deal with questions of German guilt and knowledge.

Ten Dyke, Elizabeth *Dresden: Paradoxes of Memory and History* Routledge (Studies in History and Anthropology), 2001. An anthropological (but very readable) study of Dresden and its residents confronting the changes of the early 1990s, after the collapse of communism.

Vonnegut, Kurt *Slaughterhouse-Five* 1970, available in various paperback editions. Partly an autobiographical account of the bombing of Dresden, partly science fiction, and wholly a satire on the absurdity of war.

Watanabe-O'Kelly, Helen *Court Culture In Dresden: From Renaissance to Baroque* Palgrave Macmillan, 2002. An academic study of the way in which Dresden's electors (from the mid-16th to the early 18th century) used art and culture as a tool for enhancing their power and achieving their political ambitions. It looks at topics as diverse as alchemy and August the Strong's conversion to Catholicism, as well as music, theatre and art collections.

Zumpe, Dieter and Hohmuth, Jurgen *Dresden Heute/Today* Prestel Verlag, 2003. With double-page photos (and some aerial photos), this charts the city's glorious rebirth.

There are several excellent books on the bombing of February 1945 – just avoid the one by David Irving:

Addison, Paul and Crang, Jeremy (eds) *Firestorm* Pimlico, 2006

McKee, Alexander *The Devil's Tinderbox, Dresden 1945* Souvenir Press, 1982 (paperback 2000)

Musgrove, Frank *Dresden and the Heavy Bombers: An RAF Navigator's Perspective* Leo Cooper Ltd, 2005

Taylor, Frederick *Dresden: Tuesday, February 13, 1945* HarperCollins, 2005

ART AND CULTURE

Addison, Julia de Wolf *The Art of the Dresden Gallery: Notes and Observations upon the Old and Modern Masters and Paintings in the Royal Collection* Kessinger Publishing, 2004. A reprint of a 1906 guide to Dresden's royal art collections.

Bischoff, Ulrich, Hipp, Elisabeth and Nugent, Jeanne *From Caspar David Friedrich to Gerhard Richter: German Paintings from Dresden* Getty Trust Publications, 2006.

The catalogue of an exhibition at the J Paul Getty Museum, including works by Carl Gustav Carus, J C Dahl, Otto Dix, and Karl Schmidt-Rottluff.

Harran, Jim and Susan *Dresden Porcelain Studios: Identification & Value Guide* Collector Books, 2001 (hardcover)

Harran, Jim and Susan *Meissen Porcelain: Identification and Value Guide* Collector Books, 2005 (hardcover)

Marx, Harald et al, photographs Karpinski, Jurgen *Picture-Gallery Old Masters: Masterpieces of Dresden* Art Stock, 2006. A short hardcover guide to the Old Masters Gallery.

Marx, Harald, Weber, Gregor (translator Stockman, Russell) *Dresden in the Ages of Splendor and Enlightenment: Eighteenth-Century Paintings from the Old Masters Picture Gallery* Columbus Museum of Art, 2000. A hardcover catalogue of an exhibition in Columbus, Ohio.

Princely Splendor: The Dresden Court 1580–1620 Staatliche Kunstsammlungen, Dresden, 2004. The catalogue of an exhibition at the Metropolitan Museum of Art, New York.

The Glory of Baroque Dresden: The State Art Collections Dresden Mississippi Commission for International Cultural Exchange, 2004. The catalogue of an exhibition at the Mississippi Arts Pavilion.

The Splendor of Dresden: Five Centuries of Art Collecting – An Exhibition From the State Art Collections of Dresden Metropolitan Museum of Art, 1978

Walther, Angelo *Canaletto in Dresden* Gordon & Breach, 1995. A German-language paperback on Bernardo Bellotto's work in Dresden and nearby.

MAPS

All except the Borch map have legends in English as well as German.

ADAC Dresden A 1:20,000 map by the German drivers' association, with every street and public building marked, as well as all bus and tram routes, one-way streets and car parks. On the reverse is a 1:100,000 regional map.

Borch Dresden A 1:20,000 map extending east as far as Pillnitz, with a 1:10,000 plan of the central areas and a 1:130,000 regional map (including Saxon Switzerland) on the rear.

Falk Dresden A 1:23,500 city plan with all landmarks, one-way streets and car parks, including outer suburbs. The Falk Extra version is ingeniously folded in a more user-friendly way, so that users won't find themselves fighting the map on a windy street corner. There's also a pocket-sized version, which still includes a regional map.

WEBSITES

www.dresden-tourist.de Dresden Tourist Office
www.germany-tourism.co.uk German Tourist Office
www.dresden.de Dresden City Hall
www.sachsen.de Saxony State Government
www.visitsaxony.com Saxony Tourist Office
www.schloesserland-sachsen.de The castles of Saxony

www.dresden-airport.de Dresden Airport
www.bahn.de/p/view/international/englisch/international_guests.shtml
German Railways
www.saechsische-dampfschiffahrt.de/?sprache=en Saxon Steamship Line
www.dvbag.de Dresden's public transport system

Festivals
www.musikfestspiele.com Dresden Music Festival
www.elbhangfest.de Elbe Slope Festival
www.zeitmusik.de Dresden Festival of Contemporary Music
www.dixieland.de Dixieland Festival

Listings magazines All give details of upcoming cultural events, entertainments and restaurants.

www.dresden.nu
www.frizz-dresden.de
www.cybersax.de

German embassies
www.london.diplo.de UK
www.germany.info USA
www.germanembassy.org.au Australia

Embassies in Germany
www.germany.embassy.gov.au Australia
www.kanada-info.de Canada
www.botschaft-frankreich.de France
www.britischebotschaft.de UK
www.usembassy.de USA

Order Form

Title   *Retail price*

. . . .

. . . .

Post & packing (£1/book UK; £2/book Europe; £3/book rest of world)   . . . .

Total   . . . .

Name . . . .

Address . . . .

Tel . . . .   Email . . . .

☐ I enclose a cheque for £ . . . . made payable to Bradt Travel Guides Ltd

☐ I would like to pay by credit card. Number: . . . .

Expiry date . . . . . . / . . . . . .   3-digit security code (on reverse of card) . . . .

Issue number (Switch/Maestro only) . . . .

☐ Please add my name to your mailing/e-newsletter list. (For Bradt use only.)

☐ I would be happy for you to use my name and comments in Bradt marketing material.

Send your order to
Bradt Travel Guides/DRE
23 High Street, Chalfont St Peter, Bucks SL9 9QE
☏ +44 (0)1753 893444   f +44 (0)1753 892333
e info@bradtguides.com   www.bradtguides.com

An Advent pyramid in front of the Frauenkirche (TB) page 147

Hofkirche and Residenzschloss (Royal Palace) (SF) pages 206 and 155 respectively

Salzgasse in the Altstadt (SF) page 158

The Semperoper (Opera House) and the Elbe
(SF) page 152

BRADT CITY GUIDES

Belgrade £6.99

Bratislava £6.99

Budapest £7.95

Cork £6.99

Dresden £7.99

Dubrovnik £6.99

Helsinki £7.99

Johannesburg £6.99

Kiev £7.95

Krakow £7.99

Lille £6.99

Ljubljana £7.99

Riga £6.99

Tallinn £6.99

Vilnius £6.99

Zagreb £6.99

www.bradtguides.com

Index

First published September 2007
Bradt Travel Guides Ltd
23 High Street, Chalfont St Peter, Bucks SL9 9QE, England; www.bradtguides.com
Published in the US by The Globe Pequot Press Inc,
246 Goose Lane, PO Box 480, Guilford, Connecticut 06437-0480

British Library Cataloguing in Publication Data
A catalogue record for this book is available from the British Library

ISBN-10: 1 84162 213 3   ISBN-13: 978 1 84162 213 2

Photographs Arco Digital Images (ADI/Tips), Bildagentur/Tips (B/Tips), BL Images/Alamy (BLI/A),
Tim Burford (TB), Stuart Forster (SF), Christoph Münch/Dresden Tourist Board (CM/DTB),
Tourismusverband Sächsische Schweiz/Richter (TSS), www.schloss-wackerbarth.de (SW)
Front cover Dresden skyline and River Elbe (BLI/A)
Title page Yenidze after sunset (SF), Detail from the Residenzschloss (SF)
Maps Steve Munns   **Illustrations** Carole Vincer, Dave Colton

Typeset from the author's disc by Wakewing
Printed and bound in Italy by Legoprint SpA

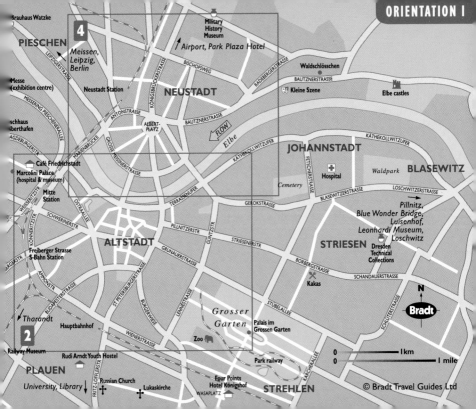

Brauhaus Watzke

PIESCHEN

4

Meissen,
Leipzig,
Berlin

LEIPZIGERSTRASSE

Messe
(exhibition centre)

MESSERING PIESCHENER ALLEE

schhaus
berthafen

AGDEBURGERSTR

Neustadt Station

Military
History
Museum

↑ Airport, Park Plaza Hotel

BISCHOFSWEG

RADEBERGERSTRASSE

Waldschlösschen

BAUTZNERSTRASSE

Kleine Szene

Elbe castles

KÖNIGSBRÜCKERSTRASSE

NEUSTADT

ANTONSTRASSE

ALBERT-
PLATZ

BAUTZNERSTRASSE

MARIENBRÜCKE

GROSSE MEISSNERSTRASSE

FLOW

Elbe

KÄTHEKOLLWITZUFER

JOHANNSTADT

KÄTHEKOLLWITZUFER

Café Friedrichstadt

Marcolini Palace
(hospital & museum)

Mitte
Station

OSTRALLEE

SCHWERINERSTR

WEISERITZSTR

KÖNNERITZSTR

Freiberger Strasse
S-Bahn Station

ARGASTR

↓ Tharandt

2

Railway Museum

TERRASSENUFER

GEROKSTRASSE

Cemetery

FETSCHERSTRASSE

Hospital

Waldpark

BLASEWITZ

LOSCHWITZERSTRASSE

BLASEWITZERSTRASSE

Pillnitz,
Blue Wonder Bridge,
Luisenhof,
Leonhardi Museum,
Loschwitz

ALTSTADT

PILLNITZERSTR

GÜNTZSTR

STRIESENERSTR

STRIESEN

Dresden
Technical
Collections

GRUNAUERSTRASSE

BORBERGSTRASSE

SCHANDAUERSTRASSE

Kakas

AMMONSTR

BUDAPESTERSTRASSE

ST PETERSBURGERSTRASSE

BÜRGERWIESE

LENNESTRASSE

Grosser
Garten

STÜBELALLEE

Palais im
Grossen Garten

SCHUBERTSTRASSE

N

Bradt

Hauptbahnhof

WIENERSTRASSE

Zoo

Rudi Arndt Youth Hostel

Park railway

KARCHERALLEE

0 ————————— 1km
0 ————————— 1 mile

PLAUEN

↓ University, Library

FRITZ-LÖFFLERSTR

Russian Church

Lukaskirche

Four Points
Hotel Königshof

WASAPLATZ

STREHLEN

© Bradt Travel Guides Ltd

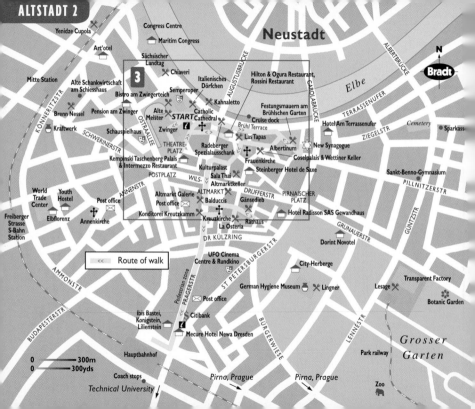

ALTSTADT 2

Neustadt

Yenidze Cupola
Congress Centre
Maritim Congress
Art'otel
Sächsischer Landtag
Mitte Station
Chiaveri
Italienisches Dörfchen
Hilton & Ogura Restaurant, Rossini Restaurant
Alte Schankwirtschaft am Schiesshaus
Semperoper
Bistro am Zwingerteich
Kahnaletto
Brenn Nessel
Pension am Zwinger
Alte Meister
START
Catholic Cathedral
Kraftwerk
Zwinger
Festungsmauern am Brühlschen Garten
Schauspielhaus
Cruise dock
Brühl Terrace
Hotel Am Terrassenufer
Radeberger Spezialausschank
Las Tapas
Cemetery
Sparkass
THEATER-PLATZ
Albertinum
New Synagogue
Kempinski Taschenberg Palais & Intermezzo Restaurant
Kulturpalast
Frauenkirche
Coselpalais & Wettiner Keller
Sankt-Benno-Gymnasium
POSTPLATZ
Sala Thai
Steinberger Hotel de Saxe
World Trade Center
Youth Hostel
Post office
Altmarktkeller
PIRNAISCHER PLATZ
Elbflorenz
Annenkirche
Altmarkt Galerie
Post office
Balduccis
ALTMARKT
DRUFFERSTR
Gänsedieb
Hotel Radisson SAS Gewandhaus
Freiberger Strasse S-Bahn Station
Konditorei Kreutzkamm
La Osteria
Kreuzkirche
Rathaus
Dorint Novotel
DR KÜLZRING
<< Route of walk
UFO Cinema Centre & Rundkino
City-Herberge
German Hygiene Museum
Lingner
Transparent Factory
Lesage
Post office
Botanic Garden
ibis Bastei, Königstein, Lilienstein
Citibank
Mecure Hotel Newa Dresden
Hauptbahnhof
Park railway
Grosser Garten
0   300m
0   300yds
Coach stops
Pirna, Prague
Pirna, Prague
Zoo
Technical University

Bradt

Elbe

ALBERTBRÜCKE
AUGUSTUSBRÜCKE
CAROLABRÜCKE
TERRASSENUFER
ZIEGELSTR
PILLNITZERSTR
GÜNTZSTR
GRUNAERSTR
KONNERITZSTR
SCHWERINERSTR
OSTRAALLEE
ANNENSTR
WILS-
POSTPLATZ
AMMONSTR
BUDAPESTERSTR
ST PETERSBURGERSTR
PRAGERSTR
BÜRGERWIESE
LENNESTR

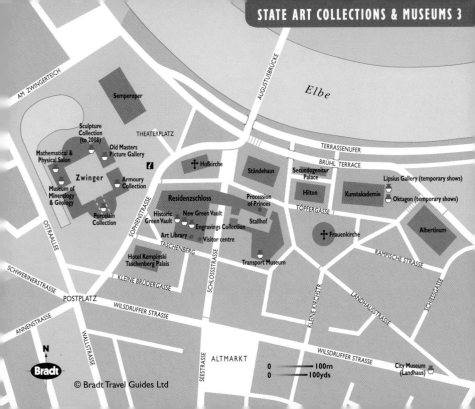

Elbe

AM ZWINGTERTEICH

Semperoper

THEATERPLATZ

AUGUSTUSBRÜCKE

TERRASSENUFER

BRÜHL TERRACE

Sculpture
Collection
(to 2008)

Mathematical &
Physical Salon

Old Masters
Picture Gallery

Hofkirche

Ständehaus

Secundogenitur
Palace

Lipsius Gallery (temporary shows)

Zwinger

Armoury
Collection

Hilton

Kunstakademie

Oktagon (temporary shows)

Museum
of Mineralogy
& Geology

Residenzschloss

Procession
of Princes

TÖPFERGASSE

Porcelain
Collection

SOPHIENSTRASSE

Historic
Green Vault

New Green Vault

Engravings Collection

Stallhof

Frauenkirche

Albertinum

Art Library

Visitor centre

OSTRAALLEE

TASCHENBERG

RAMPISCHE STRASSE

Hotel Kempinski
Taschenberg Palais

Transport Museum

SCHLOSSSTRASSE

SCHIESSGASSE

SCHWERINERSTRASSE

KLEINE BRÜDERGASSE

KLEINE KIRCHSTR

LANDHAUSSTRASSE

POSTPLATZ

WILSDRUFFER STRASSE

ANNENSTRASSE

WALLSTRASSE

SEESTRASSE

ALTMARKT

WILSDRUFFER STRASSE

N

0   100m
0   100yds

City Museum
(Landhaus)

Bradt

© Bradt Travel Guides Ltd

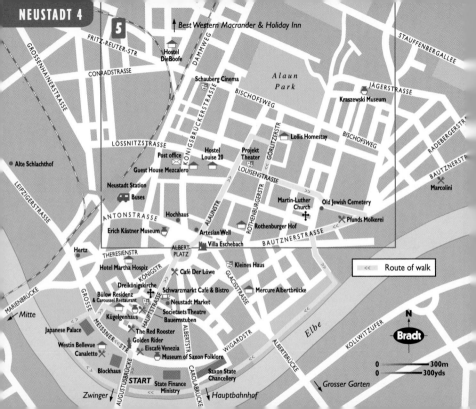

NEUSTADT 4

5

Best Western Macrander & Holiday Inn

FRITZ-REUTER-STR

Hostel DieBoofe

CONRADSTRASSE

GROSSENHAINERSTRASSE

DAMMWEG

Schauberg Cinema

Alaun Park

BISCHOFSWEG

STAUFFENBERGALLEE

JÄGERSTRASSE

Kraszewski Museum

BISCHOFSWEG

RADEBERGERSTR

LÖSSNITZSTRASSE

Alte Schlachtof

LEIPZIGERSTRASSE

Post office

Guest House Mezcalero

Neustadt Station

Buses

ANTONSTRASSE

Hochhaus

Erich Kästner Museum

Hertz

THERESIENSTR

Hotel Martha Hospiz

Hostel Louise 20

KÖNIGSBRÜCKERSTRASSE

Projekt Theater

GÖRLITZERSTR

Lollis Homestay

LOUISENSTRASSE

ROTHENBURGERSTR

Martin-Luther Church

Old Jewish Cemetery

Pfunds Molkerei

ALLAUNSTR

Artesian Well

Rothenburger Hof

BAUTZNERSTRASSE

Villa Eschebach

ALBERT-PLATZ

Kleines Haus

BAUTZNERSTR

MARCOLINI

Route of walk

KÖNIGSTR

Café Der Löwe

Dreikönigskirche

Bülow Residenz & Caroussel Restaurant

Kügelhaus

MARIENBRÜCKE

Mitte

GROSSE MEISSNER STR

Japanese Palace

Westin Bellevue

Canaletto

Blockhaus

AUGUSTUSBRÜCKE

Zwinger

START

Schwarzmarkt Café & Bistro

Neustadt Market

Societaets Theatre Bauernstuben

The Red Rooster

Golden Rider

Eiscafé Venezia

Museum of Saxon Folklore

HAUPTSTRASSE

ALBERTSTR

GLACISSTRASSE

Mercure Albertbrücke

WIGARDSTR

ALBERTBRÜCKE

Elbe

Saxon State Chancellery

State Finance Ministry

CAROLABRÜCKE

Hauptbahnhof

Grosser Garten

KOLLWITZUFER

Bradt

N

0   300m
0   300yds

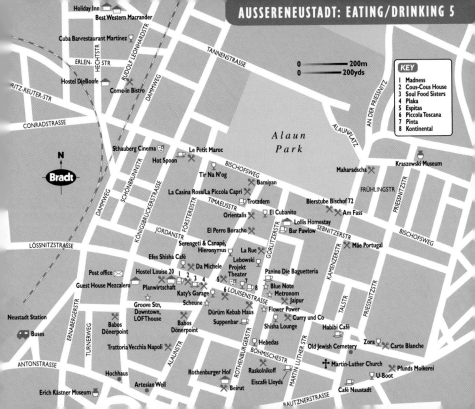

KEY
1 Madness
2 Cous-Cous House
3 Soul Food Sisters
4 Plaka
5 Espitas
6 Piccola Toscana
7 Pinta
8 Kontinental

0 ———— 200m
0 ———— 200yds

N
Bradt

Holiday Inn
Best Western Macrander
Cuba Bar-restaurant Martinez
ERLEN-STR
HECHTSTR
RUDOLF LEONHARDTSTR
DAMMWEG
TANNENSTRASSE
Hostel DieBoofe
FRITZ-REUTER-STR
Come-in Bistro
CONRADSTRASSE

AN DER PRIESSNITZ
ALAUNPLATZ

Alaun Park

Schauberg Cinema
Le Petit Maroc
Hot Spoon
BISCHOFSWEG
Maharadscha
Kraszewski Museum
DAMMWEG
SCHONBRUNNSTR
Tir Na N'og
Bamiyan
FRÜHLINGSTR
PRIESSNITZSTR
La Casina Rosa/La Piccola Capri
TIMAEUSSTR
Trotzdem
Bierstube Bischof 72
BISCHOFSWEG
Orientalis
El Cubanito
Am Fass
LÖSSNITZSTRASSE
FÖRSTEREISTR
El Perro Boracho
Lollis Homestay
Bar Pawlow
SEBNITZSTR
Mãe Portugal
JORDANSTR
Serengeti & Canapé, Hieronymus
La Rue
GÖRLITZSTR
KÖNIGSBRÜCKERSTRASSE
Efes Shisha Café
Da Michele
Lebowski
Projekt Theater
Panino Die Baguetteria
KAMENZERSTR
Post office
Hostel Louise 20
1 2 3 4
5
Blue Note
Guest House Mezcalero
Planwirtschaft
Katy's Garage
6 LOUISENSTRASSE
Metronom
Jaipur
TALSTR
PRIESSNITZSTR
Neustadt Station
Buses
Groove Stn, Downtown, LOFThouse
Scheune
Flower Power
Curry und Co
Habibi Café
Zora
Carte Blanche
ERNA BERGERSTR
TURNERWEG
Babos Dönerpoint
Babos Dönerpoint
Dürüm Kebab Haus
Suppenbar
Shisha Lounge
Old Jewish Cemetery
ANTONSTRASSE
Trattoria Vecchia Napoli
ALAUNSTR
Hebedas
BÖHMISCHESTR
ROTHENBURGERSTR
Martin-Luther Church
Pfunds Molkerei
Hochhaus
Rothenburger Hof
MARTIN LUTHER STR
Raskolnikoff
U-Boot
Erich Kästner Museum
Artesian Well
Beirut
Eiscafé Lloyds
Café Neustadt
RAUTZNERSTRASSE

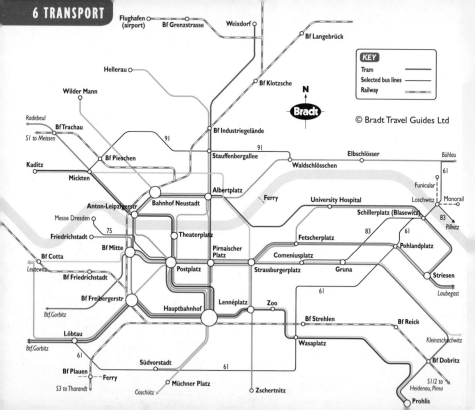

KEY
Tram
Selected bus lines
Railway

Bradt

© Bradt Travel Guides Ltd

N

Flughafen (airport)
Bf Grenzstrasse
Weixdorf
Bf Langebrück
Bf Klotzsche
Hellerau
Wilder Mann
Bf Industriegelände
Radebeul
Bf Trachau
S1 to Meissen
91
Stauffenbergallee
91
Elbschlösser
Bühlau
Bf Pieschen
Waldschlösschen
61
Kaditz
Mickten
Albertplatz
Ferry
Funicular
Loschwitz
Monorail
Anton-Leipzigerstr
Bahnhof Neustadt
University Hospital
Schillerplatz (Blasewitz)
83
Messe Dresden
Pillnitz
Theaterplatz
Fetscherplatz
83
61
Pohlandplatz
Friedrichstadt
75
Bf Mitte
Pirnaischer Platz
Comeniusplatz
Striesen
Bf Cotta
Postplatz
Strassburgerplatz
Gruna
Leutewitz
Bf Friedrichstadt
Laubegast
Bf Freibergerstr
61
Btf.Gorbitz
Hauptbahnhof
Lennéplatz
Zoo
Bf Strehlen
Bf Reick
Löbtau
Btf.Gorbitz
Wasaplatz
Kleinzschachwitz
61
Südvorstadt
61
Bf Dobritz
Bf Plauen
Ferry
Müchner Platz
S1/2 to Heidenau, Pirna
S3 to Tharandt
Coschütz
Zschertnitz
Prohlis